Delivering the People's Message

Delivering the People's Message

The Changing Politics of the Presidential Mandate

Julia R. Azari

Cornell University Press
Ithaca and London

First published 2014 by Cornell University Press

Printed in the United States of America

Library of Congress Cataloging-in-Publication Data

Azari, Julia R., 1979– author.
    Delivering the people's message : the changing politics of the presidential mandate / Julia R. Azari.
        pages cm
    Includes bibliographical references and index.
    ISBN 978-0-8014-5224-6 (cloth : alk. paper)
    1. Presidents—United States—Election—History—20th century.
2. Presidents—United States—Election—History—21st century.
3. Rhetoric—Political aspects—United States—History—20th century.
4. Rhetoric—Political aspects—United States—History—21st century.
5. Political leadership—United States—History—20th century.
6. Political leadership—United States—History—21st century.   I. Title.

    JK528.A93 2014
    324.973—dc23   2013027562

Cornell University Press strives to use environmentally responsible suppliers and materials to the fullest extent possible in the publishing of its books. Such materials include vegetable-based, low-VOC inks and acid-free papers that are recycled, totally chlorine-free, or partly composed of nonwood fibers. For further information, visit our website at www.cornellpress.cornell.edu.

Cloth printing   10   9   8   7   6   5   4   3   2   1

To Nasim and Cyrus, who will always be my little brothers and who always keep my narrative honest

CONTENTS

ACKNOWLEDGMENTS

In the course of researching, writing, and rewriting this book, I have been fortunate to have never been without the company of wonderful friends, family, and colleagues; likewise, I have never been without the support of terrific institutions that have helped to bring this project to fruition. I ask for the reader's indulgence as I enumerate a long list of those whose support was crucial to the realization of this book. All shortcomings and errors are, of course, mine alone.

I am immensely grateful to Michael McGandy and Sarah E. M. Grossman of Cornell University Press, and to the anonymous readers who provided excellent feedback and suggestions. I am also grateful to Erin Thomas, Bob Mate, Ben Stewart, and Dave Ruigh for excellent research assistance, and to Supurna Banerjee for excellent copyediting. I also owe a debt of gratitude to the talented and patient employees of the Carter, Johnson, FDR, Reagan, Eisenhower, and Nixon presidential libraries for their assistance in my archival research.

I have been fortunate to have financial and academic support from several generous institutions. I am grateful to Marquette University for a generous subvention, which aided in the publication of this book. The Center for the Study of American Politics at Yale, the Marquette University Office for Research and Sponsored Programs, and the Harry Middleton Foundation all provided funding for the research on which this book is based. More generally, I owe a debt of gratitude to the Department of Political Science at Yale and the American Politics Workshop at the Institute for Social and Policy Studies for the training and "tough love" that they provided during my years as a graduate student. My gratitude extends to the support staff as well as the faculty.

This project would not have come to fruition without the guidance and expertise of David Mayhew, Stephen Skowronek, and Jacob Hacker, faculty members at Yale whose mentorship was tough, encouraging, and deeply connected to the world of ideas. I also remain grateful to other mentors there, including Greg Huber and Susan Stokes, who also provided guidance during this project. Reaching back even further, my path to becoming a political scientist was initially shaped and encouraged by my undergraduate mentors at the University of Illinois: William Bernhard, Jeff Bosworth, Brian Gaines, and Carol Leff. My own time as an assistant professor has made me all the more appreciative of the hours they spent with me, providing guidance about formulating research questions, gathering and analyzing data, and, eventually, choosing a graduate program.

The Department of Political Science at Marquette University has been a source of intellectual and personal support during my six years in the department. My gratitude extends to our entire department, but Lowell Barrington, McGee Young, Amber Wichowsky, Paul Nolette, Risa Brooks, Duane Swank, Ryan Hanley, Karen Hoffman, Jeff Drope, and Barrett McCormick have been especially helpful in offering suggestions, reading drafts, and freely giving good advice. Their kindness, generosity, and intellectual acumen have not only helped to make this a better book but also exemplify the very reasons why I chose a career in academia.

I have also been immensely fortunate to have a wide circle of political science colleagues whose expertise and friendship have helped me through the ups and downs of researching, writing, and revising this book. I am thankful to the following individuals for their involvement at different stages of the process: Lara Brown, Sonali Chakravarti, Ken Collier, Steve Engel,

Dan Galvin, Lilly Goren, Amelia Hoover Green, Matt Hall, Andira Hernandez-Monzoy, Gaye Ilhan Demeriyol, Nancy Kassop, Harris Mylonas, Zim Nwokora, Daniela Donno Panayides, Nassos Roussias, Colleen Shogan, Jenny Smith, Justin Vaughn, Jose Villalobos, and Eric Zeemering. This diverse group of political science scholars has pushed me to consider the implications of my work in American political development, political theory, and comparative politics, as well as to be mindful of different analytical paradigms. The book also benefited from several expert discussants at conferences over the years: Robert Collins, Matt Eshbaugh-Soha, Russell Renka, Bert Rockman, and Daniel Klinghard. Outside of political science, I have been lucky to have friends who have not only provided support and encouragement but also sometimes contributed to my work by sharing insights from their own fields of study: Catherine Deibel, Heather Hlavka, Matt Krause, Allison O'Mahen Malcom, Kevin Miller, Sameena Mulla, Tipan Verella, and Michael Wert.

During the years I spent on this project, I have also been fortunate to have the support of my family: my parents, Mahmood and Sarah Azari; my mother-in-law, Nancy Hathaway; my father-in-law, Tom Osterman; and my various siblings and siblings-in-law, Nasim and Adriana Azari, Cyrus Azari, Travis and Julia Osterman, and Heather and Doug Hopek. However, only one person willingly chose to be part of my family during the time that this book was under way. Todd Osterman has not only endured the usual indignities afforded to those whose spouses are writing books: preoccupation on holidays and weekends, ever-growing stacks of books and papers that take over living spaces, and late nights of writing; he has also been patient and generous in providing love, support, food, coffee, and a simple refrain of encouragement: "You'll get it done." As usual, you were right.

DELIVERING THE PEOPLE'S MESSAGE

INTRODUCTION

Political Institutions and the Politics of the Presidential Mandate

A politician thinks of the next election. A statesman thinks of the next generation.

—JAMES FREEMAN CLARKE

Elections have consequences.

—SENATOR LINDSEY GRAHAM

Twenty-first-century U.S. presidents operate in an age of mandate politics. Compared with mid-twentieth-century leaders, contemporary presidents draw on the logic of campaign promises and election results much more frequently. The use of mandate claims is not mere rhetorical window dressing; rather, this trend represents a fundamental shift in the logic of presidential politics. In the contemporary era, presidents no longer use mandate rhetoric primarily in televised national speeches or talks addressing partisan supporters. On the contrary, the logic of electoral mandates pervades presidential speech in media interviews and news conferences, minor speeches, and remarks to other members of the government, particularly those working in the executive branch. Changes in rhetorical behavior have resulted from changing ideas about the nature of legitimate presidential governance, transformation in the political party system, and an evolving relationship between the presidency and the political parties.

   The research presented in this book examines how presidents have incorporated electoral mandates into their communication strategies from the

Progressive Era through the first decade of the twenty-first century. Distinct patterns are evident, but counterintuitive. The era of mandate politics has been building for decades, starting with Richard Nixon's insistence on speaking for a "silent majority" in 1969 and gaining strength with Ronald Reagan's case for a conservative mandate after the 1980 election. The presidencies of George W. Bush and Barack Obama, who have extensively sought to justify their policy choices in terms of the will of the electorate and the clear choices presented in their campaigns, represent the apex (thus far) of this trend.

The content of mandate rhetoric has also changed. Recent presidents have tended to tie the election result to specific policies rather than broader ideas about national or party values. Mandate rhetoric also reflects changing ideas about presidential representation. In the middle of the twentieth century, mandate rhetoric contained a mix of "delegate" and "trustee" references.

Explaining this development is the central aim of this book. In the research presented in this work, I trace variation in the use of mandate claims to corresponding changes in the institutional context. Specifically, the shift toward more frequent, partisan, and delegate-style mandate rhetoric has resulted from the intersection of two institutional developments. The first of these is the declining status of the presidency after Vietnam and Watergate. In the wake of these events, strong executive power fell out of public favor.[1] Mandate rhetoric provided a way for presidents to respond to public skepticism about the office by emphasizing their transparency and accountability. In other words, this development helps to account for presidents' increased use of rhetoric about "the promises I made in my campaign" and "the reasons I was elected"—rhetoric that stresses their responsiveness and responsibility to voters.

Legitimacy problems have coincided—and interacted—with the second institutional development in the party system, which has undergone polarization and ideological sorting. In Matthew Levendusky's account, the process of "sorting" means that voters' partisan and ideological labels have become more "tightly connected" than in the past; self-identified liberals have gravitated toward the Democratic Party while conservatives have largely aligned with the Republican Party.[2] As the parties have become less ideologically diverse within their own ranks and less cooperative with each other, the relationship between presidents and parties has been transformed. Not only do twenty-first-century presidents rely more heavily on their fellow partisans in Congress and in the electorate,[3] but they can also count on vociferous criticism from their opponents, some of which emanates from the partisan "new media." Cable news, talk radio, and online news sources transmit evaluations of news items from elites to ideologically predisposed mass audiences and allow citizens to narrow the range of ideas to which they are exposed.[4] In this way, media developments have facilitated the convergence of polarization and delegitimization.

The rise of mandate politics has shaped, as well as been shaped by, the dynamics of the party system and the contours of presidential leadership. The partisan implications of the turn in mandate rhetoric are intuitive; speeches claiming a mandate for party ideas or ideological principles (or casting the election as a rejection of the other party's beliefs) reinforce the image of the president as a party politician rather than a national statesman. All presidents must balance both of these roles,[5] but partisan mandate claims signal to supporters that they can expect the president to put the party's agenda first. Such claims also buttress the sentiment among opponents that this elected official is not "their" president (as bumper stickers during the Bush administration attested). In other words, mandate rhetoric serves to entrench the same political conditions to which it responds, contributing to a vicious cycle of presidential partisanship and illegitimacy. In a similar vein, mandate rhetoric—especially that which stresses campaign promises and the distinctions between the parties—elevates the principle of majority rule. The notion that fifty percent plus one constitutes a sufficient warrant for policy change, provided the platform's policy pledges were clear, undergirds the theory of "responsible party" politics.[6] But such thinking about majorities and policy change is at odds with the design of the American system, in which veto points abound. Contemporary presidents face considerable obstacles in this regard. With opposition parties highly motivated to defeat presidential proposals and a de facto sixty-vote requirement in the Senate, promises can prove difficult to keep. As with the polarization issue, the cycle of heightened and dashed expectations has become a vicious one for presidents and citizens alike, distorting how citizens view the political process and setting elected officials up for failure. Presidential mandate rhetoric has served to deepen the contradiction that drives this cycle.

The Construction of a Mandate: George W. Bush and the 2004 Election

Before the polls opened for Election Day 2004, conservative pundit Ramesh Ponnuru predicted that if Bush won reelection, the Republican president would "make a mandate" by aggressively pursuing his policy agenda. In a piece for the *Washington Post* on October 31, Ponnuru speculated that Bush would turn a 2004 victory into a mandate for "bold, audacious" policy moves, including Social Security reform.

A few weeks later, Bush won reelection with a clear, if slim, majority of popular and Electoral College votes. Congressional Republicans made gains in both Houses. Perhaps most importantly for the construction of a "bold, audacious" mandate, the 2004 campaign exposed major differences between the two parties on policy and political philosophy. Bush and his Democratic challenger, Senator John Kerry (D-MA), took distinct positions on social issues, economic policy, and perhaps most prominent of all, the invasion of Iraq in March 2003. However, John Kerry also failed to persuade the electorate that he would be a better leader than the incumbent. In their study of the 2004 election, Paul Abramson, John Aldrich, and David Rohde observe that "Kerry had several weaknesses, which the GOP campaign exploited," including the relative ease with which the Bush campaign was able to "portray (Kerry) as vacillating and two-faced."[7] The 2004 contest was a Republican victory, but as a conservative policy mandate, its status was more dubious. Potential explanations for the election result abounded. Furthermore, with several policy areas under consideration, it was difficult to attribute the election to one specific pledge.

Despite this ambiguity, Bush immediately began framing the election as a policy mandate. After a reporter asked whether he felt "more free" to pursue his preferred policy agenda, the newly reelected president described his plans to move forward with a policy agenda: "And after hundreds of speeches and three debates and interviews and the whole process, where you keep basically saying the same thing over and over again, that—when you win, there is a feeling that the people have spoken and embraced your point of view." He neglected to specify the policy substance of this "point of view," but the meaning of the remark was clear enough: Bush had clarified his position in the election campaign, and his majority victory signaled that the electorate approved of these policy ideas. After his second term began, Bush embarked on a national tour to promote Social Security reform. True to Ponnuru's prediction, he tied the proposal to the promises of his campaign and spoke about the election and the campaign more frequently than any modern president at the start of a term.

Bush's choice embodies what many scholars and pundits now believe about presidential mandates: that they are the products of elite construction rather than objective truths about the meaning of election results. These constructions require careful decision making on the part of presidents. Leaders can choose to interpret elections in a variety of ways. They can stress party victory or national unity; they may claim an electoral mandate for a specific policy or a broad idea; they can use language about the election to define their relationship with the electorate. They may also choose to eschew mandate language altogether, justifying their policy choices in different terms.

Faced with these possibilities, Bush chose to identify the election as a conservative, Republican policy mandate. He chose a policy position that was popular only with a deep ideological core within his party: the privatization of Social Security. He positioned himself—fancifully, as it turned out—as a responsible party leader, a politician who had run on specific policy promises and now intended to fulfill those pledges.

Revising the Theory of Presidential Mandate Claims

Intuitively, it seems that we should expect presidents to use mandate rhetoric when they can point to a decisive election victory or even high approval levels to substantiate their claims. Yet, in the example of George W. Bush and the 2004 election, the opposite relationship obtains. Existing theories about presidential mandates cannot explain the rise of "mandate politics" at the end of the twentieth century. Previous scholars have contributed to our understanding of mandates by conducting in-depth analyses of election dynamics, including Stanley Kelley's foundational study, *Interpreting Elections*, and Patricia Conley's comprehensive historical analysis, *Presidential Mandates: How Elections Shape the National Agenda*. In *Presidential Mandates*, Conley asserts, "When a president declares a mandate, he makes a claim that the people elected him to change policy in a substantial way. The task of both the president and Congress is to forecast the probability that he is right and that if conflict ensued, the mobilization of the public would result in affirmation of the president's preferred position."[8] Charles O. Jones similarly notes the "ideal conditions" for claiming a mandate: "publicly visible issues, clear differences between the candidates, a substantial victory for the winner and his party in Congress, and a post-election declaration of party unity."[9] Using these definitions, Conley and Jones both identify 1952, 1964, and 1980 as mandate elections and categorize others as partial mandates or nonmandates. Lawrence Grossback, David Peterson, and James Stimson similarly find that the 1964, 1980, and 1994 elections seem to have precipitated a brief but significant change in congressional behavior. After each of these three contests, media and political elites converged on the mandate as a way to explain unexpected election results.[10] All three of these studies conclude that when presidents can credibly claim electoral mandates, major policy change is more likely. In other words, mandates are associated with brief windows of exceptional politics. But what of the more common periods of normal presidential politics? All elections are subject to interpretation, and presidents do not have to win landslide victories in order to cite popular legitimacy for their power.[11] The emphasis on persuading Congress is also unnecessarily limited. We have ample evidence that presidents shape politics in ways that do not always involve major policy initiatives. To use Stephen Skowronek's terminology, presidents "disrupt" politics in a number of ways.[12] William Howell finds that presidents have considerable power to enact policy unilaterally through executive orders and management of the executive branch.[13] Even before policy changes occur, presidents can change the nature of policy debate through their use of language, altering the way citizens and elites discuss an issue area for decades.[14] By focusing the study of mandate rhetoric on congressional persuasion, we miss a significant part of the story.

Furthermore, existing accounts rest on several flawed assumptions. Conley's analysis presumes that the concept of the presidential mandate has carried similar meaning over time, signifying the same ideas about the relationship between the president and the public in 1860 and in 1960. In a similar vein, these studies also assume that most—if not all—presidents perceive establishing a mandate narrative to be strategically desirable and will claim an electoral mandate if they think they can do so credibly. These assumptions do not hold up to either theoretical or empirical scrutiny. We know that ideas about American democracy, the role of the presidency in politics, and the nature of presidential power have all changed over the course of American history. We also know that the ideas behind the presidential mandate were forged in the context of such ideational changes; most scholars cite Andrew Jackson or Woodrow Wilson as the first president to theorize about popular mandates.[15] Why, then, should we assume that the meaning of the mandate has been static ever since? Empirically, the findings of this research also defy these assumptions—not all presidents claim mandates, and considerable variation exists in the frequency and content of mandate rhetoric. Studies of contemporary mandates also embrace the common understanding that presidential speech choices are made in the context of isolated policy "games" with Congress, with rhetoric serving as a tool to help the executive branch maximize leverage over the legislative.[16] By considering mandate rhetoric in the context of the longer arc of changing institutional status and cross-institutional relationships, I challenge this assumption as well.

The central alternative explanation for the increased use of mandate rhetoric is the contention that presidential politics have become more "plebiscitary" over time. The plebiscitary thesis posits that absent institutional support for negotiation with Congress, public opinion leadership has become the main tool of presidential influence.[17] In other words, a plebiscitary explanation would posit that presidents perceive a need to make more popular appeals, to emphasize the link between the president and the populace as a whole, and that the expansive use of mandate rhetoric is merely a reflection of a shift toward greater use of public appeals.

However, when we try to explain the rise of mandate politics, the plebiscitary thesis falls short. The ways in which presidents talk about elections, both on the public record and within the White House, do not conform to the expectations of the plebiscitary account. Mandate rhetoric after 1969 rarely features the kinds of populist themes associated with plebiscitary politics. Instead, the emphasis is less on "the people" than on distinctions between the candidates and the campaign promises made by the winner.

Mandate rhetoric in this later period also lacks antiparty themes. A central tenet of the literature on the plebiscitary presidency is that forging a direct relationship with the people (however superficial) has happened at the expense of the political parties.[18] In this vein, we might expect that mandate rhetoric serves as a tool for presidents to build their own constituencies, separate from those of their parties. The findings of this research challenge this assertion. By contrast, mandate rhetoric appears more directly aimed at partisan supporters than at any time since the Progressive Era. As mandate rhetoric has increasingly come to depict elections as contests between different sets of ideas and policy prescriptions, partisan themes have emerged stronger, not faded into the background.

The approach of this book is to move beyond the treatment of the presidential mandate as merely about the interpretation of elections and the persuasion of Congress. When presidents claim mandates they are interpreting elections, to be sure, but these interpretations are influenced by political context and by how presidents themselves understand the office and its role in the political system. Employing a broader institutional framework allows us to explain the variation and patterns in presidential mandate rhetoric. It also helps us to understand what the presidential mandate has meant in context—what this concept has signified at different points in the post-Progressive presidency and how different presidents have viewed its relevance for their governing choices.

Similarly, the plebiscitary explanation oversimplifies the complex dynamics of institutional change. Presidential behavior is influenced by changes in ideas and by cross-institutional relationships. The relationship between the president and the public has changed, but this evolution has not been simple, nor has it occurred in isolation from changes in the rest of the political system.

Presidential Mandates and American Political Development

In response to the need to move beyond earlier frameworks, this research situates the study of presidential mandate rhetoric in the tradition of American political development. The findings of this study contribute to our understanding of how the boundaries of presidential legitimacy evolve, positing that as these boundaries contract and expand, the inclination to use mandate rhetoric ebbs and flows. These findings also have relevance for the study of presidents and parties, as they engage the dynamic of antagonism and mutual dependence and suggest that the relationship between presidents and parties shapes consequential rhetorical choices.

The Dilemma of Presidential Legitimacy

What does it mean to say that legitimacy is a recurrent problem for the presidency? The Constitution affords the office considerable power, but remains silent on the scope and boundaries of that power.[19] For example, Article I allows the president to veto legislation, but fails to specify under what conditions this power may be invoked. Early in the history of the U.S. republic, presidents contended with the question of whether they could veto legislation simply on the basis of a policy disagreement or should reserve this power for legislation deemed unconstitutional? The president's role in domestic governance is even less clear. Article II places the president at the head of the executive branch and charges him with informing Congress about the "state of the union."[20] Even in the early stages of the U.S. republic, however, presidents have played a central role in shaping the country's policy direction, often in ways not prescribed by the Constitution. In other words, for much of presidential history, the capacity of the office has exceeded expectations about its legitimate scope of responsibilities, leading to clashes with other branches of government and accusations of tyrannical behavior.

To manage and, at times, to exploit this ambiguity, presidents have developed narratives of justification. In this way, rhetoric has been central to presidential leadership throughout the history of the republic, as it has allowed presidents to formulate arguments about the legitimacy of their actions. These arguments have cited policy, emergent threats, partisan competition, constitutional interpretation, and electoral mandates. Different scholarly approaches in the study of the presidency have emphasized different aspects of legitimacy arguments. In some accounts, the construction of a "crisis" has been central.[21] Alternatively, Skowronek contends that the ability to break with the past determines legitimacy. He argues that presidents have expansive power—the ability to act unilaterally, to influence other actors, to change policy, and by engaging in some or all of these actions, to change the polity and "disrupt" the received political order. In other words, presidents frequently effect policy change, which in turn empowers some groups in society at the expense of others, creates new constituencies, and unifies or destroys political coalitions. The challenge lies in establishing the authority—defined as "the warrants that can be drawn from the moment at hand to justify action and secure the legitimacy of the changes effected" for these consequential actions.[22] Skowronek's well-known account casts these authority claims as cyclical in nature, related to the resilience of the received political order and the president's relationship to it, whether affiliated or opposed.

Although Skowronek portrays issues of legitimacy in terms of recurrent patterns, his analysis also focuses on the challenge of establishing authority for specific policies and programs. In other words, despite his study's long historical span, he depicts the project of legitimacy mostly as specific policy initiatives. To cite a few examples, he discusses the implications of Theodore Roosevelt's efforts to engineer tariff reform and antitrust policy, and of Jimmy Carter's successful bid for consumer protection legislation, in the context of a presidential necessity to balance the "ideas and interests" of their respective parties' coalitions.[23] Where leaders fall in "political time" shapes their success in this endeavor; however, Skowronek's account pays relatively little attention to the overarching dynamics of institutional legitimacy. In contrast, the research presented in this work contends that presidents engage in a struggle over the legitimacy of the office itself, in addition to their efforts to change and define public policy. Furthermore, this struggle has taken on broad temporal dimensions, receding after the Progressive Era and resurging in the final decades of the twentieth century.

Scholarship within the U.S. political development tradition also considers the expansion of presidential governing authority over time, taking into account the slackening of informal proscriptions on types of presidential behavior and the navigation of relations among the different branches of government. Victoria Farrar-Myers identifies these expansions as "changes in the informal scripts" between the president and Congress.[24] Mandate rhetoric plays a key role in these larger institutional negotiations. By emphasizing their connections with the people, presidents justify the expansion of what Adam Sheingate calls "institutional jurisdictions." In a study of the role of political entrepreneurship in institutional change, Sheingate observes that the text of Article II leaves much ambiguity about the president's role in the political system, leading to conflict because "multiple actors may legitimately claim authority over the same functions or domains of action."[25] Indeed, Richard Ellis and Stephen Kirk contend that the idea of the presidential mandate was forged during a dispute over the scope and nature of presidential power: Andrew Jackson's "bank war."[26] Jackson's presidency is widely viewed as a critical moment for the expansion of legitimate presidential action. As historian Daniel Walker Howe describes, "All the major political controversies of Andrew Jackson's two terms in the White House involved issues of authority. Jackson exercised political authority in new ways, removing competent officeholders and vetoing more bills than all his predecessors put together."[27] Jackson's willingness to use the power of the presidency clashed with the beliefs about presidential power still held by many of Jackson's fellow Jeffersonian Democrats.[28] It was in the context of this discrepancy between limited ideas of legitimate presidential authority and the expansive reality of presidential power that the presidential mandate was "invented."[29] After the 1832 election, Jackson claimed a popular mandate to destroy the Second Bank of the United States (BUS). Before the election, Jackson vetoed a bill renewing the BUS charter. Both the Democratic campaign for Jackson and the National Republican effort to elect Henry Clay made an issue of this veto.[30] Jackson won soundly and could credibly claim that the veto distinguished his view from those of his opponent. Yet, the election itself was not the central driving force behind the choice to bring electoral logic into the BUS debate. Rather, it was the incongruity between what the president could do (order the removal of the deposits) and what he might previously have been expected to do (defer to Congress or at least wait until the expiration of the bank's charter) that inspired Jackson to use the mandate as justification.

In addition to the Jackson presidency, scholars have devoted substantial attention to the Progressive Era as a turning point in the status of the presidency. Farrar-Myers identifies significant change in the president's role in both foreign and domestic policy during this period. She traces changing norms about presidential behavior to exogenous pressures; these included an industrializing economy, the debate over the relationship between the United States and Europe, and the nationalization of political issues. Jeffrey Tulis posits a reversed causal order, linking Progressive presidential thought directly to the idea of the presidential mandate. In *The Rhetorical Presidency*, Tulis cites the direct connection with the people as one of Woodrow Wilson's foundational arguments for expanded presidential involvement in policy and public leadership.

This study places contemporary presidential mandate rhetoric within the conversation about the dynamics of presidential legitimacy. One of its main findings is that presidents can and do rely on the idea of a popular electoral mandate to address the need for new legitimacy narratives to match expansions of presidential influence. At the same time, presidential authority has not steadily expanded since the Progressive Era. Rather, some events have led to declining, rather that increasing, institutional legitimacy.[31] Presidents also face different legitimacy challenges on the scale of individual policies, as Skowronek points out. In other words, as the polity changes, presidents face long-term shifts in the status of the presidency; throughout their time in office, they also face shorter-term challenges to their governing authority.

Presidents and Parties

The findings of this study also have implications for our understanding of the relationship between presidents and parties. One crucial dimension of this relationship is the balance between antagonism and interdependency. This conflict traces its roots to the early republic. The Constitution establishes the president's responsibilities as a national leader, and many founding thinkers saw political parties as potentially destructive. Yet, even one of the nation's most famous founding statesmen, George Washington, was pulled into emergent conflicts over policy, and priorities nudged the first president toward the Federalist position.[32] Presidents have been, in some sense, party politicians ever since, needing the campaign organizations and patronage networks that these organizations provide. Despite this interdependence, the relationship has still not always been harmonious and productive. Presidents seeking to effect major change have sometimes found parties to be a source of constraint. In an account of the development of the modern presidency, Sidney Milkis describes this fraught relationship. As Franklin Roosevelt tried to expand and revise White House administration, his reforms often challenged accepted practices and structures in the Democratic Party. In establishing his administration, Roosevelt avoided party machines and traditional forms of patronage to the extent possible, seeking instead to elevate "'idea men' from outside the party ranks" in order to promote New Deal policies.[33] Richard Neustadt similarly presents parties and presidents as having fundamentally different objectives that lead them into conflict. With his observation that "what the Constitution separates our political parties do not combine,"[34] Neustadt theorizes that presidents cannot count on fellow partisans for political support. In light of this argument, discord between presidents and parties took hold as the default scholarly assumption.

A more recent wave of scholarship has begun to question the prevailing wisdom and to assess the extent to which parties can be useful to presidents, particularly in the electoral arena. Lara Brown observes that presidential aspirants alter "organizational, ideological and coalitional" aspects of political parties in order to serve their own political ambitions.[35] Similarly, Daniel Galvin posits that since 1952, Republican presidents have worked to build their parties' organizations in an effort to "change their political environment."[36] In a study aimed at more recent developments, Richard Skinner claims that although tension and antagonism may have characterized the era of FDR, Dwight Eisenhower, and Lyndon Johnson, this dynamic has shifted. The electorate now perceives presidents in partisan terms, with wide gaps between Democrats and Republicans in their evaluation of presidential performance. This development has also taken hold at the elite level; Skinner observes that "the president . . . leads the battalions of a partisan army into the battlefield of contemporary Washington."[37]

Taken as a whole, the literature on presidents and parties suggests that this relationship is dynamic, changing with external political conditions, presidential governing ambition, and political opportunism, and even varying between the two political parties. I find that this relationship is linked to the status of the presidency, with high levels of polarization detracting from the status of the office. Furthermore, evolutions across these two institutions—the party system and the presidency—have influenced presidential behavior by shaping how presidents interpret elections and incorporate those ideas into their plans for governance.

Changing Institutional Norms

The changes described in this book can be construed in terms of informal expectations about presidential behavior: it has become acceptable for presidents to claim mandates even after modest victories and to act as a partisan and ideological leader. This development has implications for other institutions beyond the presidency. These implications lie beyond the scope of this book, but bear consideration. First, the presidential struggle for legitimacy creates opportunities for other actors. As presidents have come to define their electoral mandates in narrower policy terms than in previous decades, political opponents can create counternarratives about the meaning of the election result. Thus members of Congress, governors and other state-level actors, and members of the "new media" attempt to stake their own legitimacy claims in their opposition to the president and to make their own arguments about how to define the issues of the day.

Second, the presidency is hardly the only office subject to the new norms. In the partisan era, congressional leaders and even governors have invoked the logic of the responsible party mandate to justify their actions, rally supporters, and persuade others. In heated negotiations over the federal budget and the debt ceiling in 2011, members of the House Tea Party caucus pressured Speaker John Boehner not to compromise with political opponents, going so far as to threaten to "primary" the Ohio Republican—that is, to run a more conservative candidate against him in the Republican primary.[38] Mandate politics have also manifested at the state level. After the 2010 elections, a group of newly elected Republican governors pursued dramatic policy changes on the basis of a "conservative mandate."[39]

The changes described in the forthcoming chapters represent an incomplete and partial development. The presidency still carries tremendous national symbolism, and presidents face high expectations about their abilities to resolve problems. It is in this context that changes in mandate rhetoric contribute to an incongruous institutional environment. Reaching back into the history of presidential mandate rhetoric since the Progressive Era, we observe that the ideas about the relationship between elections and presidential governance often reflect incomplete institutional change. By tracing changes in the party system, in the capacities and the limitations of the presidency, and in ideas about the president's role, this work sheds new light on later developments.

Tracing the Rise of Mandate Politics

The Progressive Era provides a natural starting point, with its renewed attention to the role of ideas in institutional design. This period brought about a major shift in thought about presidential power and the relationship between the president and the electorate, making it an important turning point in the development of the presidential mandate. After the Progressive

Era drew to a close, the assumptions formed during that period (e.g., that the president should be a policy leader and engage with the electorate) have persisted, although they have been expressed in different ways. In the following chapters, I divide the period between 1929 and 2009 into two eras, the modern and the partisan, with a transition period leading up to each era. Chapter 2 covers the transition from the Progressive Era to the modern era, which lasted from 1929 to 1938; chapter 3 discusses the modern era, from 1939 to 1968; chapter 4 covers the transition era from the modern to the partisan era, which began in 1969; and chapter 5 examines the partisan era, which began in full force in 1981 with Reagan's accession to office and which continues through the present.

What David Mayhew has termed "periodization schemes" can be reductive; at the same time, such classifications can help to provide a road map for understanding the relationship between mandate rhetoric and institutional development.[40] The typology used in this research draws on many well-known characterizations of presidential eras. Its "cut points" occur around the New Deal, the end of the Johnson presidency, and the beginning of the Reagan presidency. In identifying change at those moments, my typology draws on the changing party dynamics that inform Skowronek's depiction of the political time cycle in the twentieth century as well as on classic theories of political "realignment."

The focus of the typology used in this research is institutional evolution. During the transition from each era, presidents renegotiate institutional boundaries. As such, major political conflicts encompass debates over both policy and the scope of presidential authority. In the Progressive-transition era, Franklin Roosevelt's failed effort to restructure the Supreme Court exemplifies this kind of struggle over institutional jurisdiction. Substantively, FDR's standoff with the high court concerned the future of his New Deal programs. But after FDR introduced the reorganization bill, his opponents denounced the effort on institutional as well as substantive grounds, accusing the president of trying to encroach on a coequal branch of government. Similarly, Nixon's conflict with Congress over the impoundment of appropriated funds highlighted the substantive debate over federal programs and spending, yet it also represented a renegotiation of the limits on presidential power. Of course, debate about the legal limits of executive power are not absent outside these periods. However, the modern and partisan eras have both produced significant court decisions placing limits on aspects of the presidency that range from emergency powers to the line-item veto. These transitional periods are distinguished by the combination of institutional conflict with changing party politics, leading to disruptions in the public understanding of the president's role. At these times, presidents find themselves in a position to defend not only their policy preferences but also the basis of their institutional legitimacy.

To elucidate these dynamics, I examine cases from the post-Progressive period: FDR after the 1932 and 1936 elections, Eisenhower after 1952 and 1956, Johnson after 1964, Richard Nixon after 1968 and 1972, Carter after 1976, Reagan after 1980, George W. Bush after 2004, and Obama after 2008. The unit of the analysis is the elected presidential term. Cases were selected according to several criteria. In each of the main eras and the two transition periods, the cases include presidents from both major parties. To the extent possible, I tried to include cases that were comparable in terms of election results. In general, the presidential terms included in the case studies began with elections that were amenable to mandate claims in some way. All but Nixon's election in 1968 brought the winner to office with a majority of the popular votes, and all but 1968 and 1980 resulted in unified party government. The elections of 1980, while not establishing a unified Republican government, brought a Republican majority to the Senate for the first time since 1952. Furthermore, the 1980 election is widely cited as both a mandate election and a turning point in American politics, and thus warrants inclusion in this study.

The 1968 election does not fit this criterion, as Nixon was elected in a close race with a plurality of the vote and took office alongside a Democratic Congress. However, to understand the unfolding of the transition from the modern to the partisan era, it is necessary to examine the changing institutional dynamics—of party and presidency—in the late 1960s. In this sense, the early Nixon presidency is important to the study not for its direct comparability to other cases, but for what it reveals about the evolution in thinking about the status of the presidency and the relationships among ideology, parties, and presidential leadership.[41]

The years between 1929 and 1938 carried over some of the characteristics of the Progressive period. Herbert Hoover and Franklin Roosevelt both struggled to negotiate the expectations and boundaries of an increasingly presidency-centered government. The Great Depression increased the demands on government and prompted Roosevelt to communicate directly with the electorate in order to explain and to reassure. The contours of the relationship between modern presidents and their parties also began to emerge during this time. Although the two parties remained distinct and strong, Franklin Roosevelt's new visions for the presidency went beyond party. He sought instead to strengthen bureaucratic capacity and to form a cross-partisan New Deal coalition.[42] Roosevelt's determination to work across party lines was partly derived of necessity; the traditional party of Southern conservatives and Northern bosses had, in the words of Milkis, "little use for the economic Constitutional order that FDR and his close advisors had begun to develop in the first term."[43] Dissent within his own party left the president with little choice but to foster a cross-party coalition in support of his plans. Ideological diversity within parties and the resultant need for cross-party coalitions came to be defining features of the modern era.

The Roosevelt presidency also continued the work of the Progressive Era by enhancing the president's administrative capacity and policy role, particularly through the creation of the Executive Office of the President in 1939. The presidency would become a more complex and powerful institution in addition to playing a more central role in proposing and promoting domestic policy, although negotiations with Congress over the reorganization of the executive branch also established the limits on the expansion of presidential power.[44] As questions were settled about what an empowered administrative presidency would look like, interbranch legitimacy struggles waned for a few decades and thereby lessened the need for mandate claims.

Finally, 1939 marks the official beginning of World War II. Although the United States would not participate in the war for two more years, the inception of world crisis also shaped the Roosevelt presidency. The Cold War provides a subtle backdrop for the high levels of presidential legitimacy during the modern era. After all, this era gave rise to Senator Arthur Vandenberg (R-MI)'s famous proclamation that "politics stops at the water's edge" as a frame for his cooperation with the Truman administration. Presidential scholar Aaron Wildavsky declared that, during this mid-century interlude, the office really encompassed "two presidencies," with presidents enjoying much greater success in Congress on foreign policy than on domestic issues.[45] The prevalence of these ideas about unity and deference enhanced the relatively high levels of institutional legitimacy that presidents enjoyed during the modern era.

These new, broad parameters of presidential legitimacy would not last indefinitely. Public trust in the presidency, and in government institutions generally, began to decline as the electorate became disillusioned with the Vietnam War and with Johnson's War on Poverty and its ramifications. Entering the White House in 1969, Nixon and his political advisers expressed much greater concern about the status of the presidency than did Johnson's White House team in 1965. The years during which Nixon, Gerald Ford, and Carter occupied the White House represent another transitional period for the presidency. In the wake of Watergate, the legitimacy of government, especially the presidency, declined. This period also produced major shifts in the party landscape. Taking advantage of backlash against Johnson-era policies, the Republican Party began to reach out to new constituencies, particularly in the South. The conservative movement grew stronger within the Republican Party. On the Democratic side, ambitious liberals— "Watergate babies"—joined Congress after the 1974 elections,[46] while the disintegration of the New Deal coalition has left Democratic presidents searching for mandate narratives in an increasingly partisan era.

The final era under consideration is the partisan era, a label borrowed from Skinner's assessment of presidential politics after 1980. Mandate rhetoric has become more prominent during this era. George W. Bush and Barack Obama both used more mandate rhetoric (in 2005 and 2009, respectively) than any of their predecessors, a trend that appears to be connected to the tenuous state of presidential legitimacy. The dynamics of presidential legitimacy in the partisan era reflect the depth of party polarization, with Republicans in the electorate reporting low levels of approval for Democratic presidents and Democrats registering high levels of disapproval for George W. Bush and Ronald Reagan (the "approval gap" for George H. W. Bush in 1989 was similar to Eisenhower's in 1953).[47] Polarization has prompted presidents to frame elections in a more partisan light than their earlier counterparts. However, polarization has not affected presidents of both parties in the same way. Despite the polarized politics of the era, the Bush administration occasionally proved effective at attracting support from the other side of the aisle. Antiterror efforts, including the invasion of Iraq, garnered Democratic votes in Congress. Bush also collaborated with Democrats, including the late Edward Kennedy (D-MA), to pass sweeping education reform in 2001. For the Democratic presidents, the situation has been different. Republican opposition to Bill Clinton was so intense that it culminated in the second presidential impeachment in American political history, despite his efforts to accommodate Republican priorities on issues such as welfare reform.

Congressional Republicans have also been highly organized in their opposition to the Obama administration, especially where budget issues are concerned.

Mandate rhetoric reflects the divergent experiences of Democratic and Republican presidents in the partisan era. Reagan and George W. Bush, confident in the dominance of their party's ideals, constructed focused mandate narratives around solidly conservative issues such as tax cuts and shrinking federal expenditures. Clinton and Obama also made expansive use of mandate rhetoric, but did so in connection with a wide range of issues, including the environment (in 1993), foreign policy (in 2009), and economic stimulus (in both 1993 and 2009), as well as more general themes such as "change." The net effect has been the development of two distinct conceptualizations of the presidency, a phenomenon that has some precedent in nineteenth-century history but less so in more recent times. In the 1830s, Andrew Jackson's Whig opponents objected as much to his strong presidential leadership as to the substance of "King Andrew's" policies.[48] The difference between contemporary Democrats and Republicans takes a more subtle form; Democrats remain both less organized and at least outwardly skeptical of unilateral presidential power.[49] In their mandate rhetoric, Republican presidents have been more overtly partisan and ideological, and have made bolder references to the strength of the presidency. Democrats, in contrast, have stressed particular policies as well as their commitment to carry out constituents' demands.

Finally, the division of the post-Progressive period into eras allows us to examine the evolution of the party system and the presidency, and to trace changes in the way presidents speak and think about electoral mandates. In each of these eras, this research considers institutional dynamics from a presidential perspective. Perceptions within the White House drive the progression between eras. Other temporal schemes identify a range of mechanisms for change: realignment theory points to changes in the electorate;[50] political time moves as presidents shatter old political orders and "reconstruct" new ones.[51] Standard theories of the modern presidency suggest that the enhanced capacity of the office after FDR distinguishes the modern office from its traditional counterpart. This research does not challenge the assertions that presidents themselves shape the political environment or that they also react to exogenous features of the political environment. However, the temporal scheme focuses on presidential perceptions of the political situation:

the extent of their institutional legitimacy, the expectations for performance, the limits on authority and power, and the benefits—and costs—of emphasizing party loyalty versus collaborating across party lines. These perceptions emanate from changes in objective conditions, including changes in the level of party polarization in Congress and the electorate, shifts in public opinion (especially about the presidency and the political system), and expanded institutional capacity. However, by focusing on how political conditions are perceived within the White House, this research offers a presidency-centered classification. This approach allows us to rigorously test the central claims of the book. If the primary purpose of mandate claims is to bolster legitimacy, then presidents' perceptions about their own legitimacy should predict their use of mandate rhetoric. Similarly, presidents' perceptions of party conflict and their relationships with their own parties should drive their use of mandate rhetoric, including its content. Presidential perspective is especially important to our understanding of the different definitions of mandate; if the theory is correct, then we should expect that presidents will define the mandate according to their own ideas about the challenges and requirements of presidential leadership.

Chapter 1

CHANGES IN MANDATE RHETORIC

From the Progressive Era to the Partisan Era

Between the presidencies of Herbert Hoover and Barack Obama, presidential mandate rhetoric has changed in frequency, context, and content. In the modern era, which began with a transition period under Hoover and Franklin Roosevelt, mandate rhetoric became relatively infrequent. When presidents did refer to election results, they invoked broad issues and, in many cases, presented the president as a national trustee. Modern presidents also tended to employ mandate rhetoric in major national addresses, in news conferences, or at partisan events. After the foundations of the modern era began to disintegrate with Nixon's election in 1968, it has become common for presidential communications to include mandate references (usually in at least 10 percent of the early communications), even among presidents whose victories would not traditionally be considered "landslide" elections. The contexts chosen for mandate rhetoric have expanded beyond inaugural and State of the Union addresses, with mandate references appearing in a steady percentage of news conferences, minor addresses, and remarks to members of the executive branch. Finally, a transformation in the content of mandate rhetoric has also occurred, with more efforts to present the president as a "delegate" of the people and more emphasis on specific policies and ideological themes.

The Data

The analysis presented in this chapter draws on an original data set created using the Public Papers of the Presidents (PPP) series, housed electronically by the American Presidency Project (APP) at the University of California at Santa Barbara. The data set covers presidential rhetoric during (roughly) the first seventy days of each elected term from 1929 through 2009 and encompasses 1,514 speeches, statements, and other communications from the terms of thirteen presidents: Herbert Hoover, Franklin Roosevelt (all four terms), Harry Truman, Dwight Eisenhower, John F. Kennedy, Lyndon Johnson, Richard Nixon, Jimmy Carter, Ronald Reagan, George H. W. Bush, Bill Clinton, George W. Bush, and Barack Obama. This collection includes presidential remarks and addresses from Inauguration Day through the end of the third month in office. For Herbert Hoover in 1929 and Franklin Roosevelt in 1933, the data begin on March 4 and ends on May 31. All other presidential terms in the data set began after the Twentieth Amendment moved Inauguration Day to January 20. Data collected for these terms include addresses through March 31. The data set includes six categories of communications: major addresses, minor addresses, news media, communications with other members of the government, remarks to party elites, and ceremonial communications.

Coding Procedures

Coding decisions reflect the answer to a single, crucial question: Does the president use the election result, the promises of the campaign, or the wishes of the electorate to justify policy action? Speeches or communications including a reference to electoral logic were coded "1," whereas those without were coded "0." Keywords, such as "mandate" and "election," and relevant synonyms qualified a speech as employing such rhetoric. The coding also takes into account context and meaning. Naturally, claims vary in their tone and strength. A handful of the 127 references to electoral logic in the overall data set refer to the election as a mandate. Most others draw on the idea of "doing what I was elected to do" or respecting the wishes of "the people who sent us here." A substantial number of claims defend policy choices with some variation of the statement "I campaigned on this."

In the forthcoming analysis, I use the percentage of communications with a mandate claim as the primary measure of whether a president used electoral logic rhetoric after an election. This method accounts for variation across administrations in the number of communications in the Public Papers of the Presidents and facilitates the assessment of the prominence of mandate claims in the overall communication strategy during the early, agenda-setting months of a presidential term. The continuous measurement of prominence allows for nuanced comparison between administrations over time. Evaluating how often the presidents relied on electoral logic, as opposed to other kinds of argumentation, to justify his actions clarifies the evolving priority of connecting policy and election results.

At certain times, presidents have placed great emphasis on the election result as a motivation for policy choices. At other times, presidents spoke very little about the election or the campaign. The data presented in Table 1.1 reveal substantial variation in presidents' use of mandate language. Some of this variation exists between different terms served by the same president. For example, Bill Clinton used substantially more mandate language after his 1992 victory than after his 1996 reelection, whereas George W. Bush used more mandate rhetoric after his reelection in 2004 than after the controversial 2000 election. John F. Kennedy is the only president in the data set to have used no mandate rhetoric, and Franklin Roosevelt did not use mandate claims after his reelections in 1940 and 1944. On the other end of the spectrum, George W. Bush and Barack Obama used mandate rhetoric the most frequently. More than one quarter of Bush's communications included mandate rhetoric, whereas 18 percent of Obama's included mandate references.

Changes in the Frequency of Mandate Rhetoric

The use of mandate rhetoric varies substantially across eras. As Table 1.1 shows, the percentage of presidential communications with mandate claims dropped in the middle of the twentieth century. During the FDR presidency,

Table 1.1. Presidential mandate claims, 1929–2009

Presidential term	Total communications Jan. 20–Mar. 31	Total number of mandate claims	Percentage with mandate rhetoric
Hoover	47	5	10.6
FDR1	32	1	3.1
FDR2	23	2	8.7
FDR3	17	0	0
FDR4	11	0	0
Truman	38	2	5.3
Eisenhower1	24	3	12.5
Eisenhower2	26	1	3.8
Kennedy	69	0	0
Johnson	94	2	2.1
Nixon1	101	6	5.9
Nixon2	62	5	8.1
Carter	82	7	8.6
Reagan1	68	7	10.2
Reagan2	96	8	8.3
GHWBush	85	12	14.1
Clinton1	156	14	8.9
Clinton2	135	1	.74
GWBush1	137	5	3.6
GWBush2	73	21	28.7
Obama	138	25	18.1
Total	1,514	127	

the office underwent a transition from the uncertainty and innovation of the Progressive Era to a more established pattern of strong presidential government in the modern presidency. Roosevelt's first two terms were especially important in permanently expanding the president's sphere of influence. This transition took place through the creation of a more institutionalized White House bureaucracy as well as efforts to lead—even to dominate—the policy process and to speak more regularly to the electorate. As early as FDR's third term, the power and status of the office had been altered, a development that lasted through the late 1960s.

Beginning with Nixon's first term in 1969, however, the trend was reversed. Since that time, mandate rhetoric has become a regular fixture of presidential discourse. This pattern holds for Republican and Democratic presidents, and for periods of both divided and unified government. In other words, a shift that transcends immediate political conditions appears to have occurred. What changed were the broad institutional contours of the presidency. Although the formal expansion of government has continued apace, the informal dimensions of presidential legitimacy have changed. The 1960s and 1970s revealed the possibilities for a powerful executive to deceive the public, to pursue unpopular foreign policy, and to break the law.

Election results do not explain the observed change in mandate rhetoric. In Table 1.2, we see that all three measures of election results are weakly and negatively correlated with the frequency of mandate rhetoric. In fact, when we examine presidents elected under similar circumstances in different eras, we observe change over time. Two sets of comparisons are instructive. First, changes in mandate rhetoric are evident among presidents elected by decisive margins, with strong victories for their parties in Congress and state-level races. This group includes Franklin Roosevelt in 1932 and 1936, Lyndon Johnson in 1964, Ronald Reagan in 1980, and Barack Obama in 2008. In each case, the president won with a majority of the popular vote, with at least 60 percent of the Electoral College vote, and with a margin of 7 percent or more. Each election also saw significant gains for the president's party in Congress; the 1980 elections delivered control of the Senate to the Republicans after nearly thirty years out of power, and after 2008 the Democrats briefly enjoyed a "filibuster-proof" majority. These cases, of course, are not identical. Roosevelt and Johnson won significantly larger vote shares than did Reagan and Obama. Unlike the other presidents, Johnson's landslide did not occur during an economic crisis or downturn, and the Kennedy assassination in 1963 made the context for Johnson's election in 1964

Table 1.2. Predictors of mandate rhetoric

Political factors	Correlation
Popular vote share	−.04
Popular vote margin	−.09
Electoral College vote share	−.13
Public approval (n = 16)	−.45
Polarization	.53

unique. Yet, from the perspective of conventional mandate theories, each of these cases fits the basic model.

Despite important similarities in electoral circumstances, these presidents demonstrated considerable variation in the way they used mandate rhetoric. Franklin Roosevelt's mandate claims occurred with moderate frequency; he made few claims, but had fewer communications overall compared to later presidents. Between his inauguration and the end of March 1965, Johnson had ninety-four communications compared to only fifty-five for Roosevelt during comparable periods in 1933 and 1937 combined. However, as Johnson introduced the agenda for his first elected term, he rarely invoked the result of the 1964 contest. Johnson gave news conferences and made statements and a variety of other remarks—including several messages to Congress about the key issues of the administration: voting rights and the social programs that would constitute the Great Society. Although neither Ronald Reagan nor Barack Obama attained the landslide conditions that Roosevelt and Johnson enjoyed, both presidents made much more extensive use of mandate rhetoric. At the start of Reagan's first term in 1981, the idea of the 1980 election as a mandate for conservative economic policies took hold as an important narrative, appearing in 10 percent of Reagan's overall speeches and messages. Yet, as some scholars have pointed out, the 1980 election was no more clearly a "mandate" than the 1936 or 1965;[1] on the contrary, Reagan won less than 51 percent of the popular vote. In 1984, his vote share was in the range of those enjoyed by Roosevelt and Johnson, with a 58 percent landslide, but the Republicans made modest congressional gains and the House of Representatives remained under Democratic control. Nevertheless, Reagan drew on both elections as a central justification for policy choices. The example of Barack Obama after the 2008 elections illustrates yet another variation on the general landslide theme. Obama's share of the popular vote, at 53 percent, was a more definitive majority than Reagan's in 1980, but still fell short of the landslide standard established by Roosevelt and Johnson. Similarly, Obama's margin of victory over Republican John McCain, at seven points, was respectable but certainly not a "blowout" along the lines of the 1936 and 1964 contests. Obama did not bill the election as such. However, his rhetorical emphasis on the election and campaign promises exceeded that of Reagan; nearly 20 percent of his communications in early 2009 included a mandate reference.

A similar pattern holds among presidents elected under more narrow circumstances. Let us now compare three presidents who won office with extremely narrow margins and without winning a majority of popular votes: John F. Kennedy in 1960, Richard Nixon in 1968, and George W. Bush in 2000. John F. Kennedy, after winning an extremely close contest with Richard Nixon, eschewed mandate rhetoric altogether. In this group, the turning point occurred with Nixon's own narrow victory over Hubert Humphrey in 1968. As in the 1948 election, the presence of a relatively successful third-party candidate deprived both major candidates of a majority victory. The race was also extremely close, with Nixon winning with a margin of less than 1 percent. Furthermore, Nixon's victory did not bring major coattails for congressional races. Republicans picked up a modest five House seats and a more impressive seven seats in the Senate, but Congress remained under Democratic control by comfortable margins. Yet, despite lacking the indicators of a personal or party mandate, Nixon made regular references to the promises of his campaign and the reasons for his election throughout his early first-term communications. Mandate rhetoric appeared in almost 6 percent of his overall communications between his inauguration and the end of March 1969. Finally, the case of George W. Bush's rhetoric about the 2000 election is particularly illustrative of the changing politics of the presidential mandate. By most conventional definitions, Bush had little grounds to claim a mandate. The presidential election ended in a tie and was ultimately resolved by a Supreme Court decision, more than a month after votes were cast. The divided nature of the electorate was also evident in the results of congressional races, many of which were quite close and which resulted in small margins of control in both chambers (indeed, the Senate was evenly divided between Republicans and Democrats). Despite the ambiguity of the election outcome, Bush referred on several occasions to the "reasons I was elected" and attempted to justify policy decisions in those terms. Accounting for about 3 percent of Bush's overall communications in the early months of 2001, efforts to define the 2000 election as a policy mandate were still modest compared to Bush's own response to winning a majority in 2004, or Obama's in 2008. But it is still striking in comparison to Kennedy's reserve after the 1960 election. The comparison with Nixon is more complicated. Bush used mandate rhetoric less frequently than Nixon, and Nixon arguably had a more credible argument that the election result had signaled voters' desire for a change in political direction. Although Nixon's own messages of law and order, peace with honor, and a more conservative approach to governance garnered only 43 percent of the vote, when combined with the 13 percent won by George Wallace, the presidential vote reflected a more widespread preference for change. Furthermore, the 2000 election actually brought Republican *losses* in congressional races. In sum, the 1968 and 2000 elections were among the most difficult to define objectively as mandates, for either president or party. Nevertheless, Nixon and Bush used mandate rhetoric at rates that resemble—and in some cases, exceed—those of landslide presidents in the modern era.

Mandate Rhetoric and Political Conditions

Election results do not explain which presidents have used mandate rhetoric most frequently. However, we have reason to believe that the use of mandate rhetoric varies systematically. The theory proposed in the introduction suggests that presidents use mandate rhetoric in response to changing institutional relationships; in this framework, the expansion of mandate rhetoric can be attributed to the declining status of the presidency and the polarization of the party system. The findings in this section provide preliminary support for these hypotheses.

Perceived legitimacy and status of the office are difficult to observe and to measure. Public approval of individual presidents, examined in aggregate, serves as a useful proxy, however. As we see in Table 1.2, public approval has a negative relationship with frequency of mandate rhetoric. After 1969, average approval ratings have dropped for presidents at the start of their terms. The sole exception to this rule is Barack Obama in 2009. As Table 1.3 shows, public approval has declined more or less steadily since its high point in 1961 (with the exception of a brief resurgence for Carter in 1977).

Individual circumstances help to explain these two outliers. Jimmy Carter and Barack Obama both used substantial mandate rhetoric, despite relatively high levels of popularity early in their terms (1977 and 2009, respectively). In Carter's case, although his personal popularity was relatively high, he came to office with the weight of Watergate, in addition to that of a political party divided by the bold policy action of the last Democratic president. As a result, Carter cast about for both a clear agenda and a narra-

Table 1.3. Public Approval of the President, 1949–2009

Presidential term	Average public approval from inauguration through March 31
Truman	61.5
Eisenhower1	69
Eisenhower2	70.25
Kennedy	72
Johnson	69.25
Nixon1	61
Nixon2	59.75
Carter	69.84
Reagan1	57.34
Reagan2	59
GHWBush	58.2
Clinton1	54
Clinton2	58.4
WBush1	57.8
WBush2	51.6
Obama	63.3

Source: Public approval ratings from Presidential Approval Data, APP. Averages compiled by author.

tive to reestablish presidential legitimacy, a process that is elucidated in chapter 4. Like Carter, Obama had made many policy promises during the campaign and came into office as the first Democrat since the Georgia governor to win a majority in the popular vote. In other words, Obama had to develop his own script about the meaning behind a Democratic electoral majority. Obama also faced well-organized opposition early in his presidency. In sum, both outliers suggest that although the overall trend in public opinion indicates declining legitimacy, the tasks of justifying presidential action and balancing governing imperatives with party priorities are often highly complex.

The second indicator of presidential legitimacy is the salience of foreign policy issues. The logic of foreign policy salience as an indicator of legitimacy is that concern about foreign crisis tends to rally the public to the president's side. In addition, foreign policy salience has a temporal dimension.

Examination of Gallup poll data reveals that foreign policy issues were cited more frequently during the height of the Cold War. Citizens expressed concern about foreign policy matters, such as relations with Russia—a common response when Kennedy took office in 1961.[2] For Johnson and Nixon, the Vietnam War emerged at the top of the list.[3] Starting with Carter in 1977, the public's policy priorities for new (and reelected) presidents have taken a decided turn toward the domestic, with 2005 and the Iraq War the only exception.[4] Once again, this connection helps to explain some cases, such as Kennedy and Johnson. Its logic also applies to Franklin Roosevelt in 1941 and 1944, when no mandate language was used. However, this finding also raises questions about the rhetorical decisions of Richard Nixon and George W. Bush.

Richard Nixon took office at a time when foreign policy was highly salient, and Bush was reelected while the global War on Terror remained a major factor in the minds of the electorate. Defying the pattern, both leaders made extensive use of mandate rhetoric, albeit to justify their domestic agendas. From a legitimacy standpoint, the Bush case is particularly puzzling. Terrorism and the war in Iraq were highly salient during 2004.[5] The Kerry campaign tried to challenge the administration's policies and failed to gain traction.[6] This evidence is further suggestive of the relationship between weakness and mandate claims: Nixon and Bush may have preferred to use mandate rhetoric to bolster their domestic credibility, an area in which Republicans have traditionally been weaker, rather than to connect the election result to areas in which Republican presidents have generally been strong.

Polarization

The second political condition that distinguishes the post-1969 era is party polarization. Deepening divisions between the two parties have manifested themselves in a variety of ways: ideological sorting in the electorate, party divisions in public approval of the president's performance, and changes in elite behavior. For the purposes of this analysis, I employ a simple and elite-oriented measure, using roll-call voting scores.[7] Polarization is defined as the difference between the roll-call scores of the Republican and Democratic members during a given Congress.[8] Polarization is positively correlated with the use of mandate rhetoric, as seen in Table 1.2. The connection between polarization and timing is likewise straightforward. According to the roll-call measure, congressional polarization has increased more or less steadily since the Seventy-fifth Congress, which began in 1937.

Several potential causal mechanisms connect mandate rhetoric and polarization. Under more polarized conditions, candidates may find it easier to differentiate themselves from their opponents and thus feel more justified in claiming a mandate for a specific policy or direction. We may observe an anticipatory phenomenon: as presidents anticipate polarization in the next Congress and in the electorate (and observe it as the term unfolds), mandate claiming may serve as way of defining and unifying the party agenda when bipartisan compromise seems unlikely.

Changing Audiences

Presidents use mandate rhetoric across a wide variety of audiences and contexts. Mandate claims are uttered in response to journalists' questions and in highly scripted public speeches. They are used in high-profile inaugural and State of the Union speeches and in remarks before Cabinet departments. They are included in addresses prepared for audiences throughout the country, and those written for party fund-raisers and retreats. Examination of venue and audience reveals new patterns of change over time and accentuates several distinct purposes for mandate rhetoric: setting policy priorities, persuading receptive audiences, and dealing with challenges to presidential ideas and authority.

Major Addresses

Compared with the volume of other communications, the number of major policy addresses has remained fairly low since 1929. During the first seventy days in office, presidents occasionally give televised policy addresses, including one before a joint session of Congress in January or February. Most presidents since Ronald Reagan have followed his lead in also delivering a weekly radio address. In all four eras, mandate claims were relatively uncommon in these addresses. Eisenhower, Nixon, Bush, and Clinton included election references in their respective 1953, 1973, 1989, and 1997 State of the

Union addresses. The relative rarity of mandate claims in State of the Union speeches defies common intuition. In addition to their high profile—particularly for newly elected or reelected leaders—they remain an important venue in which presidents establish priorities and frame policy initiatives. Communications scholars Karlyn Kohrs Campbell and Kathleen Hall Jamieson note that "by the sheer fact of its delivery, the address reminds the country that presidents have a unique role in our system of government. They are to view questions in the aggregate and as they pertain to the whole—to the Union. They must report to and advise Congress, the diverse representatives of the people of all states and regions, all of which implies that the presidency gives its occupant a unique, national vantage point."[9] In major addresses, presidents address broad policy priorities and establish agendas; we should expect that mandate rhetoric associated with those purposes will appear in major speeches.[10]

Minor Addresses

The minor address category consists of three types of presidential communications. First are those speeches made in the course of presidential travel, delivered to live audiences rather than a national audience through television or radio.[11] Second are those delivered to organized nongovernmental groups, such as the American Medical Association or the League of Women Voters. Third are miscellaneous statements and remarks. As with local addresses, miscellaneous statements have shown a marked increase over time. However, organized group addresses have remained relatively stable in number through the eighty-year period surveyed.

This group contains many more speeches, statements, and remarks than the major addresses category. However, these communications are more varied in purpose and certainly attract less media attention. The minor address category is an important diagnostic tool in understanding the changing use of mandate rhetoric. The use of mandate claims in minor speeches, remarks, and statements illustrates the pervasiveness of the concept in presidential rhetoric and thought. In other words, mandate claims in minor speeches and remarks are not merely rhetorical flourishes added to televised addresses. Rather, they reflect the way that the logic of the electoral mandate has become integrated into presidential narratives about why they undertake policy actions.

Media Communications

This category includes presidential news conferences as well as one-on-one interviews, appearances on news shows, and remarks to reporters. As with minor addresses, communications in this category have increased over time. From Hoover to Carter, each newly elected (or reelected) president engaged with the media ten or fewer times during the period under consideration. From Reagan through Obama, ten has been the minimum number of media exchanges during the first seventy days of each new term. At the higher end of communications, Clinton conversed with the media sixty-eight times after taking office in 1993, mostly in exchanges with reporters prior to meetings with other U.S. officials or foreign leaders.

The relationship between the president and the news media is an expansive topic that deserves much more attention than it receives in this work.[12] For the purposes of this analysis, electoral logic rhetoric in news settings has two distinctive features. First, reporters can pose questions about a wide range of topics, creating opportunities for presidents to link issues to the campaign or election outside of their usual mandate narrative. Second, presidential responses to press questions are often defensive. Reporters challenge presidential choices, sometimes echoing the objections of critics and asking presidents to respond. The presidential tendency to talk about elections and campaign promises in their responses demonstrates a previously under theorized purpose of such rhetoric.

Government Communications

The communications in this category, although part of the public record, were not necessarily aimed at a public audience. Rather than the president's efforts to guide public opinion, these communications signal the logic by which presidents sought to sway others in governing positions. This category includes remarks to various other government officials, such as governors and mayors associations and members of the executive branch, and policy messages to Congress other than the State of the Union. The category also comprises signing statements and veto messages. As with minor addresses, the use of mandate claims in these venues, directed at governing officials, reveals the extent to which mandate logic has become part of presidential governance.

Partisan Speeches

The partisan category encompasses remarks made before congressional delegations from the president's party, at party dinners and fund-raisers, and other organized party events. Like major addresses, party events and fund-raisers remain sparse in the public papers throughout the entire time period. However, in light of the posited relationship between mandate claims and president-party relationships, this group of speeches is particularly significant.

Ceremonial Speeches

The final category includes ceremonial and symbolic addresses. This category includes inaugural addresses as well as presidential speeches at events such as the National Prayer Breakfast, ceremonies honoring individuals, and dedication ceremonies. Some of these speeches—especially, but not exclusively, inaugural addresses—include some policy content, and thus warrant inclusion in the data set.

Change and Continuity

The primary theme of this analysis is change. However, some patterns have persisted across eras. These areas of continuity also contribute to our understanding of how presidents use mandate rhetoric, and ultimately to the theory about why it has changed over time. Figure 1.1 shows the proportions of each communication category that included mandate rhetoric, broken down

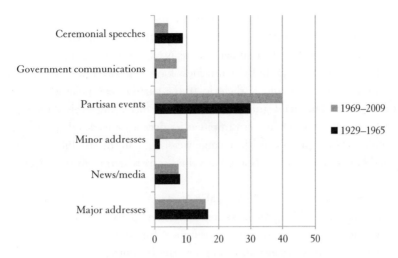

Figure 1.1. Mandate rhetoric by audience

by era. The two eras are similar in terms of major speeches and media inter-actions; in both eras, about 16 percent of major addresses included a mandate reference and around 8 percent of media interactions included one. In the other categories, the distinction between the two eras becomes apparent.

In the modern era, mandate rhetoric was mainly featured in four of the six categories: major speeches, media interactions, speeches at partisan gath-erings, and ceremonial addresses (namely, inaugural addresses). Minor ad-dresses and intragovernmental communications featured much less mandate rhetoric. Of the fifteen mandate claims made between 1929 and 1965, five occurred in the context of a news conference, two in nationally broadcast speeches, three at partisan events, and two in inaugural addresses (falling under the ceremonial heading). The major addresses that included mandate rhetoric were Franklin Roosevelt's March 1937 "fireside chat"—a major ra-dio address—and Eisenhower's 1953 State of the Union address.[13] Presidents using mandate language in press conferences included Hoover and Eisen-hower (twice each) and Johnson (once). Mandate claims directed at partisan audiences are concentrated in the earlier part of this era, when they were used by FDR and Truman at Democratic dinners. Similarly, Hoover and FDR used mandate rhetoric in their inaugural speeches in 1929 and 1933, respectively.

Several patterns have theoretical significance. First, the concentration of mandate rhetoric in news conferences and partisan events, which accounts for more than half of the mandate claims used in the modern period, suggests that partisanship and defensiveness have long been part of the way that presidents use mandate rhetoric. In the partisan era, polarization and declining institutional legitimacy have inspired increasing levels of mandate rhetoric, but the venue pattern from earlier decades suggests that this relationship existed previously; the change we observe in the late 1960s and beyond has resulted from a change in values rather than from the effects of the explanatory variables.

Second, modern-era presidents also used mandate claims in a variety of communications. Alongside news conferences and party dinners, they talked about election results, sometimes even including the word "mandate," as they introduced policy agendas and proposals. In contrast, mandate rhetoric rarely appeared in minor addresses or communications with Congress and other governing elites. In the absence of direct insight into the motivation of presidents or speechwriters, these data are merely suggestive. However, the use of mandate rhetoric in major and ceremonial addresses, along with its sparseness in minor and behind-the-scenes communication, suggests that at that time, mandate claiming served more as a rhetorical flourish than as an established tenet of institutional logic.

As in the modern era, partisan-era presidents included mandate claims in a wide variety of communication genres. However, we observe some new patterns in this era. The first major area for growth in mandate rhetoric was in major addresses. Of the 127 communications that included mandate rhetoric, only eight were nationally broadcast (via radio or television) speeches. Only three of these were State of the Union addresses: one of Nixon's five policy messages to Congress in 1973, George H. W. Bush's address to Congress in 1989, and Bill Clinton's 1997 address after his reelection in 1996.

Interestingly, all three of these speeches were addressed to a Congress controlled by the opposing party, and the content of the rhetoric reflected this difference. George H. W. Bush told the Democratic Congress in 1989, "The people didn't send us here to bicker, and now it's time to govern."[14] Similarly, Bill Clinton urged a Republican-controlled legislature in 1997 to consider "inaction" the real enemy of the country, reminding them that "we must work together. The people of this Nation elected us all. They want us to be partners, not partisans. They put us all right here in the same boat, they gave us all oars, and they told us to row. Now here is the direction I believe we should take."[15]

As a small, but politically significant, segment of the mandate claims in the data set, these statements underscore the connection between mandate rhetoric and challenging situations. After winning a solid majority against opponent Michael Dukakis, George Bush struggled to find common ground with congressional Democrats. Clinton's political circumstances were even more difficult. The 1996 contest between Clinton and his Republican opponent, Robert Dole, was not close. But Clinton's share of the popular vote fell just short of a majority, making him only the second president to be elected twice with a plurality of the vote. Turnout was low, and Clinton's second term began facing a hostile Republican Congress— one that would eventually impeach him. Under these circumstances, it made sense to highlight the national standing and influence of the presidency, in hopes of enhancing presidential stature and setting the stage to depict congressional opponents as shortsighted partisans for obstructing the agenda.

The use of the mandate claims in news media represents both continuity and change. Although the proportion of media interactions that included mandate rhetoric was similar in the two eras, partisan-era presidents have had far more media interactions (242 compared with 53), thus accounting for some of the increase in overall mandate claiming. Interviews and news conferences account for a significant portion of the mandate claims made by partisan-era presidents—twenty-five instances in all. The tone and subject of many of these claims illustrate the point about mandate rhetoric as a defense against a challenge or criticism. For example, in an interview with PBS's Jim Lehrer on February 27, 2009, Obama invoked electoral logic to respond to a question about resistance to the president's Iraq policy.

In a different context, George W. Bush similarly used mandate logic in response to a reporter's question about whether he had lived up to his promises of bipartisanship (four days after taking office). Bush replied, "It is in recognition of what a Presidential campaign is all about. I don't believe Dick and I would be sitting here had we not taken strong positions on key issues. And I told the American people if I had the honor of being the President, I would submit those positions I was campaigning on to the legislative branch, and that's exactly what I've done."[16] The role of mandate claims as defensive rhetoric is one of the important themes of the partisan era, as presidents manage a critical and increasingly omnipresent media, a polarized political environment, and fluctuating levels of trust in government.

Two categories account for most of the rise in the frequency of mandate rhetoric in the partisan era: intragovernment communications and minor speeches. Beginning with Nixon, electoral logic became a consistent feature of presidential communications with members of the executive branch. For his own part, Nixon invoked the logic of fulfilling campaign promises in remarks about the patronage and the appointment of postmasters, about increasing expenditures for science research, and about policies to promote business growth. More recently, Reagan, George H. W. Bush, Clinton, and Obama have all used the rhetoric of electoral logic in their communications with members of the executive branch, often referring to the connection between proposed policy and the fulfillment of campaign promises. By comparing the use of mandate language in messages to Congress versus that aimed at members of the executive branch, we can also assess the extent to which the mandate plays a role in presidential persuasion across institutional boundaries, as opposed to within them. In other words, the literature on presidential mandates often identifies this concept as a bargaining chip used by presidents to persuade Congress.

In addresses to subnational government audiences, we observe a variety of situations and claims. For example, Reagan addressed the National League of Cities Conference on March 2, 1981, and remarked:

> As you're well aware, rejuvenation of the American economy is the number one priority of my administration. This, I believe, was the mandate of the voters last November. It was a mandate that I sought, yet something all elected officials should understand, because it's a mandate for all of us. The election did not commission me to attempt economic reform alone, but to work with elected officials—Federal, State, and local—to put America's economic house in order. And that's why I'm here.

Before what was presumably a more ideologically sympathetic crowd, Clinton referenced the 1992 election at a Democratic Governors Association dinner on February 1, 1993:

As you and I learned from the elections last year, the American people want their political system and their Government to end gridlock, to face problems, and to make progress. They're tired of a process that's been too divided by partisanship or dominated by special interests or driven by short-term advantage of politicians instead of the long-term interests of people. They sent us to the statehouse and to the White House to change America. And they want action now. That is our mandate, and we must never forget it.

The second major growth area for mandate rhetoric in the partisan era was the minor address. In the modern era, less than 2 percent of minor and miscellaneous communications included a mandate reference; in the partisan era, 10 percent included one. The composition of this category itself has changed. As levels of presidential travel, accompanied by local speeches and interactive "town hall meetings," have increased, presidents have used these opportunities to share their interpretations of election results and to connect their policies to campaign promises. This trend has been particularly true among the later presidents in the partisan era. George W. Bush's tour of a number of cities to promote Social Security reform accounted for about half the mandate claims he made at the start of the second term. Similarly, Clinton made nearly a third of his 1993 mandate claims at town meetings and other forums while on the road.

Speeches at partisan events show a moderate increase in the frequency of mandate claims, from 30 to 40 percent. This pattern is consistent with the theory of institutional—specifically party—change. As the parties have become more polarized and more ideologically sorted, it stands to reason that presidents would offer narratives about elections as party mandates, and partisan events constitute natural venues for such stories. We observe that this connection was also true during the modern era, at least in the cases of Franklin Roosevelt and Harry Truman. Although partisan speeches were the most likely among the six categories to include mandate rhetoric, these communications do not account for the recent rise in mandate rhetoric. Presidential appearances at party dinners, gatherings for congressional delegations, and party fund-raisers have remained relatively stable throughout the period covered by the data set. Ten of the twenty-one presidential terms featured no such communications in the first seventy days—five in the modern era and five in the partisan era. Among the remaining terms, presidents made between one and three speeches to a party audience. Compared with media interactions, minor addresses, and government communications, party speeches account for a relatively small percentage of mandate rhetoric during the later period.

Finally, in one category of communications, the use of mandate rhetoric has declined over time. This change occurred in ceremonial addresses and remarks, where later presidents have increased the number of communications but have not included mandate rhetoric. Looking exclusively at inaugural speeches (for which the denominator is fixed and thus similar in both eras), the use of mandate rhetoric is more even. As in the modern era, two partisan-era presidents chose to include interpretations of the election in their inaugural addresses. One was Ronald Reagan in 1985, who said, "We must never again abuse the trust of working men and women by sending their earnings on a futile chase after the spiraling demands of a bloated Federal Establishment. You elected us in 1980 to end this prescription for disaster, and I don't believe you reelected us in 1984 to reverse course." The other was Bill Clinton, who emphasized the election's message for change after defeating Reagan's successor, George H. W. Bush:

> The American people have summoned the change we celebrate today. You have raised your voices in an unmistakable chorus. You have cast your votes in historic numbers. And you have changed the face of Congress, the Presidency, and the political process itself. Yes, you, my fellow Americans, have forced the spring. Now we must do the work the season demands. To that work I now turn with all the authority of my office. I ask the Congress to join with me. But no President, no Congress, no Government can undertake this mission alone.

As with the major address category, inaugural addresses are not the locus of the age of mandate politics. Presidents are no more—or less—likely to interpret elections in the context of a highly visible address.

The six different categories present distinct facets of the president's institutional identity. In areas where mandate rhetoric is more prominent—communications with news media, minor addresses, and most recently, communications with the executive branch—we observe several distinct political phenomena. We see how mandate claims are sometimes used defensively in presidential rhetoric to respond to reporters' questions and challenges. The political significance of mandate rhetoric is not limited to defense against criticism, however. Speeches to local crowds and remarks or memoranda to top executive officials reveal the role of mandate logic in presidential decisions, as well as in the creation of narratives about the basis of policy and legitimate executive rule. Local addresses represent the public face of these endeavors. They are also plainly political and plebiscitary, bringing the president close to the people. In the context of communications with the executive branch, presidential mandate claims reveal the extent to which electoral logic pervades governance, particularly in the partisan era.

Changing Content

We have seen how mandate rhetoric has become a more routine feature of presidential communications, and how it has grown more pervasive in government communications and minor speeches. In this section, we will see how the content of mandate rhetoric has also changed. Mandate rhetoric has become more specific in its policy content, invoking distinct policies rather than general ideas. The treatment of partisan and ideological themes in mandate rhetoric has changed as well, in a more complicated way. Mandate rhetoric has also changed in its presentation of presidential leadership; it has become more defensive and more likely to present the president as a delegate rather than as a trustee of the electorate.

These changes signify a shift in the way leaders think about elections. After an election, questions arise about whether it was won on broad governing principles, policy specifics, or idiosyncratic factors (such as campaign gaffes or candidate qualities). Election results also often invite speculation and argument about whether they conferred a party victory or a demand for cross-party cooperation. Some elections lend themselves to fairly straightforward interpretations, whereas others have more ambiguity; in all cases, some room exists for leaders to manipulate the narrative. Their choices for doing so have changed over time, irrespective of the particular details of each election. On a deeper level, the use of mandate rhetoric to justify narrow policy decisions and the increased use of "delegate" rhetoric suggest a greater emphasis on the potential for elections to inform governance.

Specificity of Policy Content

During the modern era, presidents generally linked the election results to broad ideas, including party principles. Hoover, Roosevelt, Truman, and Eisenhower all touted their victories as endorsements of basic party positions. Hoover spelled out the specific provisions in the platform that he believed had been important in the 1928 election and thus would pursue in office; the others approached the subject with varying degrees of abstraction. In keeping with the context, Roosevelt suggested that the 1932 election had been a mandate not for the specific policies of the New Deal but rather for action and a change in direction. Similarly (but without the Depression backdrop), Eisenhower framed the 1952 election in terms of a broad list of goals for the nation.

In the transition to the partisan era, this adherence to broad ideas began to change. Since 1969, electoral logic rhetoric has contained a mix of general principles (both partisan and nonpartisan, as the next section explores) and specific policies. For example, Nixon framed the 1968 election as an agreement between himself and the electorate to do the following specific and largely unrelated things: improve government support for scientific research, reform the U.S. Post Office Department, promote private ownership, listen more carefully to the preferences of North Atlantic Treaty Organization (NATO) allies, and cut the federal budget. From Reagan through Obama, mandate rhetoric generally included a mix of specific policies, such as Social Security reform (George W. Bush) or withdrawing troops from Iraq on a timeline (Obama), and general policy principles or broad goals, such as change or economic recovery. These findings are summarized in Tables 1.4 and 1.5.

Some partisan-era presidents also tend, as the Nixon example just given illustrates, to claim electoral logic behind a number of different, and often apparently unconnected, policy issues. Nixon, Carter, George H. W. Bush, Clinton, and Obama used electoral logic to defend a combination of economic, social, and even (in rare cases) foreign policy positions. Reagan

Table 1.4. Policy issues in mandate rhetoric, 1929–1965

Term	Specific	General
Hoover	Republican platform (specifically enumerated), farm relief, limited tariff reform	
FDR1		Change, general solution to economic problems
FDR2		Party victory, government protection from effects of the depression
Truman		Party platform, interests of the people over those of special interests
Eisenhower1	Farm policy, balanced budget	General goals for the administration
Eisenhower2		General party mandate
LBJ	Medicare	Fighting racism

Note: Italics signify divided government at the start of the term.

and George W. Bush, on the other hand, remained focused in their mandate rhetoric, framing their respective elections in very consistent ways. Reagan depicted both the 1980 and 1984 elections as primarily about economic issues. Bush focused his 2001 mandate rhetoric on tax cuts, and in 2005, most references to the 2004 campaign concerned Bush's position on Social Security reform. In Reagan's case, focusing mandate claims on a single, broad issue proved to be part of an effective messaging strategy. For Bush, the focus on a single policy was less successful; his plan to change Social Security never gained traction in Congress, and Bush missed an opportunity to shape and to define policy after a strong Republican victory in 2004.

The recent emphasis on smaller, more specific policy issues suggests a connection between party evolution and mandate politics. This shift has been especially noticeable among Democrats. FDR, Truman, and Johnson appealed to values such as unity, freedom, and justice, whereas Carter, Clinton, and Obama spoke very specifically about public demand for action on particular policies; these included salient issues, such as the economy,

Table 1.5. Policy issues in mandate rhetoric, 1969–2009

Term	Specific	General
Nixon1	Post Office Department reform, science research, private property ownership, listening to NATO allies, budget cuts	Represent the entire nation
Nixon2	Drug control, toughness on crime, keeping prices and taxes down, budget control	
Carter	Energy conservation, gas deregulation, zero-based budgeting, executive branch reorganization, election reform, foreign policy (toward USSR), tax reform	
Reagan1		Economic improvement, government efficiency
Reagan2	Lower taxes, lower government spending	Economic growth
GHWBush	Education, drug policy, environmental policy (acid rain), deficit and tax reduction	Strong governance,
Clinton1	Shrinking White House staff, technology policy, economic stimulus bill, White House office on environmental policy, health care reform	Economy, ending "gridlock," active and efficient government, change in direction of government
Clinton2		Working with congressional Republicans
GWBush1	Tax cuts, missile defense system and arms reductions	Leadership
GWBush2	Social Security reform, extensive enumerated party agenda (including Social Security reform, privatization of other social services, education reform)	Presidential authority
Obama	Plan for federal budget, stem cell research, support for biofuels, tax cut for working families, national service programs, TARP program, ending "enhanced interrogation techniques," removing troops from Iraq	Change in government direction, ideas about political economy

Note: Italics signify divided government at the start of the term.

foreign policy, and the environment, and more obscure procedural and administrative concerns. One plausible explanation for this change is the decline in the status of the Democratic Party. During the modern period, Democratic ideas were dominant, even ascendant leading up to Lyndon Johnson's 1964 victory. In the later period, Democratic ideas about economic justice and the potential for government programs to address society's problems have fallen out of favor. Republican mandate rhetoric about economic inefficiency, privatization, and limiting the role of government also coincides with this development.

The turn toward policy specificity in mandate rhetoric is also consistent with the hypothesis that the growth of such rhetoric constitutes a response to the declining status of the presidency. Nixon and Carter, at the nadir of the presidency's institutional status, stand out even among partisan presidents for linking the election to very narrow and specific policy issues. Neither claimed an electoral mandate for sweeping change or broad approaches to governance. Rather, institutional weakness led these leaders to focus on narrower issues and to justify these actions in terms of campaign promises and election results. Despite the low prestige of the Nixon and Carter presidencies, this logic has persisted through the partisan era, in which presidents often interpret elections more narrowly and use campaign promises to justify minor policy decisions.

Treatment of Party Themes

When interpreting election results, presidents have a choice about whether to emphasize issues that speak to the party base or to try to link the election rhetorically to more centrist and broadly appealing policies. On the whole, mandate rhetoric in the partisan era has featured about half partisan themes and half national themes, whereas the modern era has demonstrated about two-thirds partisan and one-third national themes. However, when we look more closely at the data from each era, a different picture emerges.

To assess this factor, all mandate rhetoric in the data set was classified as either partisan/ideological or nonpartisan. Claims were categorized as partisan if presidents mentioned the party directly, if they referred to the distinct positions of the two candidates or parties in the campaign, or if they invoked a policy position associated with their own party platform. If they mentioned national unity, transcending party divisions, or values explicitly labeled as national, the claims were classified as "nonpartisan." In nonpartisan mandate claims, presidents generally employed one of two forms of argument. The first was to argue that the election had demonstrated national consensus, sometimes by using a word like "unity" or "consensus" and other times by presenting the election result as a reflection of the entire nation. For example, George H. W. Bush's (abbreviated in this section as Bush 41, with George W. Bush abbreviated as Bush 43) comments to the Senior Executive Service just a few days after his inauguration included this argument:

> And there's much we need to accomplish for America. There is a mandate to fulfill, and there are problems to solve. We have work to do in promoting education, protecting the environment, and certainly in fighting crime. We have work to do in our cities and on our farms, and we have a war on drugs to win. We must provide for the common defense, strive for a lasting peace, and we must keep our economy growing so it can keep producing jobs and opportunity.[17]

The second way that presidents used nonpartisan rhetoric of electoral logic was to link the election result to issues like good governance and economic improvements, or to issues that had traditionally been "owned" by the other party. The objective of these arguments was not to highlight national agreement, but to claim a mandate for an issue outside of the traditional platform of the president's party. Bill Clinton combined these strategies in his remarks in Detroit, Michigan, in February 1993, stating, "The people demand and deserve an active Government on their side. But they don't want a Government that wastes money, a Government that costs more and does less. They voted for change. They wanted a literal revolution in the way Government operates, and now you and I must deliver."[18] Similarly, as he assumed office in 1969, Richard Nixon referenced campaign commitments to budget cuts, better cooperation with NATO allies, and funding for scientific research.

Partisan mandate claims vary in scope and focus and do not always appear after presidents or their congressional partisans win landslides. For example, Harry Truman's remarks at the 1949 Jefferson-Jackson Day Dinner included a direct reference to the party mandate: "What I feel tonight is not personal pride or elation; it is a deep satisfaction that our party has served its country so well that the people have endorsed it for the fifth consecutive time. The central issue of the campaign last fall was the welfare of all the people against special privilege for the few. When we made it clear where the Democratic Party stood on that issue, the people made it clear where they stood with us."[19]

The Democratic event was hardly a controversial venue to claim a mandate for Democratic policies, especially considering the party's sizeable congressional gains despite Truman's own narrow victory margin. As president, however, Truman had the opportunity to make a case about what the 1948 result had meant for the party, and in his address at this party event, he defined the party's agenda around the idea of "the welfare of all the people against special privilege for the few."[20]

The second kind of partisan mandate claim is exemplified by the following statement by Bush 43 at the 2005 National Republican Congressional Committee Dinner:

> In the 2004 elections, we ran on large issues. We campaigned on a platform of big ideas. We discussed those ideas at every campaign stop, and the American people responded. . . . We've given the people of this country a clear choice, and we have performed. We did that in the 2002 elections; we did that in the 2004 elections. The American people have responded to a party which sets a clear agenda, a party which doesn't want to mark time, a party which understands that we must confront problems now and not pass them on to future Presidents and future Congresses. In those elections, the American people have made it clear they want a President and Congress that understand the role of courts in our democracy.[21]

Like Truman, Bush 43 had the forgiving task of claiming a party mandate before a party audience. However, Truman integrated a variety of policies, including the repeal of the Taft-Hartley Act and the maintenance of farm price supports, into a unifying framework. Bush 43, in contrast, presented a series of major policy items, including tax cuts, tort reform, changes to health care policy, education reform, and Social Security reform. As opposed to Truman's remarks, this extensive list lacked an overarching idea or philosophy. Several themes recurred, such as private control over resources, but Bush 43 offered a separate explanation for each policy rather than connecting them all through an explicitly labeled theme. Truman claimed before his fellow Democrats that the election had been a referendum on the defense of "the people" against "the special interests."[22] Bush 43 argued in front of fellow Republicans that the election had been a referendum on a series of specific measures, on each of which the party's distinct position had been clear. This difference, while subtle, illustrates the variety of ways in which presidents can claim party mandates.

This style of rhetoric has not been entirely confined to party dinners. Obama invoked the 2008 election as a rejection of Republican economic ideas in the weeks following his inauguration. In remarks to members of the Department of Energy, he said, "So let me be clear: Those ideas have been tested, and they have failed. They've taken us from surpluses to an annual deficit of over a trillion dollars, and they've brought our economy to a halt. And that's precisely what the election we just had was all about. The American people have rendered their judgment. And now is the time to move forward, not back. Now is the time for action."[23]

This sentiment—verbatim and paraphrased—appeared throughout Obama's remarks on various policies associated with Democratic positions. Using the mandate to present the other party in a negative light is consistent with the growing polarization, especially among elites, that has characterized early twenty-first century American politics.[24] In contrast with the quotations from Truman and Obama's predecessor Bush 43, Obama's choice of mandate strategy also eschews defining the party's agenda or stances; his words portray the Democratic mandate as nothing more than voters choosing one alternative over another. Although the victory of one alternative fits the "responsible-party" idea of the mandate, it lacks the stronger images of a national movement evoked by other instances of mandate rhetoric.

Nixon's statements on crime policy illustrate the third kind of partisan electoral logic rhetoric. During a news conference in March 1973, he remarked, "During the sixties, the United States went far down the road of the permissive approach to those charged with crime, and we reaped a terrible harvest, the greatest increase in crime that this country has ever had, explosive to the point that law and order, so-called, became a great issue in

'68. It was still a great issue in '72."[25] The indictment of the opposite party is subtler than in Obama's statement, but the reference to permissiveness in the 1960s points squarely at Democratic leadership and suggests that one of the reasons for Republican victories (such as they were) in 1968 and 1972 was the party's approach to "law-and-order" issues.

Among the 127 mandate references in the data set, seventy communications emphasized the partisan dimensions of the election or campaign, whereas fifty-seven invoked nonpartisan themes or indicated intent to work with both parties. Tables 1.6 and 1.7 show how the partisan character of mandate rhetoric has changed over time.[26] During the transition from the Progressive Era, party themes pervaded mandate rhetoric. Hoover especially stressed the Republican platform in his mandate rhetoric. During the modern era, the balance shifted to nonpartisan mandate claims. Between 1941 and 1965, presidents did not use very much mandate rhetoric overall. The mandate rhetoric they did use was generally split between partisan and nonpartisan. Although all but one began with unified party government, covered in Table 1.6, the balance of claims emphasized nonpartisan themes. Strikingly, these three terms began following three of the most decisive party victories of the period: 1932, 1952, and 1964.

The partisan era displays a different pattern. In the eleven terms covered in Table 1.7, five featured more nonpartisan than partisan mandate rhetoric. These five terms fit intuitive predictions: Nixon in 1969 entered office under

Table 1.6. Party versus nation in presidential mandate rhetoric, 1929–1965

Term	Partisan	Non-partisan	Total
Hoover	5	0	5
FDR1	0	1*	1
FDR2	2	0	2
Truman	2	0	2
Eisenhower1	1	2*	3
Eisenhower2	1	0	1
LBJ	0	2*	2
Total	11	5	16

* Denotes more partisan than non-partisan claims.
Note: Italics signify divided government at the start of the term.

Table 1.7. Party versus nation in presidential mandate rhetoric,
1969–2009

Term	Partisan	Nonpartisan	Total
Nixon1	2	4*	6
Nixon2	4	1	5
Carter	0	7*	7
Reagan1	5	2	7
Reagan2	6	2	8
Bush	3	9 *	12
Clinton1	5	9*	14
Clinton2	0	1*	1
GWBush1	4	1	5
GWBush2	15	6	21
Obama	15	10	25
Total	59	52	111

* Denotes more partisan than nonpartisan claims.
Note: Italics signify divided government at the start of the term.

divided government after having eked out a narrow victory with a plurality
of votes; Carter won a very close election; Bush 41 faced a Democratic Congress in 1989; and Clinton's promises to be a "new kind of Democrat" in 1992
won him only 43 percent of the vote, and in 1996 he returned to office with
a plurality victory and a Republican Congress. Although the period between 1969 and 2009 lacked party blowouts like those seen in 1932, 1952,
or 1964, the contests of 1980, 2004, and 2008 demonstrated clear partisan
directions. After these elections, Presidents Reagan, Bush 43, and Obama,
respectively, framed the elections in partisan terms.

These patterns offer a tentative generalization worthy of further consideration: modern presidents responded to party victories with rhetoric about
unity and consensus—even after strong party victories such as those of
Johnson and the Democrats in 1964. In the late twentieth and early twenty-
first centuries, presidents defined party victories—even narrow ones—in
party terms, whereas mandate rhetoric about common ground remained
the preferred strategy of plurality presidents and those leading divided
party government. Nonpartisan mandate rhetoric arises in predictable circumstances. Presidents facing divided government and seeking common
ground with the opposite party have sought to frame their elections in

terms of bipartisan issues. Presidents who assumed "preemptive" leadership stances, in Skowronek's political time formulation, have also sought to reconcile the priorities of their parties with those of their opponents.[27]

Previous sections illustrate how the electoral mandate has pervaded the logic of governance. By examining the content of these statements, we have learned more about the ideas contained therein. Contemporary presidents have defined elections in increasingly partisan and ideological terms and shared these interpretations with audiences other than attendants at party events. The resulting model for governance can be summarized in Barack Obama's words to a gathered group of Republican congressional leaders in 2009: "I won."[28]

Challenges to the legitimacy of the presidency and the political system have also inspired mandate rhetoric that emphasizes neutral good governance. Nixon, perceiving the diminished status of the office, began to emphasize reform during his first term. After Nixon's own scandals exacerbated public distrust, his Democratic successor, Jimmy Carter, deliberately emphasized campaign promises in his effort to rehabilitate the image of the presidency. Carter contended that by choosing him in 1976, voters had responded to his promises for reorganization of the executive branch and proposals to reform the electoral system. In 1981, Reagan connected the ideas of change and economic recovery to government efficiency, citing the mandate of the election in a memorandum calling for the resignation of noncareer federal employees.[29] Echoing reform themes from the Carter administration, Obama remarked to White House senior staff on the second day of his presidency, "In a few minutes, I'm going to be issuing some of the first Executive orders and directives of my Presidency. And these steps are aimed at establishing firm rules of the road for my administration and all who serve in it, and to help restore that faith in Government, without which we cannot deliver the changes we were sent here to make."[30] Ideas about governing were not limited to efficiency and upright practices. George H. W. Bush and his son George W. Bush both claimed more general mandates to "govern" and to "act."[31]

In aggregate, the partisan-era mandate rhetoric actually demonstrates more balance between party and national themes. However, when we analyze these data further, we see that some of the most notable party victories of the modern era were not presented in party terms, whereas the presentation of later contests, including the 1993, 2004, 2008, and even the 2000 elections, has been considerably more partisan. At the same time, presidents in the later period have also introduced substantial "neutral accountability" rhetoric into their communication strategies. These changes highlight both the ubiquity of mandate logic and the spreading impulse to interpret elections and present presidential leadership in party terms.

Defensiveness

Presidential mandate rhetoric can also be classified in terms of its defensive or opportunistic tone. Opportunistic mandate rhetoric is defined as claims to an electoral mandate made in the context of introducing a policy stance. Instances of opportunistic mandate rhetoric have largely dominated previous studies; presidents claim mandates, as we have seen, in major and minor policy addresses. However, defensive claims also make up a significant percentage of mandate references, as Table 1.8 shows.

Mandate references were classified as defensive if they were offered in response to a challenge or a criticism. Sometimes the challenges and criticisms were concrete, usually offered in the form of a question from a journalist or occasionally from an audience member at a live event. In other instances, the president alluded to the criticism in his own speech, quoting the flaws that others had identified in a plan or a policy. In either case, the response included "I am doing what I was elected to do" or "I am doing what I promised I would do in the campaign." In contrast, opportunistic claims were those that simply introduced policies or offered statements about the meaning of the election.

The use of defensive mandate rhetoric follows the temporal pattern of mandate rhetoric in general; it is more common in the transition period from the Progressive Era and in the partisan era, and less common in the modern

Table 1.8. Defensive and opportunistic mandate rhetoric, 1929–2009

Period	Defensive	Opportunistic	Total
1929–1937	4	4	8
1941–1965	1	8	9
1969–2009	24	86	110
Total	29	98	127

era in between. The main source of the earlier defensive claims is Herbert
Hoover, who used mandate rhetoric to defend his farm policy choices (fellow Republican Dwight Eisenhower would do something similar in 1953, as
chapter 3 discusses). Defensiveness resurged in the partisan era, with Clinton,
Bush 43, and Obama citing election results and campaign promises in
response to media questions about their decisions. Obama, in particular, has
brought up campaign promises when his foreign policy choices have been
questioned.

The connection between mandate rhetoric and defensiveness is intuitive, if largely absent from the contemporary mandates literature. By maintaining that a difficult policy choice fulfills an election mandate, presidents
can respond to criticism in a way that appeals to venerated democratic
values. This kind of response also allows presidents to avoid actually defending their priorities or decisions. In this sense, defensive mandate rhetoric
takes the delegate position even further, suggesting that their decisions
reflected not their own careful consideration, but rather their commitment
to put the judgment of the electorate into effect.

Finally, a methodological note is in order. The coding scheme used in
this section almost certainly undercounts the instances of defensive mandate rhetoric. From the data presented in this work, we do not know if
defense against criticism played a part in the speechwriting process. As we
see in later chapters, these themes sometimes emerge in the preparation of
speeches. They also emerge in the course of defending the administration to
elite critics in exchanges that are never seen by the public and in response to
scandal accusations. The data set does not cover the Watergate period, but,
in chapter 4, we learn that Nixon's defense strategy included citing the mandate of the 1972 election. In sum, the analysis of speeches tells us only part of
the story; archival sources provide us with more insight about the defensive
role of mandate rhetoric.

Presentation of Presidential Leadership

Mandate language contains implicit arguments about the nature and legiti-
macy of presidential leadership. The literature on the development of the
American presidency acknowledges this purpose; Richard Ellis and Stephen
Kirk discuss Andrew Jackson's claim to an electoral mandate as a critical

expansion of the legitimate basis of presidential power.[32] Similarly, the popular mandate has been cited as a pillar of Woodrow Wilson's reconceptualization of the president's role.[33] Yet empirical studies of modern presidential rhetoric and mandate claiming largely neglect this dimension of the mandate, focusing instead on election results and policy agendas.

This oversight has led scholars to gloss over a major development in the way that presidents have used mandate language to describe the role of the office. Specifically, this speaks to the president's relationship to the electorate. A classic formulation of political representation involves the dichotomy between delegate and trustee styles of representation. The trustee model suggests that governing officials base decisions on their own judgment. In the words of Edmund Burke, "Your representative owes you, not his industry only, but judgment; and he betrays, instead of serving you, if he sacrifices it to your opinion."[34] At times, presidents have combined the ideal of trusteeship with claims to an electoral mandate by asserting that the election revealed demand for strong, decisive leadership. In this case, the ideal type would say something like, "By electing me, the people have entrusted to me to make this decision." Trusteeship is often overlooked in scholarship on presidential mandates, as trusteeship and mandates have traditionally been considered to be separate, competing paradigms. However, the concept of a "personal mandate" overlaps substantially with the idea of trusteeship. Claims to a mandate for the candidate specifically implicate the candidate's judgment and decision-making skills as well as—or instead of—his policy positions. For the American presidency, this difference constitutes a crucial distinction about the source of authority. Without mandates, presidential authority emanates from the Constitution. With a personal or trusteeship mandate, authority emanates from the people and allows the president to exercise independent judgment. With a delegate-style mandate, the people authorize the president on a more specific range of issues.

The trustee model highlights the president's role as a decision maker and leader. Only twenty-four of the 127 instances of mandate rhetoric in the data set depicted the president as a trustee of the electorate rather than as a delegate acting out the public's will. The period between 1941 and 1965 accounts for less than 7 percent of mandate claims in the entire data set. Yet, six of the twenty-four trusteeship claims—more than 20 percent—come from this era.

The distinction between assertions of trusteeship from assertions of delegation is a fine one. Generally, the language that distinguished trusteeship rhetoric included references to trust, responsibility, and leadership. For example, Eisenhower introduced the four major goals of his administration in his 1953 State of the Union address by stating, "It is manifestly the joint purpose of the congressional leadership and of this administration to justify the summons to governmental responsibility issued last November by the American people."[35] The four goals, which Eisenhower calls "ruling purposes" were broad and uncontroversial: peace, integrity in government, economic productivity, and equal opportunity and well-being for citizens. Claims that invoked trust and elite leadership were not always separate from partisanship. For example, Reagan's second inaugural address in 1985 referred to the trust of the electorate, but placed it in the context of Republican ideas, maintaining "we must never again abuse the trust of working men and women by sending their earnings on a futile chase after the spiraling demands of a bloated Federal Establishment. You elected us in 1980 to end this prescription for disaster, and I don't believe you reelected us in 1984 to reverse course."[36] In this speech, Reagan presented trust as an essential component of leadership. At the same time, he made the argument that the 1980 and 1984 elections fit into a broad, cohesive narrative of conservative politics, thus depicting the president as a leader in this movement, combining trusteeship and partisan themes.

Trusteeship claims were not limited to Republican presidents. Johnson referred to the 1964 election as an expression of the electorate's "trust" in a speech before the Anti-Defamation League and in remarks to the press about the development of Medicare.[37] Whereas Clinton laid out the idea of trusteeship in his 1997 State of the Union address, Obama used a mix of trustee and delegate rhetoric. In remarks on the federal budget, the newly elected president said, "The American people sent us here to get things done, and at this moment of great challenge, they are watching and waiting for us to lead. Let's show them that we are equal to the task before us, and let's pass a budget that puts this Nation on the road to lasting prosperity."[38] Similarly, Obama cited responsibility and problem solving in his address at a Democratic Party fund-raiser: "To kick these problems down the road 4 years from now, 8 years from now, for the next President, for the next generation, that would be to duplicate the irresponsibility that led us to this point. That's not why I ran for office. That's not why you worked so hard during this election. You didn't send me here to pass on problems to somebody else. You sent me here to solve them, and with your help, that's what I intend to do."[39]

What unites these claims is their suggestion that the essence of the connection between president and people lies in the president's capacity to resolve problems and exercise sound judgment. The trustee model of representation reiterates older ideas about executive leadership. As Ralph Ketcham explains in *Presidents Above Party*, early American ideas about the presidency emanated from the ideal of the "patriot king" and placed high priority on "patriotism" and "disinterested commitment to the general welfare."[40] In the trusteeship claims, presidents assert their right to determine the nation's best interests and to make decisions, sometimes with reference to party and ideology, and other times in connection to more transcendent national values.

Although presidents in the modern era presented themselves as trustees of the public, presidents in the partisan era have claimed a delegate relationship with their constituents, attuned to their preferences rather than their long-term needs. The delegate model posits that elected representatives should behave as if they have received instructions from their constituents about how to proceed in the policy process. As Andrew Rehfeld describes, this idea of representation binds the representative to "the dictates of one's constituents."[41] The changes in mandate rhetoric over time suggest that as institutions have evolved, presidents have edged closer to the delegate end of the spectrum. Most presidential mandate claims—around 80 percent—fit the delegate model. Many, but not all, of these statements involve a reference to the promises of the campaign. While promoting his Social Security plan in 2005, George W. Bush told a Westfield, New Jersey, audience, "See, here's the thing about this issue. I actually ran on it. I said, 'Vote for me, and I'm going to do something about Social Security, and I'm going to try to put out some innovative ideas to fix it.'"[42] Unlike trusteeship claims, which often underscore broad directions and major policies, delegate-style mandate claims were often associated with very specific policies. Sometimes these were major agenda items, such as Bush's Social Security proposal. In other instances, however, presidents used campaign-fulfillment rhetoric to defend lower salience items, such as George H. W. Bush's plans for child-care legislation and Jimmy Carter's ideas about zero-base budgeting.[43]

Delegate language not only provides electoral justification for relatively minor policies. It also offers a way to construct an electoral mandate from a close or otherwise indecisive election. Yet, a paradox exists with regard to presidential leadership. This style of rhetoric does little to enhance the president's image as a decisive, independent leader. Although delegate-style representation is often naturally associated with the electoral mandate, the American presidency was not designed with this in mind. Presidents are often expected to respond to public opinion,[44] but this responsibility is balanced by the demand that presidents exercise independent leadership. Such leadership, in the words of presidential scholars Thomas Cronin and Michael Genovese, requires presidents "to use the bully pulpit to promote a moral and political vision in support of change."[45] Claiming a mandate to act as a delegate of the people requires that presidents try to reconcile these competing ideals of leadership and representation. Despite this dilemma, delegate rhetoric accounts for much of the increase in overall mandate claims since the decline of the modern era. Statements about campaign promises and electoral accountability appear in major and minor speeches, in news conferences, and in comments to other governing elites. In other words, keeping campaign promises and making choices about "what we were elected to do" have become more pervasive in the logic of governance. The prevalence of "delegate-style" mandate claims in the partisan era indicates a shift in thinking about the nature and constraints of the presidency, as well as the underpinnings of its legitimacy.

Evidence for Systematic Change

Presidential mandate rhetoric has changed in frequency, venue, and content. Alongside these changes are continuities that suggest linkages between mandate rhetoric and institutional dynamics. For example, we have seen that news conferences and other media interactions have long accounted for substantial percentages of mandate rhetoric, underscoring the connection between defensiveness and mandate claiming. We have also seen that the increase in mandate rhetoric has tracked closely with the evolving institutional environment. High levels of polarization and lower levels of public approval are strongly correlated with mandate rhetoric, whereas decisive election results are not.

These data leave us in a position in which we can only infer strategy and motivation, however. We have observed patterns and relationships, and examined the content of mandate rhetoric. These patterns lend substantial support to the theory proposed in the introduction. However, these data stop short of actually revealing the causal relationship between institutional change and presidential mandate claims. In the next four chapters, we will take advantage of presidential documents, interviews, and other sources in order to trace the relationship between institutional evolution and changing patterns of presidential mandate rhetoric.

Chapter 2

THE CHANGING PRESIDENTIAL SCRIPT

Hoover, Roosevelt, and the Politics of Transition

One week after he took office in 1933, Franklin Roosevelt received a telegram urging him to act quickly to resolve the nation's economic problems. Invoking the election as a mandate for swift action, the telegram read, "Mr. President the people of the United States have elected you. The people of the United States stand solidly behind you. Whereas Congress may only grant you official permission to act drastically the people have given you a moral sanction. Congress failed. God and success be with you."[1] It is intuitive that elites and citizens alike might see the 1932 election as a mandate for a new economic program. However, Roosevelt's own interpretation of the election's meaning was shaped by more than the immediate politics of the moment.

Franklin Roosevelt sits atop nearly every list of "greatest presidents."[2] Among the reasons for his indelible mark on presidential history is the connection he forged with the electorate through a carefully crafted communication strategy. Roosevelt succeeded in changing the national conversation about economic policy by invoking fundamental American ideals. Stephen

Skowronek describes Roosevelt's central message: "Change was possible, indeed imperative, he [Roosevelt] claimed, because the values that held sway in American government were not the values on which American civilization rested."[3] He also used a relatively new medium, the radio, to invent a new form of address, the "fireside chat." Fireside chats not only allowed the president to shape public thinking on policy matters, they also established a direct relationship between the president and the mass electorate. Formidable electoral success buttressed this relationship. His first two elections were landslides in the popular vote and in the Electoral College. He also won an unprecedented third and then fourth term. Yet, as we saw in chapter 1, Roosevelt's public communications placed relatively little emphasis on the idea of the presidential mandate, despite his strong election victories and clear connection with the electorate. Understanding FDR's approach to electoral logic has intrinsic value for understanding this important presidency. The Roosevelt case study also contributes to the larger narrative of the presidential mandate after the Progressive Era. During the Progressive Era, enthusiasm for a strong presidency led to greater emphasis on the mandate. As we shall see, mandate rhetoric became a standard feature in inaugural addresses during this time, and presidents saw their connections with the electorate as central to their authority to lead. Roosevelt, Woodrow Wilson, and other Progressive leaders envisioned significant reforms to the political structures set forth by the Constitution and by the Jacksonian party system. In these endeavors, they succeeded in amending the Constitution to allow a federal income tax, extend suffrage to women, provide for the direct election of senators, and temporarily, to enshrine a social crusade in the letter of the Constitution. But the formal boundaries around the presidency and Congress remained unclear. Questions about how these boundaries might change and about the expansion of the president's informal role went unresolved. Similarly, with regard to party politics, the Progressive Era successfully chipped away at new structures and introduced new rules, most notably presidential primaries. The relationship between presidents and parties changed as presidents began to cultivate their own bases of political support[4] and as a previously regional party system became more nationally integrated. However, changing political circumstances and stymied efforts to change the party system and the executive branch ultimately brought about a less optimistic and reform-minded period: the modern presidency. Beginning during FDR's second term and lasting through the presidency of

Lyndon Johnson, the modern era was distinct from the Progressive and partisan periods. Mandate rhetoric became far less common, and presidents largely jettisoned the notion of delegate-style representation. As we examine in this chapter, the FDR presidency played a significant role in the transition from the Progressive Era to the modern era.

Contested Institutional Boundaries

The transition era, dominated by the Roosevelt presidency, shared characteristics with both the Progressive and Modern periods. Like his Progressive predecessors, Roosevelt stepped into an office with expanded powers and unclear institutional boundaries. Between 1880 and 1929, presidential politics had changed substantially.[5] The creation of new cabinet departments, such as Commerce and Labor (created together in 1903 and separated in 1913) increased the regulatory capacity of the executive branch. Perhaps more importantly, ideas and informal norms about presidential behavior were transformed. Jeffrey Tulis identifies a major innovation in constitutional doctrine in this era, which resulted in shifting norms about presidential use of policy rhetoric and engagement with popular audiences. In a similar vein, Victoria Farrar-Myers finds evidence for new informal norms, or "scripts," that afforded presidents expanded authority in foreign and domestic policy.[6] Presidents made greater use of their persuasive capacity than in the past, delivering public speeches in order to gather public support for policies.[7] The responsibilities of the federal government also expanded to match growing demand for economic regulation. These changes inspired new arguments for the legitimacy of a strong presidency—one that would play a different role than that described in the Constitution. In contrast with the nineteenth-century presidency, Peri Arnold argues, "We can see the Progressive Era's presidency as an ill-structured role with a loosened script."[8] The influential presidencies of Theodore Roosevelt and Woodrow Wilson illustrate this development.

For both TR and Wilson, one of the central goals was expanding the legislative influence of the presidency. In practice their approaches to the office sometimes appeared similar; both undertook public campaigns to promote policy, sought to increase federal regulation of the economy, and contended with isolationist politicians over foreign policy. However, Roosevelt's vision of a strong presidency differed from Wilson's; the Progressive Republican was not as concerned about the need for democratic legitimacy to undergird executive power. Historian Sarah Watts observes that in Roosevelt's view, "Representative government . . . not only bred ineffectual leaders, it weakened the manhood of the entire population."[9] In this sense, the presidency actually served as an antidote to the inherent "weakness" of democracy. Because the people could not be relied on to make difficult decisions, especially where war was concerned, the leadership of "strong men" was necessary.[10] This thinking informed Roosevelt's ideas about the expansion of presidential power as a natural effect of the continued expansion American influence in the Western Hemisphere.[11] Roosevelt's ideas about presidential strength also informed his innovations in the use of what he termed the "bully pulpit." The essence of this linkage was that Roosevelt, in Peri Arnold's words, "associated his public image with his policy agenda."[12] The public campaign to promote his signature Hepburn Act (1906) drew on his considerable political skills in using resonant ideas such as corruption and public interest.[13] Thus he led public opinion and achieved legislative victory.[14] As the events surrounding the Hepburn Act illustrate, the first President Roosevelt pushed against the established boundaries of presidential legitimacy. Fusing an ambitious policy agenda with the cultivation of a personal political following, he sought a stronger and more dominant office.

Wilson shared his Republican rival's thirst for influence. His conception of democracy and representation differed from Roosevelt's, however. Wilson envisioned a "parliamentary" style of leadership, in which the president would guide congressional Democrats through the legislative process.[15] This approach reflected the responsible-party ideal that had informed some of the president's earlier political ideas. Wilson's vision of himself as a "prime ministerial" party leader anticipated the modern, legislatively active presidency. Yet the former New Jersey governor hoped that presidents might be able to exert meaningful leadership over their congressional parties, and he theorized about breaking down the "parchment barriers" between the branches of government.[16] Initially, Wilson made progress in this direction. He was heavily involved in "his legislative party's deliberations" on tariff reform, breaking a wall of separation between the branches.[17] As Tulis notes, Wilson "preferred that the president and Congress be fully integrated into, and implicated in, each others' activities."[18] Later on, Wilson also made use of the "bully pulpit" to persuade the Senate to ratify the Treaty of Versailles

(1919), which encompassed the League of Nations covenant. Wilson's ideas about the presidency, however, included more than the changing relationship between the executive and legislative branches. Wilson also envisioned a qualitatively different relationship between the president and the public. At the same time that he worked closely with Congress behind the scenes to shape tariff reform, he also took a strong public stance on the issue, which pushed the boundaries of accepted presidential authority and attracted criticism from some legislators.[19] Despite his detractors' accusations that he was usurping authority that rightfully belonged to the legislature, Wilson believed that political leaders had an opportunity and an obligation to "interpret" public opinion—to "sift through the multifarious currents of opinion to find a core of issues that he believed reflected majority will even if the majority was not fully aware of it."[20] In other words, Wilson's image of a reformed presidency envisioned deeper integration with Congress and more interaction with the public, but with the president in an authoritative position.

At the time of FDR's inauguration, the president's informal role had expanded, yet the efficacy of a more active and more public presidency remained in doubt. Theodore Roosevelt and Woodrow Wilson both experienced the limits of direct popular leadership. The Hepburn Act passed, but in a much weaker form than TR preferred.[21] The Senate did not ratify the League of Nations treaty, thus rendering Wilson's last initiative a failure. The shortcomings of the public rhetoric strategy, particularly in Wilson's case, were not solely attributable to a failure of persuasion.[22] Rather, the expansion of presidential influence encroached on the prerogatives of other branches. When FDR took office, the extent to which Congress (and later, the courts) would tolerate the presidential impulse to dominate the national conversation had yet to be determined. The Progressive vision of an active and public presidency was bound to upset the balance of the system eventually (and the negotiations over the Treaty of Versailles perhaps approached this threshold), but in 1933 that point had not yet been reached. FDR renegotiated the limits of presidential legitimacy in the context of pressing and acute crisis. The FDR presidency was shaped not only by extraordinary events in domestic and international politics, but also by the unfinished transformation of presidential legitimacy that occurred before he took office. The formal and informal capacities of the office had grown, the boundaries loosened, and yet the polity did not have limitless tolerance for a powerful executive.

Parties in Transition

Progressive ideas about reforming government and reshaping the presidency were closely linked to the role of political parties. As with presidential legitimacy, however, Progressive efforts brought about reconsideration but not complete transformation. Throughout the nineteenth century, parties served as both decentralized electoral operations and as vehicles of social provision, but by the 1930s, they had become more nationally integrated and programmatic.[23] Some of this change resulted from reform efforts: civil service reform deprived parties of federal patronage, and voter registration efforts and direct primaries began to chip away at electioneering and nominating practices. After decades of relative disadvantage in the localized, patronage-based system, presidents in the 1880s began to cultivate independent bases of political support and to lead their parties on the issues of the day.[24]

Theodore Roosevelt's relationship with congressional Republicans foreshadowed the tension between presidents and parties that characterized the modern era. His clashes with the Republican Party began during his career as governor of New York, where his antitrust priorities challenged state party leaders.[25] Chosen as William McKinley's second vice president after the death of Garret Hobart, the New York Republican was not a favorite among top Republicans. McKinley adviser Mark Hanna disliked Roosevelt for a number of reasons, including his "impulses" to reform civil service and party politics.[26] After becoming president, Roosevelt continued to forge independence from the party and to engage in policy conflict with Republican congressional leaders.[27] Yet Roosevelt was not completely unmoored from party as an idea; his struggles with established party figures occurred in the context of competition over who could best articulate Republican principles. As Skowronek describes, "the meaning and context of Roosevelt's response to industrialism was inextricably bound up with his earnest quest for a *Republican* response."[28] This dilemma would carry through to the modern era; presidents sought independence from parties and yet depended on them to provide political support and grounding ideas.

Progressive leadership was also characterized by willingness to question the rules of the system, and Theodore Roosevelt embodied this reformist spirit. Seeking the Republican nomination in 1912, he took aim at party nominating practices. Building on an antiparty critique that had taken on patronage, corruption, and "bossism," he had competed in the first presidential primary and bested his opponents in most contests. After the Republican Party nominated incumbent president William Howard Taft despite the primary results, TR ran on the Progressive ticket, which underscored the possibility that parties and presidential leadership could be decoupled.[29]

Wilson, too, believed that American political parties were in serious need of reform. During the 1912 campaign, he openly denounced the "boss" system, implicating leaders in his own party and promising not to reward "special interests" in his own administration.[30] He maintained that parties could better serve the nation by "articulating more coherent and timely political visions."[31] In the absence of a plan for enacting such a reform, Wilson instead "arrived at strong presidential leadership as a solution."[32] In this regard, Wilson's approach resembled Roosevelt's; parties were useful (at least in theory) for programmatic and ideological bedrock, but it was desirable for the president to break free of their corrupt and hierarchical practices.

The legacy of this incomplete transition influenced Franklin Roosevelt's campaign and presidency. In the early 1930s, the Democratic Party was still caught between a Progressive reform vision and the power structures of the old "boss" system. Throughout the 1932 campaign, FDR found that substantial numbers of voters, especially in Western states, had begun to harbor Progressive objections to the labor intensive, patronage-oriented "machines." Along with campaign manager James Farley, Roosevelt sought to mobilize these reform-minded voters in support of his bid for the nomination and, later, the presidency. However, for many of these voters, the Roosevelt-Farley campaign style, coupled with their New York origins, evoked machine politics.[33] In the 1932 campaign, Roosevelt successfully offered "programmatic appeals" to the Western voters.[34] However, this tension was not merely a question of campaign tactics; Roosevelt had inherited an unrealized and contradictory set of ideals from his Progressive predecessors. Progressives had challenged the status quo about how parties did business, but fallen short of completely replacing the system with something new. As a result, presidential candidates expected to be able to act independently of party, and cultivated this expectation in others. In practice, presidential candidates still depended on party labels, structures, and resources.

FDR tried to reconcile the contradiction between countervailing ideas of the president as party leader and as an independent political voice. As the nominee from a party divided over the repeal of Prohibition and between cultural, religious, and regional groups,[35] Roosevelt made good use of the candidate-centered strategies pioneered around the turn of the century. He offered a message that appealed across party lines and devoted considerable effort to campaign speeches and reaching out to voters.[36] However, even as a candidate seeking to make a broad appeal, Roosevelt's tactics did not amount to an effort to rise above party; rather, he used the new candidate-centered campaign norms and his own political gifts to unite supporters around a central message that resonated with older Democratic themes.[37] In *Electing FDR*, Donald Ritchie notes that FDR's campaign speeches sought to "appeal to a broad coalition of liberal and conservative Democrats and progressive Republicans. He presented general themes that audiences found readily understandable. He scattered enough clues about where he would lead that his speechwriters later insisted he had outlined almost every program of the essential New Deal."[38] Roosevelt also read from the Democratic Party platform during a radio speech in July and referred to the platform as a "covenant" between government and citizens.[39] FDR's campaign strategy reflected the unfinished reforms of the Progressive Era and anticipated the tension between presidents and parties in the imminent modern presidency. Although modern presidents would face expectations that they could act boldly, independent of party constraints, the need for party organizations and ideas would persist. This fraught relationship, combined with the rising status of the presidency that continued for several decades after World War II, shaped mandate rhetoric during this time.

Mandate Rhetoric in the Progressive Era

We have established that the Progressive Era was one of significant, if stymied, institutional evolution and reform. As early as the 1890s, these changes began to manifest themselves in presidential mandate claims, a departure from nineteenth-century patterns. Although Andrew Jackson was a central figure in the development of the presidential mandate, mid-nineteenth-century presidents rarely invoked electoral logic in their speeches. Starting with Grover Cleveland in 1893, however, mandate rhetoric became a much more regular feature of inaugural addresses. Cleveland claimed an electoral mandate for tariff reform in his second inaugural address, remarking that, "The people of the United States have decreed that on this day the control of their Government in its legislative and executive branches shall be given to a political party pledged in the most positive terms to the accomplishment of tariff reform."[40] Similarly, in 1897, William McKinley "define[d] the election outcome as a mandate for his policies."[41] Defending tariffs as the main source of federal revenue, McKinley noted in his inaugural address that, "To this policy we are all, of whatever party, firmly bound by the voice of the people—a power vastly more potential than the expression of any political platform." In contrast to Cleveland's claim to a party mandate, McKinley's words indicated at least a small measure of independence from party.

As McKinley's successor, Theodore Roosevelt likewise used popular rhetoric to present himself as a leader, not a follower, of the people and of the party. As Milkis describes, "Roosevelt styled himself a friend of popular rule but insisted that a sincere and effective democratic leader had to lead, and not slavishly follow, public opinion."[42] According to Colleen Shogan, Roosevelt's rhetoric to promote the Hepburn Act of 1906 identified the legislation as "a fulfillment of electoral expectations." She posits "the electorate clearly expected and anticipated moral leadership from Roosevelt, who believed deeply in the importance of strong individual and national character in a democracy."[43] In other words, Roosevelt offered his own vision for the relationship between the public, the party, and the president, suggesting that his own victory obligated him to unify the party around a reform agenda. This conception of electoral mandates, in other words, defines them in terms of leadership, not party responsibility. As a leader and a trustee, presidents could use the election to enhance their authority, but not as a core justification for their actions.

Not all presidents asserted their independence in mandate rhetoric as clearly as McKinley and Roosevelt, however. Mandate rhetoric typically emphasized both partisan themes and presented presidents as delegates of the public interest. For example, in Wilson's first inaugural address, he sought explicitly to interpret the election as a "change of government," with Democrats now controlling the House of Representatives, the Senate, and the executive branch. In this speech he suggested "success of a party means little except when the Nation is using that party for a large and definite purpose. No one can mistake the purpose for which the Nation now seeks to use the Democratic Party. It seeks to use it to interpret a change in its own plans and point of view."[44] While Wilson shared Roosevelt's conviction that presidents could best serve by leading and educating the public, his belief in responsible-party government is also evident in his first statement as president.

In the 1920s, the Progressive reform agenda gave way to plans to cut taxes and government expenditures.[45] Ironically, the use of mandate rhetoric by Republicans in this decade bears resemblance to that of Wilson and of Cleveland. Calvin Coolidge invoked the idea of "responsible party" in his 1925 inaugural, suggesting that "when the country has bestowed its confidence upon a party by making it a majority in the Congress, it has a right to expect such unity of action as will make the party majority an effective instrument of government. This Administration has come into power with a very clear and definite mandate from the people." In the 1924 election, Coolidge maintained, the electorate demonstrated its rejection of "public ownership of railroads and certain electric utilities," and its support for judicial repudiation of expanded regulation.[46] In his disavowal of Progressive policy stances, Coolidge drew on the responsible-party paradigm that Progressive Democrat Woodrow Wilson had espoused.

Herbert Hoover also claimed a Republican policy mandate in his inaugural address, as well as in two news conferences, a message to Congress, and a statement about farm relief. Hoover's ideas about Progressive government included faith in expertise, specifically social science, as a basis for good governance.[47] He also believed in the ideals of his political party. As Skowronek writes, "For all his apolitical sensibilities, Hoover took the field in 1928 as an earnest booster of the Republican regime. Hoover's leadership project covered deep political divisions within the coalition, and his call for a New Day mustered what enthusiasm there was for the completion of the work of the 1920s."[48] Yet, contrary to popular belief, the former bureaucrat initially approached the country's economic collapse by playing an "independent, active role."[49] Hoover also became the major target for public frustration when conditions did not improve. After his name became synonymous with suffering and want, Hoover attained the dubious honor of being the third president since 1832 to be renominated by his party and subsequently lose the general election. With these simultaneously held values of programmatic leadership and impartial expertise, Hoover's presidency represented the beginning of the transition from the Progressive to the modern presidency. Progressive presidents sought to shape their parties' ideas, whereas modern presidents sought to transcend them, either by building extrapartisan coalitions or by claiming to neutrally administer broad national goals.

The sense of optimism that Progressive presidents shared about shaping their parties—Cleveland and McKinley's successes in defining policy positions, Roosevelt's quest to bear the Republican standard, Wilson's ideals of party responsibility—faded considerably in the modern presidency. Hoover's difficult political situation made it difficult for him to influence his own party, but even his successor Franklin Roosevelt, a lucky and talented politician, found his efforts to lead his party thwarted. FDR's efforts to transform the Democratic Party and to "purge" the party of New Deal opponents demonstrated the limitations of even the most politically skilled presidents to unify parties around policy. As leaders tempered their expectations about changing the president-party relationship, they began to work within the confines of the new dynamic. Presidents had managed to forge some independence from party and yet had been unable to either fully shed the constraints of party or to take charge of their party. In the modern presidency, we observe presidents who appeared simultaneously adhere to party ideals and espouse the idea of being above party, seemingly resigned to live with that contradiction—and perhaps inspired to exploit it.

Although Hoover's presidency embodied the tension between neutrality and party, he is most often remembered as a staunch adherent to Republican principles. Mandate rhetoric in early 1929 foreshadowed this legacy. Hoover's efforts to interpret the 1928 contest stressed his fealty to the Republican platform and, months before the economic collapse that took down his presidency, used the platform to rebut criticism of his policies. This interpretation of the 1928 election did not emerge spontaneously, however. Hoover's defense of his policies in mandate terms built directly on a bipartisan legacy from the preceding era. Like Cleveland and McKinley in the 1890s, Hoover drew directly on the idea of an election mandate to justify his governing vision. By invoking the Republican Party platform, Hoover also exemplified the "responsible-party" ideal expressed in Woodrow Wilson's critique of the political system. However, Hoover's statements differed crucially from Wilson's idea of presidential leadership in a reformed system. Wilson advocated for parties led by presidents, instead of the reverse. In James Ceaser's words, Wilson envisioned the party as "an instrument at the leader's command helping to further the principles and programs for which he had won approval in his direct appeal to the people."[50] In statements about the party's policy pledges, Hoover conveyed the idea of principled policy appeals. Yet his statements and actions failed to convey the sense of leadership that was central to Wilson's vision. Instead, their defensive character under-mined the idea that Hoover was in charge and leading the policy agenda. In light of the association between party mandate and political inflexibility, it is unsurprising that Hoover's modern successors were not drawn to this kind of rhetoric.

The partisanship, frequency, and defensiveness of Hoover's mandate rhetoric resembled that of the partisan era that began forty years later. The emphasis on "pledge politics" and the use of the mandate to respond to chal-lenging questions anticipated how a diverse group of later leaders—Nixon, Carter, Clinton, George W. Bush, and Obama—would employ mandate rhetoric. In contrast with Hoover's successors who departed quickly from this mold of mandate claiming, presidents in the partisan era have em-ployed it as a rhetorical norm. Political and institutional conditions account for this difference.

Interpreting the 1932 Election

The historical significance of the 1932 election can hardly be mistaken. Herbert Hoover was turned out of office and his Democratic rival, Franklin Roosevelt, was elected with more than 57 percent of the popular vote. The new president offered a "New Deal," which contained a mix of new and old ideas, packaged in terms of national values as well as economic necessity.[51] Roosevelt also engineered changes in the Democratic Party's nomination rules, was the first president inaugurated under the Twentieth Amendment (which moved Inauguration Day from March to January), and became the first (and last) president elected to more than two terms.

In the evolution of mandate rhetoric, the FDR presidency was also a turning point. FDR neither embraced Wilson's vision of the party mandate, nor did he use mandate logic frequently when promoting New Deal poli-cies. Both the 1932 and 1936 elections could easily have qualified as party landslides, yet Roosevelt's mandate rhetoric reveals a more complicated pic-ture. In 1933, when his position was strong and national crisis bolstered the legitimacy of his initial agenda, mandate rhetoric was sparse. After the 1936 election, Roosevelt invoked the election mandate in the context of an insti-tutional clash: the "court-packing" plan of 1937.

Even with the Great Depression as a backdrop, the meaning of the 1932 election was contested. Newspapers offered a range of interpretations. The superintendent of the Anti-Saloon League, Scott McBride told the *New York Times*, "If the party misinterprets the election as a mandate for beer and a demand for repeal it need not hope to succeed. Most of the wet Democrats who won in this landslide were elected because they were Democrats and not because they were wets."[52] Coverage of the election offered a number of possibilities for its meaning: some emphasized the Democratic victory; some gave the numbers a central place in the narrative; and still others directed attention toward voter anger, suggesting a negative referendum on the incumbent administration rather than a positive one on Roosevelt or the Democrats.[53] Charles Hurd reports in the *New York Times* that "7,000,000" cast their votes in favor of the New Deal and emphasizes both the magnitude of the victory and the party and policy implications of the result, suggesting that the "Democratic triumph entails an implied command to solve the problems of economic dislocation, of prohibition, and the foreign affairs of the United States as they are related to war debt and tariffs."[54] By contrast, the *Wall Street Journal* questions the partisan and ideological terms in which the victory had been cast by the president and sources sympathetic to him; an article with the subtitle "Strange Bedfellows Made Up the Mass Movement Which Elected Roosevelt" questions Roosevelt's claim to a "victory of liberal thought" in the postelection radio address and further ponders the role of electoral majorities in the design of the Constitution.[55]

Roosevelt's own efforts to interpret the 1932 election were varied. FDR's inaugural address did not mention the promises of the platform, in contrast to several of his predecessors' inaugural addresses. He also appeared to veer away from some of the ideas that Progressives, particularly Woodrow Wilson, had advanced about the potential for presidents to act as delegates in a "responsible-party" system. After taking office in March 1933, Roosevelt began to promote his plans to the Congress, the news media, and the electorate. During his first seventy days in office, FDR issued twelve messages to Congress, held six press conferences, and gave two fireside chats. He also issued several signing statements and gave miscellaneous remarks. Throughout the rest of 1933, the president continued to communicate regularly with citizens, giving two more fireside chats and addressing groups such as the Third Annual Women's Conference, the American Legion Convention, and a number of religious groups. Throughout his first year in office, Roosevelt only occasionally invoked the 1932 election result as a justification for his actions, only twice in eighty-four communications during that year.[56]

Roosevelt's interpretation of the 1932 contest also reflected an ambivalent relationship between president and party, a stark departure from Hoover's claims to a Republican mandat." At the same time, the campaign's emphasis on policy experimentation clashed with the idea of a specific policy mandate.[57] By asking for a chance to try different policy approaches in hopes of repairing the economy, Roosevelt implicitly declared his intent to take a trusteeship approach to the presidency, leaving decisions about policy content to experts rather than placing them before the electorate. This idea was consistent with FDR's separation of the policy team—the "brains trust"— from the fray of politics. Furthermore, as presidential rhetoric scholar Elvin Lim has pointed out, FDR's signature New Deal speeches—the fireside chats—engaged the people directly, but their content suggested hierarchy and command.[58]

On the few occasions when Roosevelt publicly referred to the election, these references remained short on policy specifics. Roosevelt did not often argue that the election had constituted an endorsement of Democratic principles and policy rather than an expression of frustration with Hoover. The delicate balance between party—a source of crucial ideas and resources— and the imperative of national leadership influenced Roosevelt's mandate rhetoric. Unlike some of his predecessors, the newly elected Democrat did not invoke a partisan mandate; rather, he suggested in his inaugural address that the people had called for "direct, vigorous action." Although clearly a response to Hoover's perceived inertia on economic issues, Roosevelt's more general claim differed from the specific issue references made by Cleveland, Coolidge, and Hoover. However, when Roosevelt addressed different audiences, his narrative of the election took on a more partisan tone. In his remarks to a group of relief administrators, Roosevelt reminded them:

> All during the campaign I think both parties made it fairly clear, especially, I might add, the Democratic Party, that there was a certain principle involved that is just as sound today as it was last year. It is this: The first responsibility of taking care of people out of work who are lacking housing, clothing or food—the first charge is upon the locality; then, if the locality has done everything that it possibly can do, it is the duty of the State to step in and do all the

State can possibly do; and, when the State can do no more, then it becomes the obligation of the Federal Government. That is why we have the present relief bill.[59]

Roosevelt's ambivalence remains evident in these remarks. He includes a brief nod to bipartisan spirit, but he ultimately makes an assertion of Democratic superiority on the issues. In a communication with an even narrower audience, Roosevelt placed the Democratic platform at the center of his letter to Judge Leon McCord about the repeal of Prohibition, stating, "I have received your telegram of July 3rd in reference to the repeal of the Eighteenth Amendment. I think I have made it abundantly clear that the platform of the Democratic Party adopted last year should be carried out in so far [*sic*] as it lies in our power. The Special Session of the Congress has already translated into law a great majority of the pledges made."[60]

In the 1934 State of the Union address, Roosevelt moved back to nonpartisan rhetoric. He began the speech with electoral logic rhetoric, telling the senators and representatives:

> I come before you at the opening of the Regular Session of the 73rd Congress, not to make requests for special or detailed items of legislation; I come, rather, to counsel with you, who, like myself, have been selected to carry out a mandate of the whole people, in order that without partisanship you and I may cooperate to continue the restoration of our national wellbeing [*sic*] and, equally important, to build on the ruins of the past a new structure designed better to meet the present problems of modern civilization.[61]

Roosevelt's indeterminate statements about the meaning of the 1932 election defy common perceptions of his rhetorical style. Famous for memorable phrases (such as the label "New Deal" for his slate of policy reforms) and compelling reapplications of long-held national values, Roosevelt spent little time translating the people's message. On the few occasions that the president did refer to the election and campaign, he offered disparate interpretations. For broad audiences, Roosevelt offered a unifying message; with other elites, he emphasized adherence to party principles and promises. The combination of partisan and nonpartisan interpretations of the election matched the contradictions of the era and of the campaign itself. This rhetoric likewise framed New Deal policies as part of a party agenda, even as

Roosevelt pulled away from the machine politics of the traditional Democratic Party.

Roosevelt's use of mandate rhetoric in 1933 reveals his distance from his Progressive predecessors. Whereas Wilson emphasized the possibilities for presidents to represent the nation and the importance of that relationship for legitimizing a strong presidency, Roosevelt took the strength of the office as a given. He does not appear to have been especially concerned about legitimacy. His attitude about party government also differed from theirs; Roosevelt sought to invoke principles that encompassed the Democratic Party platform but also went beyond it, speaking to the fundamental values of the American founding. Questions surrounding the legitimacy of strong presidential leadership had also dissipated in response to crisis. The dire economic situation inspired demand for strong, decisive leadership—not party mandates. Absent the need to establish legitimacy for robust executive action, mandate rhetoric played a relatively small role in the president's communication strategy.

Court Packing and the Will of the People

During Roosevelt's second term, efforts to expand presidential power reached the boundaries of what the system would tolerate. Court challenges to the New Deal brought the presidency into conflict with the judicial branch. After the 1936 election, debates about substantive outcomes, partisan principles, and institutional authority began to merge. This combination of debates initially seemed promising for FDR, who could accuse his opponents of not only backing failed policies but also of thwarting the will of the people. However, the politics of the court-packing episode revealed both the limitations of the informal dimensions of the Progressive presidency and the pitfalls of using the mandate to establish legitimacy for presidential action. Policy debate took place on both substantive and procedural levels, with arguments about the best ways to fix the economic situation and about the proper roles of the executive branch and of the federal government. Senator William Borah of Idaho expressed his view of the debate in pointed terms, remarking "You can't eat the constitution."[62]

Despite these emerging debates, Alfred Landon, the Republican candidate in 1936, offered little in the way of substantive criticism of Roosevelt's central policies. Indeed, the Kansas governor "had endorsed any number of New Deal projects in words that were to come back to plague him during the campaign."[63] In his history of the Democratic Party, Jules Witcover notes that the business community was increasingly alarmed and frustrated by FDR's policy choices, but "Roosevelt's personal popularity in the country . . . led prudent Republicans to question the political wisdom of waging the fight against his reelection on such premises."[64] Although Roosevelt's political advantages may have stemmed mainly from his personal popularity, he strove to integrate party themes into his campaign rhetoric. Jean Edward Smith tells the story of a rally in Madison Square Garden in which "FDR all but proclaimed victory." First, Roosevelt maintained "no man can occupy the office of the President without realizing that he is President of all the people." Then, so as not to "disappoint the partisan crowd," the president attacked Republican criticisms of Social Security and described the abuses of previous Republican administrations. The description of "nine mocking years at the ticker and three long years in the breadlines" evoked not only Hoover, but also Harding and Coolidge before him.[65]

If 1932 was a decisive victory, 1936 was a veritable landslide, with Roosevelt winning the Electoral College votes of all but two states, Maine and Vermont. Democrats also improved their margins in Congress. At the same time, the 1936 election exemplifies why policy mandates are deceptively difficult to establish. Despite consistent and substantial Democratic victories, party victory remained only one of several plausible explanations for the election result. The incumbent's personal popularity could not be disentangled from the popularity of his New Deal policies. On a few occasions, however, Roosevelt tried to construct a policy mandate from the election victory. A few days after the election, Roosevelt referred to the victory in an address to the National Conference on Labor Legislation. In contrast with the more general depiction of policy meaning following the 1932 contest, this mandate claim incorporated specific policy outcomes, delivered to an audience assembled for specific policy purposes:

> The sessions of the National Conference on Labor Legislation in 1934 and 1935 formulated a program for the raising of labor standards which commands my whole-hearted sympathy and approval, and that of my Administration. Furthermore, I believe the country has this last week given a mandate in unmistakable terms to its legislators and executives to proceed along

these lines until working people throughout the Nation and in every State are assured decent working conditions, including safe and healthful places of work; adequate care and support when incapacitated by reason of accident, industrial disease, unemployment, or old age; reasonably short working hours; adequate annual incomes; proper housing; and elimination of child labor.[66]

After his second inauguration, Roosevelt communicated somewhat less frequently with the public than in 1933, although he still held four press conferences and gave a number of ceremonial and local speeches, such as a radio address marking the thirty-first anniversary of the Boy Scouts and remarks at a schoolhouse dedication in Georgia. He also issued ten messages to Congress. These communications remained devoid of references to the election result or to the campaign. However, Roosevelt invoked mandate rhetoric twice during the first seventy days of the second term. One instance came during a speech at Democratic Party dinner. The second mandate reference was included in a much more widely received address. Roosevelt delivered one fireside chat in February 1937, in the midst of controversy over the proposed Judiciary Reorganization Bill, or "court-packing" plan. After the New Deal had faced several years of legal challenges, Roosevelt responded with a proposal to expand the court by appointing one new justice for each sitting justice who neglected to retire after reaching the age of seventy.[67] By offering a plan to restructure the high court, Roosevelt prompted accusations that he sought to dominate a coequal branch of government. Throughout the crafting of the New Deal, Roosevelt was attentive to constitutional limits at least some of the time. In his study of Roosevelt's attempts to reshape the court, Jeff Shesol reports that although FDR was sometimes "cavalier" about presidential power, he "had gone to some lengths to ensure that his executive order declaring a bank holiday . . . rested on constitutional grounds."[68] Boundaries on executive power were delimited by the written rules of the Constitution as well as informal limits to curb presidential involvement in the policy process.

The story of Roosevelt and court packing parallels that of Andrew Jackson and the Second Bank of the United States. In the summer of 1832, Jackson made the controversial decision to veto a bill renewing the bank's charter. Jackson later drew on his veto as evidence that the electorate had known about his position on the bank before reelecting him and thus endorsed his stance. However, throughout the presidential campaign of 1832, Jackson's National Republican opponents emphasized the president's earlier veto of the bank recharter because of their belief that "it was they who had the most to gain from shifting the election onto the grounds of policy— particularly a policy that badly split the Democratic party—rather than have to run against a popular hero."[69]

Roosevelt, too, downplayed constitutional issues during the 1936 campaign because he was reluctant to give Republicans the opportunity to "rally their supporters around the Constitution."[70] Nevertheless, the possibility that Roosevelt might try to alter the court was well established during the 1936 campaign, not by the president himself but by his opponents. The deeper parallel between Jackson's bank war and Roosevelt's court packing involves the institutional legitimacy at stake. After the election, Jackson ordered the secretary of the treasury, William Duane, to remove deposits from the national bank and place them in state banks—and fired Duane when he refused to do so. By way of justification for this decision, Jackson maintained that his reelection signaled the people's opposition to the bank, and held that this popular mandate formed the basis of his power to destroy the bank by removing the deposits. In other words, the mandate was not simply about policy positions but also about elections as the basis of presidential authority.

Similarly, FDR tried to frame the debate about judicial reorganization in terms of the will of the people versus the power of an unelected court. This lens matched with the economic message of the early New Deal, which linked economic reforms to the preservation of essential American ideals. When Roosevelt first introduced the plan to congressional leadership, he received a positive response from his fellow Democrats.[71] In the spring of 1937, for every piece of mail the administration received in support of the plan, it received eight letters in opposition.[72] Many of the objections were on institutional rather than substantive grounds. William Leuchtenburg maintained that "in attempting to alter the court, Roosevelt had attacked one of the symbols which many believed the nation needed for its sense of unity as a body politic. The Court fight evoked a strong feeling of nostalgia for the days of the Founding Fathers."[73] The president defended his legitimacy by claiming a mandate for his actions, drawing on his connection to the people and his fulfillment of campaign promises.

When FDR introduced the plan to Congress in a message on February 5, 1937, the only mandate he referred to was constitutional.[74] A month later, he defended the plan to the electorate in a fireside chat, emphasizing the power of the people and castigating the court for interfering with the elected branches. In this address, Roosevelt drew on the exigencies of the Depression as well as the presidential mandate:

> The American people have learned from the depression. For in the last three national elections an overwhelming majority of them voted a mandate that the Congress and the President begin the task of providing that protection— not after long years of debate, but now.

> The Courts, however, have cast doubts on the ability of the elected Congress to protect us against catastrophe by meeting squarely our modern social and economic conditions.

> We are at a crisis in our ability to proceed with that protection. It is a quiet crisis. There are no lines of depositors outside closed banks. But to the far-sighted it is far-reaching in its possibilities of injury to America.

Ultimately, the winner of this debate remains unclear. Roosevelt never mustered serious public support for the plan, even immediately after the fireside chat in March.[75] Yet, the overall outcome of the struggles during 1937 led to a shift in jurisprudence on New Deal issues, with "switches" and resignations producing a stable majority in favor of New Deal reform.[76] Scholars will continue to debate about what this episode meant for the Roosevelt presidency and for American politics. For understanding the evolution of the presidential mandate, however, the court-packing story has several important implications.

The first lesson of Roosevelt's efforts to justify the court-packing plan with mandate rhetoric is that mandates are constructed according to political necessity rather than strictly around the results of the election. As John Sloan writes, "by not addressing the question of Supreme Court reform during his campaign, he could not honestly claim an electoral mandate to do so. Still, after winning the election by a landslide, the president was ready to retaliate against a Court that had rebuked his policies."[77] Sloan's observation underscores the element of construction in presidential mandate narratives: even after a party landslide like that of 1936, a clear mandate message is rarely, if ever, obvious. Presidents and their communications teams craft these messages according to their political needs once the president has taken office, if they choose to emphasize electoral logic at all. In this case, Roosevelt did not directly claim a mandate to reshape the Supreme Court; rather, once the plan met resistance, he formulated his interpretation of the election in response. His election references did not anticipate conflict with Congress; nor did they emerge as an organic response to the election result in 1936. They were reactive. By talking about the election result in his March 1937 fireside chat, he underscored popular support not only for the policies in question but also for the right of the president (and Congress) to do what was necessary to bring the people's will to fruition.

Political context and necessity help to explain FDR's different strategies of mandate claiming after the 1932 and 1936 elections. After the 1932 election, Roosevelt's appeals to the popular mandate drew on broad ideas of national unity. In the first inaugural address, the newly elected president presented himself as the electorate's trustee, someone elected to act decisively. More partisan and specific claims were reserved for other audiences. Although the 1936 campaign also ended with a crushing victory for FDR and another round of substantial gains for Democrats in Congress, the political needs were different afterward. Not only had the Supreme Court overturned several important New Deal programs by 1936, but the court-packing plan eventually created a political problem of its own. Once Roosevelt introduced the plan to Congress, the president needed a narrative to respond to the backlash and to explain the heavy-handed role he had embraced toward the judicial branch.

The court-packing debate also illustrates how even the outsized expectations placed on FDR had limits. Ultimately, the failure of FDR's claim to popular authority was also the refusal of Congress and the electorate to accept the expansion of presidential power into judicial affairs. In the context of 1937, Roosevelt's stumble with the court-packing plan was the first of several defeats that delineated the limits of institutional growth.

The next of these major setbacks was Roosevelt's efforts to "purge" the party of New Deal opponents in the 1938 primaries. By trying to rid the Democratic Party of anti-New Deal conservatives, Roosevelt inspired fears that he wished to lead an ideological party.[78] These efforts failed, however, and the Democrats remained an ideologically varied party well into the twentieth century. This diverse nature of American political parties has shaped how modern presidents—particularly Democrats—have approached the idea of the mandate. Constructing a party mandate has proven particularly difficult for presidents charged with leading a party divided on key issues. As we will see in later chapters, this challenge has also applied to Lyndon Johnson, Jimmy Carter, and Barack Obama.

Finally, FDR's efforts to reorganize the executive branch fared slightly better than his attempts to change the judiciary and the Democratic Party. New Deal legislation such as the National Industrial Recovery Act (NIRA) in 1933 and National Labor Relations Act (NLRA; also known as the Wagner Act) in 1935 created new administrative capacity in the executive branch. In the White House itself, the problems identified in the Brownlow Report eventually prompted the growth and institutionalization of White House staff. Although these changes altered the way the presidency and the federal government functioned thereafter, efforts to expand the formal capacity of the executive branch eventually met resistance. Marc Landy and Sidney Milkis describe how the expansion of executive power encountered both legal and political obstacles: the Supreme Court's decision to strike down the National Recovery Administration (created by the NIRA) "declared that the discretionary authority that Congress had granted, at Roosevelt's request, to the National Recovery Administration, the leading economic agency of the New Deal, was an unconstitutional delegation of legislative power to the executive."[79] On the political side, they note that Roosevelt's initial proposal to reorganize the executive branch inspired "the cry of 'dictator,' a charge that had special meaning because of the rise of fascism in Germany and Italy."[80] Nevertheless, significant restructuring eventually occurred on FDR's watch, including the creation of the Executive Office of the President (EOP) and the subsequent transfer of the Bureau of the Budget from the Treasury Department into direct White House control. But these changes were produced by a "watered-down version of FDR's original reorganization bill, largely re-written by legislators."[81] By illustrating both the potential and the limits of presidency-centered government, executive reorganization punctuated several decades of fierce and focused debate over the role and power of the institution and thus marked the transition into the modern presidency. The struggle over national and party leadership per-

sisted, but the moment of responsible parties had—at least temporarily—
passed.

Mandate Politics at a Time of Transition

Between 1929 and 1939, the Progressive period of "loosened scripts" gave
way to the growing demands of the modern presidency. Theodore Roosevelt and especially Woodrow Wilson pushed the limits of the president's
role and contemplated new justifications for expanding presidential power.
The legacy of Progressive politics shaped Hoover's and FDR's approaches to
governing and administration as well. They also inherited unresolved tension between party and nation from the Progressives.

With Hoover's presidency and the onset of the Great Depression, the
search for justification took a backseat to the demand for action. After replacing Hoover in 1933, Franklin Roosevelt often acted as if political conditions
supplied all the necessary justification for presidential strength. Roosevelt's
apparent hesitance to proclaim the 1932 election a Democratic mandate—
in contrast with earlier presidents—signaled a shift into a new presidential
era. Just as FDR conceptualized his New Deal leadership as a national project,
his modern successors would largely see themselves as leaders of a nation
first and a party second.

In Roosevelt's failures and shortcomings, we can also see the Progressive Era coming to a close. Attempts to transform the Supreme Court, the
Democratic Party, and the executive branch signified the end of major negotiations over presidential jurisdiction. In the most politically salient of the
three failures, Roosevelt invoked the electoral mandate as a justification for
his actions. Roosevelt's declaration of a mandate in response to a political
confrontation rather than to the triumph of election victory fits into a recurrent pattern of presidential mandate rhetoric. One of the central goals of
Progressive presidents Wilson and the earlier Roosevelt had been to expand
presidential involvement in the policy process, but FDR took this development to a new level. In pushing the New Deal and inventing the "First
Hundred Days" benchmark for presidential achievement, Roosevelt con-
firmed the legitimacy of a legislatively active presidency. In the modern era,
conflicts over institutional legitimacy occurred less frequently. As national

leaders, modern presidents managed Cold War foreign policy, the pursuit of economic prosperity, and the growing demands for civil rights protections and racial equality. In the face of these demands, electoral logic played a small role in presidential rhetoric, diminished significantly from Progressive ideals about how popular leadership would buoy presidential strength. Presidential strength in the modern era, it seemed, emanated from an ability to both fulfill and temper the demands on the office.

Chapter 3

President of All the People?

Eisenhower, Johnson, and Leadership in the Modern Era

Between 1939 and 1968, presidents were elected and reelected with land-slide majorities and with excruciatingly close margins. Both groups, how-ever, demonstrated restraint in their use of mandate rhetoric. When they did refer to the elections that installed them in office, they often shied away from divisive or ideological themes and described the presidency in trustee, rather than delegate, terms. In this sense, this era was distinct from the Pro-gressive period, when mandate claims—clear, specific, and partisan—were more common. Nearly all inaugural addresses between 1893 and 1933 con-tained some sort of mandate reference; in contrast, during the period be-tween 1941 and 1965, few inaugural speeches included mandate rhetoric. Generally, this period represents a low point in the prominence of electoral logic rhetoric. Examining the cases of Dwight Eisenhower and Lyndon Johnson reveals that choices about how to publicly interpret elections were shaped by a combination of political strategy and visions of the office. Un-like Progressive Era presidents who sought to expand their role in the politi-cal system, modern presidents contended with high expectations about what they would be able to accomplish. Neither Eisenhower nor Johnson appears to have seen mandate rhetoric as a useful tool in dealing with high expectations. Furthermore, both concluded that remaining above party politics (or at least appearing to do so) would help them cultivate a more "presidential" image. As a result, claiming a party mandate became a much less popular communication strategy during this era.

The relatively sparing use of mandate rhetoric is especially puzzling given the wide acceptance of the elections of 1952 and 1964 as mandates in the popular and scholarly consciousness. Few elections have received more attention in the mandate literature than 1964. Charles O. Jones counts it among several "mandates for change."[1] Patricia Conley identifies 1964 as a "popular mandate." She cites Johnson's victory speech as evidence that "Johnson interpreted his victory as a 'command' to build on the principles and policies of the Kennedy-Johnson administrations."[2] Lawrence Grossback, David Peterson, and James Stimson also count the 1964 result among three major, unexpected victories that later came to be classified by the media and by political actors as mandates.[3] From an elections and policy perspective, these assessments are quite intuitive. However, they neglect institutional dimensions of the mandate. Despite the considerable scholarly attention the election has received, none of these accounts look directly at how perceptions of election results within the Johnson White House shaped communications and policymaking. Internal memoranda from the Johnson White House in 1964 and 1965 suggest that the President's top political advisers had reservations about using mandate logic to justify the policy agenda, and that maintaining a "presidential" image—above party politics—remained an important priority.

Scholars have also included the 1952 election among popular mandates and mandates for change. Yet, like much of Eisenhower's presidency, the actual significance of the election remains difficult to pin down. At first glance, 1952 appears to have the traits of a party mandate. After twenty uninterrupted years of Democratic presidents, and only a brief Republican interlude in Congress, the idea of a mandate for fundamental changes in policy direction fit the circumstances. However, the early months of the Eisenhower presidency reveal a different approach. Eisenhower's own references to the campaign and the election sometimes refer to party positions and at other times cite general goals. He was often at odds with his own party, and the partisan, delegate-style concept of representation implied by party mandates conflicted with Eisenhower's attitudes about the presidency.

Conventional theories of mandate claiming predict that both Eisenhower and Johnson would frequently highlight their election victories as a source of political advantage. The other presidents in this era, Truman and Kennedy, both approached electoral logic in much the way we might expect, given that Truman's splintered party contributed to a plurality victory and that Kennedy, too, fell short of a majority and beat Richard Nixon by only two-tenths of a percent in the popular vote. In contrast with later winners of narrow or plurality elections such as Nixon, Clinton, and George W. Bush, neither president made electoral logic central to their communications. Truman's references to Democratic victory harkened back to the partisan logic of Progressive Era inaugural addresses. However, instead of in major national speeches, Truman's claims about the 1948 election as a party victory were confined to a partisan audience at the 1949 Jefferson-Jackson Day dinner. Truman's inaugural address made reference to the American people in a kind of watered-down version of Roosevelt's ideas: "The American people stand firm in the faith that has inspired this nation from the beginning. We believe that all men have the right to equal justice under law and equal opportunity to share in the common good."[4] Kennedy's communications in 1961 were essentially devoid of any electoral logic rhetoric. Presidential scholar George Edwards quotes Kennedy as responding to a question about the mandate with the following: "Mandate, schmandate. The mandate is that I am here and you are not."[5] This attitude seems natural given the election result, but it also exemplifies a broader truth about the relationship between mandates and presidential authority during the modern era. Unlike other presidents at different points in history, these presidents did not need to use the idea of mandate to expand the scope of their legitimate influence. The presidency had been established as a seat of power and a source of policy solutions.

Eisenhower and Johnson are useful cases to consider not only because of the election results that brought them to office. The presidents themselves also provide a "most different" case comparison.[6] Eisenhower had spent his career in the military and had held no previous political office or prior record of service within the Republican Party. This background is often credited with Eisenhower's appeal as a "nonpartisan" president.[7] Lyndon Johnson, in contrast, was an established party politician. First elected to Congress in a special election in 1937, Johnson championed Democratic priorities in the House of Representatives and then in the Senate, first as minority leader and then majority leader. After more than twenty years in the Senate, Johnson unsuccessfully pursued the presidential nomination in 1960, instead becoming John F. Kennedy's running mate.[8] In other words, it would have seemed absurd to suggest in 1964 that Johnson, as a candidate or a president, represented the same nonpartisan values as Eisenhower. Yet, we observe some similarities in the way that Eisenhower and Johnson framed their respective elections. Despite their apparent political differences, the political circumstances and ideas that shaped the attitudes about mandates held by these two leaders had important similarities: both valued the ability to appear "above politics," they conceptualized the office as a seat of political power and strength, and they saw the high expectations placed on the presidency as both an opportunity and a burden.

Legitimacy and the Modern Presidency

Compared with the later partisan period, presidents in the modern era also enjoyed a higher level of institutional status and legitimacy. Therefore, they had no need to define and justify the office in mandate terms, particularly those which draw on delegate notions of presidential representation. Eisenhower and Johnson inherited a political environment in which Progressive reformers had cultivated high expectations of the presidency. The emergence of a more candidate-focused style of presidential politics also placed the onus of fulfilling these expectations on the individual occupying the office. Franklin Roosevelt's presidency solidified this new set of expectations. FDR's extensive accomplishments and political successes set an impossibly high standard for his successors.[9] His highly personal approach to leadership—from the "fireside chats" to his organization of the White House—also shaped the legacy of expectations in the modern presidency. These expectations did not fade as the memory of FDR receded further into history. To the contrary, several foundational works of scholarship on the modern presidency find that the public's expectations of modern presidents far outpace their actual capacities and identify this factor as defining and shaping presidential behavior. This contention was central to Richard Neustadt's analysis, which posited that presidential success depended largely on personal leadership qualities: reputation, consistency, and ability to make the most of strategic bargaining situations.[10] Similarly, George Edwards observes in *At the Margins* that presidents themselves encourage unrealistically high expectations about their influence on Congress and in the policy process. In the decades between the New Deal and the end of Lyndon Johnson's effort to create a "Great Society," the legacy of expectations diminished the need for presidents to use mandate rhetoric to justify their actions.

Political Parties in the Modern Era

In retrospect, the modern period is most readily defined by what was absent: party polarization and distrust of government. Compared with later eras, modern presidents enjoyed relatively high levels of approval among citizens who identified with the opposite party. During Johnson's second year in office, the Gallup Poll revealed that 49 percent of Republicans approved of Johnson's performance in office; likewise, Eisenhower enjoyed about 50 percent support among Democrats during his second year. This number was roughly double Reagan's approval among Democrats at a comparable point in his presidency and about equal to George W. Bush's average approval among Democrats immediately following the September 11, 2001, attacks—a time of exceptionally high patriotism and trust.[11] Also absent during mid-century was the "new media" to reinforce partisan objections to presidential proposals.[12] As a result, presidents in the modern era had more opportunities to maintain broad support in the electorate than their later counterparts would, thus shaping their perceptions about the relationship between the president and the public.

Cultivating support among members of the opposite party was also a political necessity. Low levels of party discipline in Congress meant that Eisenhower and Johnson could not always count on fellow partisans to advocate for White House priorities. Characterizations of mid-century elections as party mandates glide past the complex party dynamics of the time. Eisenhower's victory in 1952 brought some Republican coattails, but congressional Republicans did not always align with the president. As Milkis observes, "Eisenhower's leadership of Congress held up the modern presidency rather than his party," and this treatment ran in both directions. For example, some members of Congress—including Republicans—remained suspicious of growing executive power. On the heels of the successful Twenty-second Amendment, which limited presidents to two terms, Eisenhower's fellow Republican John Bricker introduced an amendment to give Congress the power to "regulate all treaties and executive agreements."[13] The votes to defeat the amendment came mostly from the Democratic Party; less than one-third of the Republican senators who voted on the amendment supported Eisenhower's position.[14] This dynamic of cross-party cooperation characterized major legislation in the modern era; although bipartisan coalitions still form to pass legislation, congressional party behavior has undergone a striking transformation.[15]

Conflict over how to react to the expanding administrative state was a key source of division within Republican Party, culminating most forcefully in the fight over whether to nominate the more moderate Eisenhower or the more staunchly conservative Robert Taft in 1952. Tensions between conservatives and the more moderate faction (sometimes called "modern Republicans") persisted throughout the Eisenhower presidency. Hostility between the two factions was exacerbated by the president's tempered approach, which did not yield electoral gains for the party.[16]

While the Republican Party cast about for an identity, the Democratic Party appeared, on the surface, to be firmly rooted in foundations of the New Deal coalition and ideas. Electoral success gave the coalition a powerful incentive to stay together. Yet, internal divisions over policy and ideology were apparent early on, as Northern liberals embraced a civil rights plank in the party's platform and Southern conservatives held fast to segregation and opposed federal action on civil rights. As a result, Johnson's relationship with the party was complex. On the surface, the 1964 election would appear to have been a clear Democratic mandate, yet this label is deceptive. Sean Savage describes the dominant political force leading up to the 1964 election as a "suprapartisan, centrist policy consensus."[17] Policies associated with Johnson's Great Society drew on support from both parties. These policies, along with the Civil Rights Act (1964) and the Voting Rights Act (1965), ultimately proved anathema to the Southern wing of the Democratic Party. Johnson won some support among Southern Democrats by using shrewd bargaining tactics, such as asking a conservative House Democrat to sponsor the Economic Opportunity Act (1964) in the House in order to defuse Southern opposition.[18] Despite these efforts, Johnson's central agenda items divided the party. In the words of Stephen Skowronek, "the liberal commitment to civil rights had never fit very comfortably into the political consensus that Johnson had determined to preserve."[19] Johnson touted the 1964 election as a mandate for national unity. Scholars and commentators have often understood it as a Democratic mandate. Closer examination reveals that neither narrative fully captures the politics of the moment.

Balancing Party and Nation in the Modern Presidency

Within the Eisenhower and Johnson White House operations, a shared presidential philosophy is apparent. Both believed in strength and in conveying the image of a leader above the fray of party politics. This objective informed their rhetoric about election results and about their relationships with the public. Balancing party and nation posed a challenge for both leaders, partly because of the party dynamics outlined in the previous section. They also struggled to define what it meant to be above partisan politics and yet still take meaningful policy stances, how to keep their broad (and often cross-party) coalitions together and still lead the nation's policy conversation.

Eisenhower's relationship with the Republican Party has stymied and fascinated recent scholars. Scholarship on Eisenhower's political views, strategy, and attitudes have been the subject of much recent rediscovery in the wake of Fred Greenstein's seminal book, *The Hidden-Hand Presidency.* Since Greenstein's revelation that Eisenhower possessed far more refined political skills than anyone had previously believed, scholarly attention to the many layers of the Eisenhower presidency has steadily developed. His underexplored skill as a politician and party leader has been of particular interest. Skowronek identifies Eisenhower as a "hard case" for classification in the political time framework; coming into office as a Republican during a Democratic political order, "he demonstrated extraordinary sensitivity to the resilience of the previously established regime."[20] Daniel Galvin finds evidence that, despite Eisenhower's lack of party credentials prior to 1952, he "worked tirelessly behind the scenes to build a new Republican Party that could appeal to a majority in the electorate and serve as a durable testament to his legacy."[21] Yet, Eisenhower's vision for the party did not lend itself to a clear interpretation of the 1952 election. His ideas about the direction of the party met resistance from congressional Republicans who preferred a more conservative approach. Furthermore, although Eisenhower was in many ways a committed party leader, the ideal of the nonpartisan president still influenced his outward political strategy.

Before he had to worry about defining his presidency, however, Eisenhower had to win the Republican nomination. Eisenhower's assumption of party leadership was somewhat unusual insofar as he had not been previously affiliated with the party and had been recruited as a candidate by both parties. In the course of a nomination contest fought against Robert Taft, however, Eisenhower became a party standard bearer of sorts. Taft, in the words of Eisenhower biographer Jim Newton, "was a leader of the U.S. Senate and an ideological archetype, a sharp critic of labor unions and the New Deal, an isolationist so committed to American nonintervention that he opposed war against Nazi Germany until the U.S. was attacked at Pearl Harbor."[22] Eisenhower provided contrast across the board: he advocated a softer and more "pragmatic" approach to New Deal programs[23] and served as "the logical choice for internationalist-minded Republicans."[24]

In his extensive documentation of Eisenhower's presidential philosophy, Greenstein observes that "the unique characteristic of Eisenhower's approach to presidential leadership was his self-conscious use of political strategies" that allowed him to reconcile the competing roles of "chief of state and the nation's highest political executive."[25] Further documentary evidence suggests that Eisenhower and his political staff viewed his relationship with the electorate primarily through the lens of trusteeship. A memo from Press Secretary Jim Hagerty to the president in 1958 illustrates the trusteeship idea in the Eisenhower White House. Hagerty, addressing concerns about how to maximize political influence under the new term limits, suggests the following stance to Eisenhower:

> It seems to me that during the next two years it might be wise to follow the old Roman idea of "The Tribune of the People" and place repeated public emphasis of the Office of the President on what you have always done— work for the welfare of the American people without regard to partisan politics. Everyone in the country realizes that you cannot succeed yourself. But I do not think that there is a general realization that the programs the President proposes are not for his own personal aggrandizement or political gain but rather for the American people as a whole.[26]

This advice reflects not only Eisenhower's need to position himself as a national leader but also his unique place in history as the first president to face formal term limits under the Twenty-second Amendment. Although the implications of Eisenhower's "lame duck" status were never clear,[27] term limits were a concrete example of a question about presidential power and legitimacy that had been settled as the modern era began; a boundary that had been firmly and formally delineated.

These ideas were not limited to the final years of the administration, however. In 1953, with a strong victory behind them and another election ahead, Eisenhower's speechwriters and policy advisers contemplated the president's role as a national trustee. A lengthy note in the papers of speechwriter Bryce Harlow observes,

> There are two ways of winning elections:
>
> 1. To promise particular favors to particular groups in hopes of putting together an active majority of beneficiaries without making the general public mad at the expense or the favoritism.
> 2. The other way is to promise a program that has overall advantages to the vast majority sufficient to overcome people's disappointment at not getting particular favors.
>
> The president was elected because the people had profound confidence that he would follow the second course.[28]

This note, which was included among drafts and memoranda about the president's major address in August 1953, deals with one of the fundamental dilemmas of mandate claiming: whether to emphasize party or nation. Eisenhower's communications team continued to be mindful of these questions as the first term progressed; in January 1954, C. D. Jackson, special assistant to the president, sent a message to Harlow from a friend suggesting that the president use the expression "your administration" instead of "my administration" in order to underscore that "the keynote of his attitude is one of harmony between political groups, and that he is president of *all* the people of the United States." A note from Harlow written on the memo reads, "He is completely right, I think."[29] Eisenhower's advisers not only stressed the importance of claiming a national mandate; they also sought to frame the election as a personal mandate for the president, a concept distinct to the modern presidency.

Papers from the Johnson administration reveal less about his philosophy of the office itself, but communications among high-level staff convey that consensus and unity played an important role in how the Johnson White House approached politics. After a long career in Congress, Johnson was defensive about appearing "presidential," especially during the campaign. For example, Johnson aide Bill Moyers attached a note to a draft of a campaign speech that read, "This speech is an effort to meet the President's desire for remarks that steer away from the strictly political and maintain instead the posture of a 'presidential address.'"[30] The juxtaposition of "presidential" and "political" as mutually exclusive categories echoes a recurring theme of the modern presidency. Modern presidents have largely been party creatures, and Johnson was no exception. Unlike Eisenhower, Johnson had been a party politician for almost thirty years when he first appeared on a national ticket as Kennedy's running mate in 1960. Like Eisenhower—and Roosevelt and nearly every other previous president—Johnson also espoused policy stances that appealed to his party in the electorate and were consistent with the party's overarching philosophy. Yet, despite his indisputable party credentials, Johnson often shied away from party themes in his policy and campaign rhetoric in an effort to appear "presidential." A memo from speechwriter Richard Goodwin to foreign policy advisor to the president McGeorge Bundy discusses mandates and foreign policy. Goodwin suggests the following:

We aim at two things specifically on the foreign policy side of the campaign: (a) get votes, (b) shape the outlines of a policy which we want to follow, and which we can, after November, say we have a mandate to follow. This is the best chance to get a foreign policy mandate a President has ever had.

In all of this we must concentrate on the single greatest weakness of our campaign and that is the doubt that Johnson is a world statesman, capable of dealing with the great issues of peace and war. The Republicans will concentrate on this very heavily, trying to make him a wheeler-dealer, a slick politico, etc. That is why foreign policy is very important in this campaign.[31]

Johnson also believed in consensus in the domestic policy arena. Although the American electorate's views on racial progress or social welfare programs were never unanimous, Johnson's held fast to his belief about consensus as a guiding concept in American politics. As Johnson biographer Doris Kearns Goodwin notes, Johnson believed that Americans shared a basic set of values, and he sought to preserve the broad consensus that he believed was embodied in the 1964 vote.[32] This attitude permeated campaign strategy. Moyers suggested in September 1964 that a possible theme for campaign speeches might be "a choice between the center and the fringe"; he offered a speech draft calling on people to "reject the fringe" and endorse the administration's "bipartisan policy."[33] In addition to Johnson's political values, these ideas also had campaign purposes; focusing on centrism and bipartisanship allowed the Johnson camp to further paint Barry Goldwater as a dangerous extremist, a narrative that proved to have traction, if not truth.

As we shall see in the examination of Johnson and mandate rhetoric that follows, the "centrism and fringe" story was less than conducive to making a distinct claim to a mandate—much less so than ex post evaluations of the 1964 election have suggested. In this sense, the extent to which electoral logic shaped policy and communications within the Johnson White House was determined by both leadership style and context. The same is true of Eisenhower. The absence of mandate rhetoric in these two cases appears to stem mostly from the fact that political context and leadership styles called for other kinds of justifications and rhetorical tropes. When these leaders did talk about election results, they often emphasized national unity and presented themselves as trustees charged with leading the electorate.

Eisenhower Interprets the Election of 1952

In 1952, Eisenhower won nearly 55 percent of the popular vote, beating Democratic opponent Adlai Stevenson by ten percentage points and winning Electoral College votes from all but nine states. Despite the early appearance of a "mandate for change" (also the name of Eisenhower's memoirs of the 1952 campaign), the Republicans lost control of Congress in the 1954 midterms and did not regain it in 1956, despite Eisenhower's popular appeal. The main issue of the campaign between Stevenson and Eisenhower appears to have been foreign policy, namely Eisenhower's promise to end the Korean War.[34] However, looking more closely at the President's rhetoric along with exchanges and notes among advisers and White House staff, we see that electoral logic appears also to have been employed in a limited way to domestic policy problems.

How did political actors at the time react to the 1952 election? What were the prevailing impressions about why Eisenhower won by such a landslide, and what did it mean for governance? Although scholars have decided in retrospect that this election result was not a party mandate and that the election's primary purpose was to justify Eisenhower's foreign policy leadership, other interpretations were apparent in late 1952 and early 1953. The day after the election, the *Chicago Tribune* reported:

> The Republican campaign was based on the necessity for a change. Eisenhower led the Republicans in attacking the administration's conduct of the Korean War, saying that if he should be elected he would go to the front himself and seek means of ending the conflict with honor.
>
> Republicans also made communism and corruption twin campaign issues. They attacked the economy of the Truman administration with its inflation and rising taxes.[35]

Eisenhower's 1952 campaign illustrates some of the common problems that arise when leaders seek to construct mandates for change. Chief among these is the assortment of possible issues to link with the election result. Another challenge is the fine line between emphasizing differences between the parties and running a mostly negative campaign. As the *Tribune* article also notes, Republicans were generally victorious in 1952. Soon after the election concluded, however, clues began to mount that the dominant narrative would not be a party mandate. On November 9, 1952, an Associated Press article declared that "the decision of the voters Tuesday came in one of those tidal sweeps that mark American political history," and compared the election to the ones that brought Thomas Jefferson, Andrew Jackson, Warren Harding, and Franklin Roosevelt to power. Unlike those contests, however, the piece maintains "it was an Eisenhower triumph rather than a party triumph."[36] A *New York Times* editorial titled "The Landslide" similarly touts Eisenhower's "mandate" but emphasizes the candidate's popularity with "'independent' voters" and emphasizes that the victory was "national" rather than "sectional."[37]

The national-versus-sectional theme had appeared in Franklin Roosevelt's mandate rhetoric in 1937, specifically in a speech at a Democratic victory dinner. In the context of court packing and increasingly intense contention over New Deal policies and presidential power, this theme fell by the wayside.

By contrast, national unity and the idea of serving as "president of all the people" figured prominently into the discussion of communication strategy within the Eisenhower White House. At the same time, there is no evidence that the president or his speechwriters were particularly preoccupied with developing a cohesive narrative interpreting the election as a mandate for any particular policy or idea. Some reactions underscored the narrative of the 1952 election as a "personal mandate" for Eisenhower himself. After the election, the president-elect received a memo on economic policy issues from White House assistant Stephen Benedict about the circumstances surrounding the victory:

> That you won by a landslide in the face of such (positive) economic readings on the economic indicators is phenomenal. There have only been four changes of party in power in this century. In 1912 the Taft-Roosevelt split gave the White House to Wilson. In 1920 several factors, including a downturn in business, turned the Democrats out. In 1932, it was the depression that beat Hoover. You, and you alone, have bucked good times and won![38]

Eisenhower's philosophy of the office is evident in exchanges with his speechwriters during the drafting of his first State of the Union address, delivered on February 3, 1953. A memo from presidential adviser Harold Stassen to speechwriter Emmet Hughes stressed the theme of bipartisanship, critiquing the piece of the speech draft that refers to "'outs' and 'ins'" as "undesirable in the atmosphere of bi-partisanship with which President Eisenhower will be starting his administration."[39] Stassen also offered his comments on an early draft of the message:

> I feel that it needs more 'lift' and more 'warmth.' It is too matter of fact, and does not bring out the humanitarian quality in President Eisenhower's approach to the people.
>
> On specifics, I would like to see it include a strong statement on the basic concept of Mutual Security, expressing the elementary premise that America cannot be secure unless other free peoples are secure, and that they cannot be secure unless America is secure.
>
> Further expression of intention to bring forward a program for Asiatic Development and Trade, and for a sound long-term approach to insure [*sic*] adequate raw materials supply for all non-Communist nations, including America, would appear to be desirable.

The message might also anticipate the better coordination and consolidation of America's economic, financial, and military aid relationships to the non-Communist countries so that with fewer employees overseas spending less money we can obtain better results and make more friends.

Earlier drafts of this message reveal stronger wordings describing the electoral logic of the 1952 election. For example, the first circulated draft of the speech included a line about the "overwhelming majority" of the people who voted for the administration.[40] A later draft also includes this phrase but provides a slightly more specific picture of what the "overwhelming majority" had demanded in the election: "a true and constructive change in their leadership's approach to our basic problems, both national and international."[41]

The State of the Union address, delivered on February 2, 1953, less than two weeks after inauguration, opened with a pledge to govern according to the broad purposes and principles established during the campaign:

> It is manifestly the joint purpose of the congressional leadership and of this administration to justify the summons to governmental responsibility issued last November by the American people. The grand labors of this leadership will involve: Application of America's influence in world affairs with such fortitude and such foresight that it will deter aggression and eventually secure peace; Establishment of a national administration of such integrity and such efficiency that its honor at home will ensure respect abroad; Encouragement of those incentives that inspire creative initiative in our economy, so that its productivity may fortify freedom everywhere; and Dedication to the well-being of all our citizens and to the attainment of equality of opportunity for all, so that our Nation will ever act with the strength of unity in every task to which it is called.
>
> The purpose of this message is to suggest certain lines along which our joint efforts may immediately be directed toward realization of these four ruling purposes.[42]

What are we to make of the disappearance of the claim to an "overwhelming" mandate in the beginning of the address? None of the accompanying memoranda explained why the final version eliminated this phrase.[43] However, the change is consistent with the general avoidance of mandate claiming during the modern era, and the Eisenhower presidency specifi-

cally. Although merely suggestive, rather than conclusive, it seems possible that the stronger mandate language was omitted at the behest of a later contributor to the speech draft—possibly Eisenhower himself. What we can tell from the available evidence is that State of the Union that the president delivered included a reference to the election that was compatible with "hidden-hand" ideas of politics and ideas about being president of all the people.

In addition to the State of the Union (and, of course, the inaugural address), Eisenhower gave five press conferences in the spring of 1953 between January 20 and March 31. He also issued three messages to Congress and gave seven addresses to groups such as the American Legion, the Boy Scouts, and the American Medical Association.

Eisenhower's only other election references (besides the State of the Union) took the form of mentioning campaign promises during news conferences. Before opening up for questions on February 17, 1953, the president read a statement about farm prices:

> I merely show—and I must emphasize here—that it is a very complicated problem. But above all things, let me emphasize this: *all through the campaign I stated—and promised—to the farmers of America: we will support the present law which goes, as you know, to December 1954, and in the meantime, we will convene commissions* [emphasis added]. We have one now—the Advisory Commission, Department of Agriculture, has on it representatives of all branches of agriculture, and we try, of course, to put on people representing the public. So, any plan devised to take effect after the expiration of the current law, will represent the thinking of America—not only of the producers but of the consumers and everybody else—so as to get as broadly based a program as it is possible to get.
>
> *Everybody, of course, sympathizes with the farmer's plight, with the special difficulties he has in his industry; and I refer you again to that sentence of the Republican Platform, which I certainly intend to do my best to carry out* [emphasis added].

The farm price support issue illustrates one of the key challenges that Eisenhower faced in claiming a mandate for his brand of "New Republicanism." The Republican platform, to which the president referred in his opening statement to reporters, made a clear and unequivocal case against federal price support programs for agriculture. Eisenhower began his own statement with a sentence from the platform: "A prosperous agriculture with free and independent farmers is fundamental to the national interest." However, this relatively innocuous and ambiguous sentence was followed by a much stronger statement:

> We charge the present Administration with seeking to destroy the farmers' freedom. We denounce the Administration's use of tax money and a multitude of Federal agencies to put agriculture under partisan political dictation and to make the farmer dependent upon government.[44]

Caught between a popular program and the convictions of conservatives in his own party, Eisenhower offered what Edward L. Schapsmeier and Frederick H. Schapsmeier call a "cagey and carefully delimited promise" during the campaign.[45] The February 1953 news statement refers back to that promise, which held that the administration would maintain the current policy for its first year in office. Other actions and statements were similarly equivocal. Eisenhower saw the necessity to be cautious with federal programs in order to maintain political support, perhaps most famously summarized in a letter to his brother, Edgar: "Should any political party attempt to abolish social security and eliminate labor laws and farm programs, you would not hear of that party again in our history."[46] Nevertheless, the newly elected president appointed the conservative Ezra Taft Benson to the post of agriculture secretary, underscoring Eisenhower's own preference to eliminate price controls.[47] In this sense, Eisenhower's references to the campaign and the election are consistent with what we already know about his circumstances and leadership style. The politics of the time required Eisenhower's balancing act between conservative ideas and prevailing standards of post–New Deal governance. His own political style was to strategically obfuscate and maintain a centrist, sometimes vague message.[48]

By using the electoral logic of campaign promises to defend the administration's policy efforts, Eisenhower appeared to follow the responsible-party model by citing the promises of the platform as a means of addressing a difficult issue. Yet, as he referred to the party platform, he obscured the platform's actual statement about farm policy. In contrast with the State of the Union address, which claimed electoral justification for a much broader set of goals, Eisenhower attempted to frame his approach to farm policy in terms of a party mandate narrative. In true Eisenhower form, the missing element was the actual content of the party's position.

Electoral Logic and Eisenhower's Mandate for Change

In the Eisenhower White House, the idea of the "president of all the people" remained a speechwriting priority through all eight years in office. At the same time, the president's policy positions derived very much from conservative ideas.[49] This tension is evident in the way Eisenhower's communications treated the 1952 election. It also helps to explain why electoral logic was used so infrequently despite the substantial election victory.

The paucity of mandate rhetoric in 1953 may also stem from an idiosyncratic feature of the election itself: almost immediately after the election, the narrative of the "personal mandate" emerged for a number of reasons—not the least of which was the gap between Eisenhower's landslide and the narrower margins by which Republicans regained control of Congress. Nevertheless, Eisenhower could have worked toward constructing a more policy-based or partisan mandate narrative. He appears to have chosen not to do so, which brings us back to the contextual and individual factors that explain why electoral logic was not an important political idea in his administration. Context weighed against the usefulness of the party mandate narrative, given the highly divided state of the Republican Party. Furthermore, Eisenhower came to office as an opponent of the dominant "regime," coming from outside what Skowronek has defined as Roosevelt's New Deal "political order,"[50] and David Crockett termed the "reigning governing philosophy."[51] As such, efforts to claim a Republican mandate might simply have run contrary to public sentiment on the issues of the day. On top of contextual factors, Eisenhower's own political style helps to explain his approach to electoral logic. Not only did he appear to value unifying rhetoric, but he also usually embraced a trustee-like approach to the presidency. When his speeches and statements did draw on the election or the campaign, they placed less emphasis on "doing what I was elected to do" than on a general sense of responsibility for the country's well being.

Overall, the Eisenhower White House did not go to great lengths to incorporate interpretations of the 1952 election into rhetoric or policymaking. The election victory appeared to be cause for some congratulations and some basic speculation. When Eisenhower did invoke electoral logic, he avoided strongly partisan or potentially divisive themes. Ultimately, the administration had other priorities in crafting its communication strategy and other means of justifying the policy agenda.

Expectations and the 1964 Election

Confidence about winning in 1964 did not obliterate political anxiety in the Johnson White House. Historian Paul Conkin notes that Johnson's goal was "not just victory but the largest mandate in history."[52] In addition, memoranda from high-level White House staff reveal concern about the high expectations created by poll results. For example, Johnson aide Douglass Cater alerted the president to the latest changes in Gallup Poll numbers: "Since early August you have lost only 3 pints [*sic*]—from 65 to 62. If you can hold this degree of slippage for the remaining period, you won't be at all unhappy. You don't want to see any headlines on Gallup, 'The President Losing Ground.'"[53] In a similar vein, Cater wrote a memorandum on October 2, urging Johnson to engage in campaign activities that show his concern for American communities and their problems as a means of counteracting implications that Johnson was merely the "lesser of two evils."[54] Cater also passed along advice from the then president of Swarthmore College Courtney Smith in a separate memo two weeks later. The president's aide added to the advice, which warned Johnson to be wary of receiving a "grudging mandate" in which he won by a landslide but without much enthusiasm, by noting, "At this point in the campaign, it seems obvious that Goldwater has no hope of victory but means to detract from your victory as much as possible." Smith also draws attention to the question of election polls and magnitude, arguing, "The effect of polls has been to create expectations that you will get well over 60% of the vote. I believe it would be useful for you to repeat what you told the bureau chiefs at the beginning of the month—that you consider 56% of the vote a decisive victory. Otherwise, I predict anything less will be treated by the press as 'Goldwater Shows Surprising Strength in Defeat.'"

These communications shed some light on the challenge of interpreting election results, even before the election had occurred. In the late stages of the campaign, the need to manage expectations began to shape the administration's considerations of a mandate. Furthermore, as the election drew near, Johnson and his aides confronted the fact that the public's high expectations had been driven in part by the perception that Goldwater was an extremist (an image the Johnson campaign had actively promoted). Their concerns also contradict the idea that electoral mandates are simple and straightforward; favorable election returns may not be enough to construct a compelling narrative.

After the election, news media contributed to the task of constructing a mandate. However, these accounts contributed to the burden of expectations that the administration now faced. As an article in the *New York Times* from November 15, 1964 states, "Even in the old Congress, Mr. Johnson was regarded as having achieved a number of lesser measures. Now he should have even smoother sailing as he presses ahead with medicare [*sic*], the Appalachia antipoverty bill, and other aspects of the Administration program on which Congress failed to act this year."[55] Similarly, James Reston of the *New York Times* declared, "How he deals with this opportunity will tell us quite a lot about the quality of his new Administration."[56] An analysis of the election in the *Chicago Tribune* lays out Johnson's circumstances in more detail, listing the ambitious policies that would be expected to pass after stalling in the previous session. The article also notes:

> House reaction remains problematical despite the increased Democratic majority. The same 1936 election sweep that Johnson approached yesterday did not produce a House that went along with many of the Roosevelt proposals. In 1938, voters removed 71 Democrats from their seats.[57]

Other news reports emphasized the weakness of Johnson's opposition. An article in the *New York Times* on November 4 introduces a potential drawback from the exceptional election victory: "the sterility of the choice offered by the opposition prevented any meaningful discussion of the real issues that confront the United States." Nevertheless, the piece maintains that the election could be interpreted as a resounding rejection of "the thesis that the challenges of an era of dynamic, relentless change in domestic and foreign affairs can be met by dismantling the Federal Government or by shaking a nuclear fist at the rest of the world."[58]

Interpreting the Landslide

Because of the election result, it is possible to assume that the mandate was obvious and thus did not need much introduction or framing. The 1964 election clearly yielded a much wider margin of victory than most elections. However, this assumption is not the same as a clearly articulated story about the policy implications of the victory. Such stories require deliberate construction, and Johnson's advisers knew this. The narrative that emerged stressed broad ideas, such as justice and progress, and de-emphasized the president's role as a delegate of the electorate's preferences. These choices offered flexibility (in contrast with later presidents who would claim an electoral mandate for specific policies), but may also have contributed to the perception that Johnson had "overreached" by pursuing such an ambitious policy agenda.[59]

As the Johnson team transitioned from campaigning back to governing, they had several options for constructing the 1964 mandate. One possibility was to emphasize the election outcome as a policy mandate, touting both the party victory and the incumbent's clear policy positions during the campaign. This first approach would have been compatible with the forming media narratives, but the administration had good reason to develop its own story. Emphasizing party politics would have both violated Johnson's own belief in the importance of consensus and common ground and presupposed a state of disciplined and unified parties that did not actually exist. In addition, the administration would now need to balance its policy ambition with the management of expectations.

The need to temper expectations also taps into Johnson's own impressions of electoral mandates. He saw them as ephemeral and unreliable ways of justifying policy. As Robert Dallek describes, Johnson "doubted that his smashing victory was a mandate or any unqualified national commitment to any specific legislative program."[60] D. K. Goodwin observes "Johnson's optimism and energy were accompanied by an intense anxiety that his popular mandate might be swiftly eroded."[61] This attitude spurred the president to work quickly, and also, it appears, to generally avoid grounding his policy agenda in the idea of an electoral mandate. Johnson instead opted for a combination of two other frameworks. Instead of stressing party victory, the president and his speechwriters cast the election in terms of Johnson's own belief in consensus and unity. But these references were also quite infrequent, especially considering the magnitude of the victory. In other words, Johnson chose not to place much emphasis on electoral logic at all.

Instead of electoral logic, Johnson frequently rooted his approach to major changes in terms of enduring and unifying values—the same values that would come into question in the political developments of the late 1960s and beyond. Johnson's inaugural address in 1965 reintroduced the idea of the Great Society in terms of "justice, liberty, and union."[62] Similarly, after the Senate passed the Medicare bill on July 9, 1965, Johnson linked the bill's passage to a fight for justice rather than to a satisfaction of campaign promises or electoral demands:

> For these long decades bill after bill has been introduced to help older citizens meet the often crushing and always rising costs of disease and crippling illness. Each time, until today, the battle has been lost. Each time the forces of compassion and justice have returned from defeat to begin the battle anew. And each time the force of increased public understanding has added to our strength.[63]

When the president did make reference to the election victory, he framed it in very broad and general terms. In an interview with the *U.S. News & World Report*, the newly reelected President maintained that his victory had been due to "a strong and broad consensus" and that he interpreted the election as a "mandate . . . for responsible, constructive, and progressive programs to meet the problems of American's agenda." [64] This brand of mandate logic also permeated advice on the 1965 State of the Union, as political aide Horace Busby expressed in a memorandum to Richard Goodwin, which suggests that "a Johnsonian tone should be struck immediately, perhaps characterizing the election outcome: i.e., the people gave all of us the mandate of their own unity—it is now for all of us, ob [*sic*] both parties, to nurture that unity and to use it for great purposes, rather than allowing it to be lost in small causes or needless divisions. As the first 'consensus' and 'unity' President of the times, I believe the President should begin on this note—with an applause line." [65] This precise logic, along with Busby's "applause line," was notably absent from the 1965 State of the Union,[66] although Johnson did allude to the "choice of the people" in his remarks on policy toward the Soviet Union.[67]

As with Eisenhower, Johnson's sparing use of electoral logic seems to have reflected a mix of attitudes about presidential governance and strategic considerations of the political constraints of the time. In a different political context, Johnson's assertions about consensus might have seemed misplaced. During 1965, Johnson enjoyed high approval ratings (between 60 and 70 percent) and a modest gap between Democrats and Republicans.[68] Between November 1964 and November 1965, the difference in average ratings was 31 percent, less than half of Barack Obama's "approval gap" in year two. As a result, Johnson could emphasize unity and make claims about national values without meeting the kind of resistance that later presidents would face. The political context of the mid-1960s meant that the consensus narrative could be persuasive, at least immediately after the election. At the same time, had Johnson's own beliefs and particular situation been different, the election narrative might have taken a different tone. Between the strategic concern about appearing "presidential" and the core belief in the possibility of national consensus, Johnson was unlikely to embrace a partisan narrative. Would a different mandate story have influenced the course and outcome of policy debate? Of course, it is impossible to know for sure. We do know that Johnson's assessment of the national consensus for a racial equality and for a slate of "Great Society" programs may have been a stretch. Johnson himself predicted that civil rights legislation would, as his famous quotation suggests, alienate Southerners from the Democratic Party for the foreseeable future. Johnson's Great Society programs, as the next section explains, changed the political conversation and invited a conservative backlash about race, culture, and the role of government that still shapes politics nearly fifty years later.

Consensus Breaks Down

Going into his first elected term, Johnson had great opportunities and also faced tremendous pressure to produce policy results. The media's construction of the 1964 election as a chance to enact an extensive agenda, Johnson's public rhetoric about fundamental principles, and Johnson's own expectations for his presidency converged to shape his Great Society programs, including the extensive and controversial War on Poverty. David Zarefsky and Jeffrey Tulis have noted the impact of rhetorical frames on Johnson's policy choices. Zarefsky observes that the "war on poverty" label, introduced prior to the 1964 election, "partook of the habits of thought that characterized the crisis presidency under the impact of the Cold War. Simply put, a crisis (such as war) rearranges the rhetorical ground."[69] Similarly, Tulis describes the link between rhetorical framing and policy:

> In place of an argument indicating why poverty should be considered a national problem, why it required a coordinated program, why present efforts were insufficient or ill-conceived, and why the kinds of legislation suggested by the president fit together as a single program—instead of this, the president offered a metaphor, whose premise provided the answers. If we were at *war* [emphasis in original] with poverty, such an effort would require a national mobilization, coordination, extensive executive discretion, and the potential involvement of virtually any social program as vital to the war effort. Wars require these things.[70]

In the context of electoral logic, the Johnson presidency generates a profound irony. In haste to claim legitimacy rooted in consensus, the administration produced policies that divided the electorate. Measures intended to alleviate poverty and racial injustice contributed to the lasting reorganization of party politics around cultural and social issues. As Johnson's War on Poverty expanded, the debate shifted from a tug-of-war over spending and federalism toward a deeper disagreement about the nature and causes of poverty. The policies to combat poverty carried implicit arguments about the causes of poverty, usually citing social and structural factors.[71] In response to liberal arguments about the historical and structural reasons for poverty, the conservative legal and intellectual movement promoted alternate, often cultural, explanations for widespread poverty. Historians Maurice Isserman and Michael Kazin suggest that Johnson's policy choices, particularly in the areas of welfare and race, engendered a backlash among members of the white working class who were "already fearful about blacks moving into their neighborhoods, [and] resented the war on poverty as a payoff to rioters, 'welfare queens,' and 'poverty pimps.' In a nation long obsessed with the automobile, it was only fitting that the earliest and pithiest statements of new political trends were to be found attached to rear fenders: when 'I Fight

Poverty, I Work' bumper stickers began appearing in the mid-1960s, it was clear that the nation's brief honeymoon of concern and goodwill with the poor was coming to an end."[72]

Similarly, crime began to heat up as a national political issue. According to Robert Dallek, "the Johnson administration was seen as more the cause than the solution to the problem. Crime increased six times faster than population during the Kennedy-Johnson presidencies, Richard Nixon asserted in 1966."[73] This backlash did not always aim directly at Johnson's programs; Supreme Court decisions about the rights of accused criminals and cultural touchstones like prayer in school also fueled conservative thinking.[74] Naturally, race played a role as well. Marc Landy and Sidney Milkis describe how Johnson's pursuit of fair housing policies created new dimensions of political conflict, noting that "LBJ's rhetorical message of integrated workplaces and neighborhoods clashed with rights and quasi-rights that many people held dear. For the most part, Americans acknowledged that everybody should be able to eat, drink, and travel where they liked. They did not view a right to live and work where one wanted in the same absolute terms."[75]

The most obvious lesson from this story concerns the dangers of over interpreting a policy mandate. This kind of error is usually associated with partisan mandate narratives. However, in this case it seems to have emanated from Johnson's sense that he was responsible not only for a few key party agenda items but for an extensive agenda. The repercussions, however, extend beyond the Johnson presidency. The Johnson backlash ushered in the reformulation of the political conversation around "law and order" issues (which encompassed racial resentments) as well as questions of culture and society. Debates about race, poverty, and rights infused policy discussions with culture and morality, making stakes high and common ground elusive. For presidential efforts to develop coherent policy narratives, this shift is significant. As chapters 4 and 5 show, presidents have rarely gone so far as to connect policy mandates to the most divisive issues. However, in a context in which these issues help to define political alternatives, narratives of unity and consensus have proven less advantageous for presidents. In campaigns and in office, presidents have also contributed to this state of affairs by stressing "wedge issues" for political gain.

Another major source of division, the escalation of conflict in Vietnam, represented a campaign promise that Johnson did not keep. Splintering over this issue led Johnson to lose the left, and a major source of presidential authority—the sense that foreign policy issues were outside the boundaries of partisan conflict. According to Skowronek, "the touchstones of the prior consensus—the containment of communism, the incremental expansion of the welfare state, and an economy managed by the federal government to secure stable growth—had all been thrown open to question by (Johnson's) concern of action on all fronts."[76]

The political salience of the Vietnam conflict increased after the 1964 election, in which Johnson was perceived to have made (and betrayed) a commitment to peace. Peace was also emphasized as a campaign theme that united disparate groups and had broad appeal. One instance of this emphasis came in the preparation for a speech at a fund-raiser in Harrisburg, Pennsylvania, in September 1964. After the topic of unemployment, Johnson aide Bill Moyers suggests peace as an issue with broad appeal:

> Quakers like it. So do the Dutch. So do the essentially conservative people who live around Harrisburg. So do Jews. So do women. Goldwater scares all these people and more on the peace issue. They fear he has an itchy finger on the nuclear trigger. Nearly everyone agrees that a simple, straightforward sincere statement on peace by the President would be his best speech line. Some would elaborate it with strength and preparedness, with references to Genevieve Blatt and women, with readiness to go the extra mile in negotiation until the arms burdens can be lifted. Governor Lawrence recalls FDR's simple 'I hate war.'[77]

The story of Johnson and Vietnam is now familiar. The conflict escalated, divided the Democratic Party, and captured public attention. Forty-eight percent of respondents in an October 1966 Gallup Poll identified the Vietnam War as the most important problem facing the country, and about a third of respondents suggested that the conflict was the "main reason" that the Republicans would likely gain seats in the midterm.[78] Mary Dovel of Freeport, New York, summed up the frustration of voters who felt betrayed in a letter written on February 14, 1966, which stated, "I voted for you because, during your campaign you advocated peace in Viet Nam. However since you took office, you seem to have allowed Hawk McNamara to take the reins from your hands and to escalate the war at his will. Therefore unless you find a way to keep your promises of peace, I shall not vote for you again."[79]

Electoral Logic and the Modern Era

We may never have a conclusive understanding about why Eisenhower was elected in 1952 and Johnson reelected in 1964. Disentangling the relative importance of all possible factors—the policy positions and personal characteristics of the winners, the flaws of the losing candidates, campaign choices, and economic conditions—would defy practical and conceptual limitations. However, we now know something about what Eisenhower and Johnson—and their advisers—thought about the victories of 1952 and 1964. From the available evidence, we can surmise that the 1952 victory was perceived in the Eisenhower White House as a result of the president's personal political style, particularly his ability to represent the national interest. Once in office, however, Eisenhower found himself balancing the national trustee narrative with the more ideologically driven promises from the party platform. Eisenhower and his advisers drew connections between the election result and the basic principles of the governing agenda, but these connections played a very small role in the president's rhetoric. Furthermore, the Eisenhower presidency was generally free from institutional disputes on the level of Roosevelt's court-packing plan. The absence of conflict over institutional legitimacy appears to have meant less reliance on electoral logic rhetoric. Nevertheless, Eisenhower still fits the basic pattern of using mandate rhetoric at a moment of political weakness; the president deflected criticism by citing the Republican platform in response to a question about the controversial issue of farm price supports. In sum, the case of Eisenhower in 1953 illustrates the role of electoral logic in the modern era. Although the 1952 election could have been molded into a party mandate, the Eisenhower White House did not perceive the result in party terms. Furthermore, the absence of major conflict over the role of the president meant less need for legitimacy narratives.

Johnson's use of electoral logic in 1965 followed a similar pattern. The policy consequences were quite different, but the underlying logic of parties, mandates, and rhetoric reflected the ideas and values of the modern presidency. Although Eisenhower and Johnson approached the presidency from drastically different political backgrounds and styles, some commonalities emerge in their characterizations of the office. As in the Eisenhower White House, Johnson and his advisers appear to have viewed the 1964 result in broad terms. They saw the result as an affirmation of New Deal values, without committing themselves verbally to any particular idea about which New Deal values were most at stake. In framing his sweeping domestic policy agenda, Johnson talked about enduring American values rather than the specifics of the campaign. It is not clear that Johnson or anyone working within his White House thought that they had received an electoral mandate to pursue voting rights or the War on Poverty—or even that they thought about the issue in those terms. Instead, Johnson and his political team saw the election result as a source of political leverage that could help them achieve their goals, not the provenance of the goals themselves. The one issue on which the team had clearly campaigned was peace. And yet it was on this issue that the administration lost its political bearings and saw its outsized coalition splinter apart. In other words, electoral logic and institutional legitimacy appeared not to concern the Johnson White House very much. They spun relatively little of their agenda in terms of the campaign or election result. The administration pursued policies on which it had not campaigned, publicly justifying these policies on the grounds that they would serve national values and the national interest.

The Eisenhower and Johnson cases reveal three major differences between the mandate politics of the modern era and that of the preceding Progressive and transitional periods. First, unlike the Progressive period, presidents of the modern era were not engaged in a negotiation over the legitimacy of the president's expanding role in the political system. In contrast, they enjoyed wide acceptance of their prominent role in politics—but also contended with high expectations about their potential for achievement. In addition to the absence of protracted legitimacy struggles, this period was also mostly devoid of major confrontations over presidential legitimacy. This factor not only distinguished modern period from the growing pains of FDR's presidency, but also from the impending struggles over executive power that would characterize the next transitional era.

Finally, the conceptualization of the presidency as an office beyond partisan politics—as idealized as that construct was—reflects a line of thinking that dates back to the founding of the United States. Yet, in the Progressive Era the idea of the president as a "responsible-party" leader was included among the possible visions of presidential leadership. Presidents regularly claimed party mandates in their inaugural addresses. During the transition, Roosevelt talked about party as he built administrative structures to replace the old party organizations and faced fierce opposition from within

Democratic ranks. Eisenhower and Johnson perceived and framed their election results in ways that acknowledge the disconnection between party and presidency. Neither made much effort to claim a party mandate. Ironically, however, Johnson's policy agenda inspired the backlash that produced lasting divisions between the parties and pushed the ideal of the bipartisan president even further out of reach.

Chapter 4

The Presidency in Crisis

Nixon, Carter, and the Decline of Consensus

In April 1969, Leonard "Len" Garment, one of Nixon's domestic policy advisers, wrote a memorandum to Chief of Staff H. R. Haldeman describing the decline in presidential status and the growing concern in the White House about public and media hostility. Garment expressed the view that "public dissatisfaction with government" was the "most important contemporary political fact." However, he also offered some more optimistic comments about the Nixon's administration's ability to handle the situation:

> The president's perception of the importance of reducing the scale and *impersonality* of the presidency (i.e. the Inaugural theme), and his success in doing so through President-to-person press conferences, are the outstanding achievements of the Administration so far. At dinner the other night, [journalist] Hugh Sidey described the process as a "demilitarized zone" for the presidency, and in his opinion, this has been more important than anything else that has occurred since January 20.[1]

Garment's optimism may have been premature. Describing the general decline in citizens' trust of government since the mid-1960s, political scientist Gary Orren observes that "a belief that government is getting worse instead of better, and that today's public officials simply do not measure up, has become a hallmark of contemporary politics."[2] During the transition period between 1969 and 1981, this distrust was felt acutely in the realm of presidential politics. Andrew Rudalevige notes "the 'presidential government' that seemed imminent and desirable in 1944 and even 1964 seemed horrifying in 1974."[3] Even before the fallout from Watergate, Nixon took office under difficult circumstances. In addition to the drop in public confidence,[4] the president's own personal stock was down. His 59 percent approval rating was the lowest of any newly inaugurated president since Truman.[5] Furthermore, Nixon would have to find common ground with a Democratic Congress. In the search for legitimacy, Nixon often came back to rhetoric about the election, the campaign, and his role as the people's representative.

Despite differences in party, ideology, and leadership style, Jimmy Carter's approach to rhetoric about the 1976 election took on a similar tone. This similarity makes sense in light of the circumstances that defined and constrained both presidencies. Nixon's involvement in the Watergate scandal and subsequent resignation contributed to the loss of institutional prestige, and Carter dealt with the fallout from these events. However, as the memo from Garment to Haldeman illustrates, Nixon also felt the effects of the institutional decline that his presidency would eventually exacerbate. Furthermore, as a leader in this transitional period, Carter also contributed to the institution's woes by projecting an image of weakness and appearing flummoxed by political setbacks. In sum, although the changing politics of the presidency affected Nixon and Carter differently, both leaders experienced the frustrations of a powerful but increasingly distrusted office and leaned on mandate rhetoric as a means of conveying legitimacy to the public as well as within the executive branch. Similarly, although the substantive issues and specific problems were quite different for the Republicans and Democrats, both parties experienced significant setbacks during this period. For the Republicans, the 1974 midterm elections, just months after Nixon resigned in disgrace, represented a low point in party history, although the party would rebound within a decade. The Democrats did not experience a dramatic low point comparable to Watergate. Nevertheless, the party had weathered major internal division in the late 1960s and would begin a long period of relative decline compared to their dominance in the New Deal era. Cultural issues had become a divisive force not only across but also within each of the two parties. It was against this backdrop that Nixon and Carter began to redefine the presidential mandate.

The presidential mandates literature has paid little attention to the mixed results of the 1968, 1972, and 1976 elections. Nixon's narrow plurality victory in 1968 and the divided government hardly fell into the same category as 1964. In 1972, Nixon's margin of victory was matched by more modest gains in Congress and ultimately was overshadowed by the disgrace of Watergate. The 1976 election struck few commentators as exceptional because of "the closeness of the race, the traditional breakdown of section and group bases of candidate support, and the short coattails of the new president." [6] Despite inconclusive election results, Nixon and Carter both offered ideas about their relationships with the electorate. As the New Deal coalition unraveled, mandate rhetoric served as part of a larger effort to reconceptualize presidential leadership.

Throughout his turbulent presidency, Nixon mainly spoke about campaign promises and election results as a response to attacks and challenges. Under different circumstances, Carter also used defensive mandate rhetoric. After winning a close election against Nixon's successor, Gerald Ford, Carter initially took a humble approach to the question of interpreting the election result. However, as resistance to Carter's plans mounted in Congress and public approval waivered, Carter's communications team embraced electoral logic as a response to criticism. Carter's struggles for legitimacy and definition were not limited to the particular circumstances of his presidency; this period represented a turning point in mandate rhetoric. The transition period between the modern and partisan eras saw an increase in "campaign promise" references by newly elected presidents. Nixon and Carter referred more often to the election campaigns that brought them to office than their predecessors did. They also talked about elections differently from the way Eisenhower and especially Johnson talked about them. In addition to the emphasis on keeping campaign promises, mandate logic also emerged during this period as a way of speaking *to* and *about* the executive branch. In this way, we can understand mandate rhetoric as a means to reestablish democratic legitimacy for a discredited institution.

In addition to the fight for legitimacy, the other critical change in the transition period occurred in the relationship between presidents and parties.

Parties fell in the public's estimation along with other governing institutions. In the late 1970s and early 1980s, observers greeted a new era of "candidate-centered politics."[7] Scholars eulogized the collective responsibility of parties and hypothesized the causes of voter "dealignment."[8]

Parties and partisanship proved anything but moribund, however. The ideological divisions of twenty-first-century politics began to emerge in the transition period. One feature of this new political landscape was the emergence of "the social issue." This term, introduced in order "to describe the complicated cluster of issues relating to the problems of permissiveness,"[9] has come to be nearly synonymous with polarization and divisive politics. Nixon sought to cultivate middle-class voters concerned about crime and angry about busing as a method of school desegregation.[10] These issues did not fundamentally alter the Republican agenda on economic or foreign policy. Rather, the underlying values of tradition and patriotism anchored the conservative position across a range of issues and tied together policy on crime, Vietnam, funding for social programs, and later, opposition to abortion and the Equal Rights Amendment. These changes—especially the cultivation of a Southern voter base—eventually opened the door for the conservative movement to become more prominent in the Republican Party.

The clash between new issues and old coalitions affected the Democrats as well. Liberal activists clashed with the traditional working-class and white ethnic constituencies within the party. This tension was particularly pronounced in the 1972 presidential election. Under new rules designed to shift power from party elites to rank-and-file members, the party nominated South Dakota senator George McGovern to challenge Nixon. McGovern embraced what Bruce Miroff calls an "old-fashioned liberalism" that embraced "the tradition of anti-imperialism and anti-militarism," and rejected the idea that "economic growth would, by itself solve the central dilemmas of American domestic life."[11] McGovern's attempt to reformulate the Democratic message ended with unambiguous defeat in the general election, but the need to revisit the party's strategy and commitments outlived the McGovern campaign.

The changing party landscape posed a dilemma for newly elected presidents as they created public narratives about the elections that brought them to power: to frame the election as a party mandate or to stress more inclusive themes? On the comparatively rare occasions when they did invoke electoral logic, Roosevelt, Eisenhower, and Johnson demonstrated a tendency to frame election results as expressions of fundamental values, beyond party conflict. New political conditions changed the contours of this dilemma. The emergence of divisive social issues forced leaders to reconsider the strategic advantages of these kinds of claims. For Republicans, the new and potent politics of the "silent majority" required a target for resentment, a message incompatible with claims of national unity. Democratic presidents weighed different considerations. For a party internally divided between reformers and traditional New Deal groups and troubled by the disintegration of old alliances in the wake of civil rights, constructing a party mandate was not an obvious choice. Yet national unity, too, remained an elusive ideal. Mandate rhetoric during the transition period reflects this ambivalence.

The elections of 1968, 1972, and 1976 were difficult to cast as party mandates. Timing worked against the possibility of sweeping, comprehensive policy agendas. Instead, Nixon and Carter both acted in response to the changes enacted during the Johnson years. Several of Nixon's central agenda items—budgetary restraint, reforming government welfare programs, crime—were direct rejoinders to the perceived excesses of his predecessor. Nixon also wrestled with the question of how to use the backlash against civil rights for political gain while maintaining the support of moderates.

The path between Johnson and Carter is somewhat more attenuated, but nevertheless traceable. In Skowronek's "political-time" formulation, Carter belongs to the disjunctive category, coming at the end of the New Deal "regime" but unable to sever ties with it.[12] In this sense, Carter shared a political heritage with Johnson. But while Johnson represented the middle of the "New Deal regime," Carter came at its end. His political reality was a fractured Democratic coalition and an unclear direction to follow up on the Great Society, the War on Poverty, and civil rights. Furthermore, because these policies had divided core groups in the Democratic constituency—African Americans, Southern whites, and urban working-class whites—against each other, Carter would have to piece together a policy agenda, and a coalition to support it, on his own.[13]

Because of these constraints, Nixon and Carter experienced greater difficulty justifying their choices, and thus relied more on mandate rhetoric. More than previous presidents, they defended their choices in terms of campaign promises rather than election results. In this regard, Nixon and Carter were alike despite their obvious political differences. The choices that both leaders made in order to defend their own political territory had a lasting impact on the way subsequent presidents perceived and framed mandates. This appears to have set a significant informal precedent. Campaign references have been a prominent form of electoral logic ever since, allowing presidents to employ mandate justifications even without winning a landslide.

Reimagining the American Presidency

Nixon's postelection rhetoric attempted to define a political agenda after an ambiguous election in a changing polity. In using this rhetoric, Nixon also sought to reestablish presidential legitimacy. For modern presidents, confrontations over the limits of presidential power had mostly concerned war actions.[14] Perceptions that the Johnson administration had overreached in Vietnam cast doubt about the trustworthiness of the nation's leaders. Objections that he had "overreached" in domestic policy inspired backlash about the government's ability to bring about social progress.[15] As the example at the beginning of this chapter suggests, discussions about political strategy in the Nixon White House regularly came back to questions about how to restore the dignity and prestige of the office. In February 1969, policy adviser Len Garment observed approvingly to speechwriter James Keogh that media coverage of the president emphasized "the way the president is reestablishing respect for the presidency."[16] However, not everyone in the Nixon White House was so optimistic about Nixon's ability to reverse the trend of declining trust. Daniel Patrick Moynihan, serving as domestic policy adviser to the president, wrote to him in July 1969 to suggest that the administration propose a constitutional convention for the nation's bicentennial in 1976. Moynihan drew inspiration for this suggestion from "the feeling that the structure of American government has not been working well of late, and that more and more persons have come to see this. It seemed to me that somehow our contemplation of this—the crisis of confidence, the erosion of authority—had to be raised to the highest levels of policy concerns, and that a constitutional convention was one way to do it."[17] Moynihan's remarks illustrate how concerns about the fundamental legitimacy and effectiveness of the political system, in addition to ordinary worries about policy and public support, had crept into White House strategizing. Earlier presidential advisers had been preoccupied with meeting high expectations and about crafting policy messages in order to maximize persuasive potential. Nixon's team, in contrast, appeared less concerned about meeting high standards for legislative achievement. Instead, staff members contemplated how to overcome growing public skepticism about government effectiveness and trustworthiness.

Concerns about legitimacy and authority existed alongside the Nixon administration's infamous views on strong executive power. Chief of Staff Haldeman went so far as to tell a writer that "the nation's constitutional design did not call for cooperation between the legislative and executive branches."[18] In other words, the administration shared some of the public's skepticism about government, insofar as this doubt pertained to the legislature. Divided government added to Nixon's doubts about working with Congress. One manifestation of Nixon's interest in working unilaterally and expanding policy influence was his plan for executive reorganization. In response to the failures of the previous administration, Nixon sought to expand the president's ability to shape policy in the implementation stage, after Congress had passed the laws.[19] The reorganization plan represented an effort to reimagine the president as a more powerful policy actor and to gain greater control over domestic affairs. Nixon's expansive view of presidential power combined with growing public skepticism to create the ideal conditions for a confrontation over the scope of presidential authority.

As their internal memoranda reveal, Nixon's team was acutely aware of the public skepticism toward government, although responses to the circumstances varied across staff members. Some advisers seemed confident about Nixon's ability to transcend difficult circumstances. Others, like Moynihan, insinuated that public skepticism might reflect deeper problems, and thus be more than merely a political obstacle. The reorganization effort revealed an ongoing interest in expanding executive power, despite flagging legitimacy. Although some of the specific conditions were new, this dilemma was essentially familiar. Nixon was simultaneously compelled to press at the boundaries of executive power and to contend with reservations about the nature of presidential strength. These are the kinds of conditions that prompt presidents to think about and to use electoral logic.

The 1968 election concluded a dramatic campaign season. Amid the trauma of Robert F. Kennedy's assassination and clashes between police and protestors at the Democratic convention, two distinct political ideas contended for the electorate's approval. Yet, the election did not result in a clear victory for either side. Democrats maintained control over Congress, and Nixon beat Democrat and incumbent vice president Hubert Humphrey by only two-tenths of a percent. The candidacy of right-wing Democratic populist George Wallace, winning more than 8 percent of the vote, deprived either side of a majority. On taking office in 1969, Nixon tried to develop a narrative about his narrow victory. The result had been extremely close, but Nixon and Humphrey had taken distinct positions as candidates. This narrative gained some traction with the news media, but not everyone was convinced. Media interpretations generally fell into one of three categories: those that made an argument for a mandate on specific issues; those that made an argument for a mandate on more general issues (i.e., "centrism"); and those that argued against the possibility of an electoral mandate. James Reston of the *New York Times* called for Nixon to "redeem his promises to bring about a workable majority in the nation and the Congress for more military arms and lower taxes, more police and more understanding in the cities, more prosperity and less inflation, better relations with the allies and larger military budgets in the allied capitals."[20] Also in the *New York Times*, an editorial pointed to the "plurality in the popular vote and a clear majority in the Electoral College" as evidence of Nixon's unquestioned legitimacy in office. An Associated Press piece suggested Vietnam had been the "overriding issue of the campaign,"[21] while another editorial suggested that the election result could be most readily attributed to "fiscal irresponsibility in the Johnson administration" rather than the many other issues of the day. Yet other accounts attributed the mandate to a more nebulous "direction" preferred by voters. These included a mandate for a "fresh start,"[22] a "conservative turn,"[23] and suggestions that the "sum and substance of a Nixon administration will be the defense of the political center against assault from the right and the left."[24] Finally, an editorial in the *Daytona Beach Morning Journal* proclaimed, "There Is No Mandate," while arguing that Nixon should maintain progressive domestic policies.[25]

Nixon's own rhetoric also reflects the multiple possibilities for the mandate of 1968. The newly elected Republican gave few major addresses in the early months of his presidency, but communicated frequently in other venues. Between his inauguration and March 31, 1969, Nixon held five news conferences and gave sixteen addresses to local audiences while traveling (several of which were outside the United States). He also issued thirty-eight communications with other government officials, including twenty-four sets of remarks to members of the executive branch and twelve messages to Congress, as well as a number of ceremonial addresses and other miscellaneous remarks and statements. Mandate logic, in its various forms, appeared in a handful of these communications, framing several of the administration's signature issues as campaign promises. These issues included U.S. Post Office Department patronage, budget austerity, and the lingering questions of civil rights.

A few weeks after taking office in 1969, Nixon announced reforms in the appointment of postmasters. Citing a campaign pledge, he announced his intent to "take politics out of the Post Office Department . . . and improve postal service."[26] This idea was not received warmly by the Republican Party. As Post Office official Nyle Jackson wrote to Harry Dent, "The announced elimination of politics from the appointment of postmasters and rural carriers was a body blow to Republican members of Congress and state and county organizations. But, here again, this was not the worst part of the plan. Most Republican members of Congress could live with a merit system of making these appointments, if they were, in fact, made strictly on the basis of merit."[27] As this suggests, the Republican establishment had two objections to Nixon's reform plan. The elimination of patronage would disrupt an entrenched practice in rural areas and thus dispense with an important tool for attracting political support. Party leaders also maintained that the new system weighed heavily in favor of Democrats. As a result, congressional Republicans and as well as national committee leaders saw the reform plan as a serious threat and political blunder.

The Post Office reform mistake illustrates Nixon's strained relationship with the Republican Party. But this strain, its manifestation in abortive efforts at reform, and its relationship to electoral logic are all part of a larger pattern endemic to the transition period. The changing political environment motivated presidents to search for new ways to claim legitimacy, including mandate rhetoric—particularly that which emphasized campaign promises—and commitment to governmental reform. At the same time, attempts to "clean up" government practices often amounted to attacks on parties and thus prompted commensurate opposition. This opposition in itself created an impossible situation for Nixon and Carter, who could succeed politically neither by embracing party politics nor by rejecting it. In the realm of interpreting elections, this tension between party reform and party opposition also proved to require a delicate balance. Invoking campaign promises automatically casts the president in the role of a delegate rather than a trustee; such a claim places decision making in the hands of the electorate. The logic of delegate-style representation is often paired with a partisan campaign message, as we saw in the mandate rhetoric of nineteenth- and early twentieth-century presidents. However, in the case of Post Office reform, Nixon attempted a different kind of mandate narrative: the nonpartisan delegate. Past efforts to interpret elections in nonpartisan terms tended to depict the president as a national trustee, prepared to apply a broad set of values to public policy (as with Johnson in 1965). Faced with political trouble like the court-packing incident or challenging issues like farm price supports, Roosevelt and Eisenhower fell back on the argument that they were simply channeling the preferences of the electorate. They presented those preferences in unmistakably partisan terms, citing party victory and quoting from party platforms. In contrast, the idea of the nonpartisan delegate combined these elements in a new way, responding to a demand for more transparency and accountability in politics. These issues, linked explicitly to the 1976 election and campaign, became frequent tropes in Carter's rhetoric in 1977. For Nixon, the fallout from the Post Office plan appears to have discouraged him from trying that type of argument again. The experience did not prompt him to abandon electoral logic rhetoric, however.

Early in 1969, Nixon suggested that budget issues had also been a key part of his 1968 campaign. In a news conference on January 27, he stated "at this time I cannot say where and how the budget can be cut. I will say that we are taking a fresh look at all of the programs and we shall attempt to make cuts in order to carry out the objectives that I set forth during the campaign."[28] Unlike the Post Office question, budget reform served to establish a Republican priority and to emphasize a key distinction between the parties. Budget politics would eventually become a central locus for conflict between Nixon and congressional Democrats. These disagreements encompassed both institutional struggles over budgetary authority and partisan struggles over priorities.

The dilemma over how to approach the civil rights question contributed to the challenge of interpreting the 1968 election. The narrow result meant that Nixon could hardly claim an overwhelming mandate for himself or for the party. However, the issue differences between the two candidates had been clear, particularly on the interconnected questions of civil rights, welfare, and crime. Nixon's speech accepting the 1968 nomination identified his opposition to federal antipoverty programs as "the clearest choice among the great issues in the campaign."[29] After Nixon took office, however, the substance of the issue proved to be more complicated than the campaign speech had suggested. Backlash against civil rights measures, informed in part by racialized perceptions of federal antipoverty programs, still provided tempting political opportunities. But Nixon's desire to appease conservative constituents (particularly in the South) conflicted with his constitutional obligation to uphold existing law. As a result, Nixon's approach to these issues was ultimately muddled. Nixon promised to obey the law regarding the established deadline for school desegregation. This pledge prompted a strong reaction from Georgia Governor Howard "Bo" Callaway, who responded, "The law . . . the law, listen here. Nixon promised the south he would change the law, change the supreme court [sic], and change this whole integration business. The time has come for Nixon to bite the bullet, with real changes and none of this communicating bullshit."[30] Callaway's comment about Nixon's promises to the South highlights the nature of Nixon's representation dilemma. Acting as the delegate of frustrated conservatives, the president might have taken a much stronger position against federally mandated desegregation (among other issues).

However, reaching out to racial conservatives was not the only way for Nixon to imagine his constituency as president. In a news conference in February 1969, a reporter asked, "Mr. President, do you agree with those who say that you and your administration have a serious problem with distrust among the blacks, and whether you agree that it is one of your more serious problems or not, could you tell us specifically what you are doing to deal with what some consider to be this distrust among the blacks?"

Nixon's response channeled the values of Eisenhower and Johnson:

> I can only say that, by my actions as President, I hope to rectify that. I hope that by what we do in terms of dealing with the problems of all Americans, it will be made clear that the President of the United States, as an elected official, has no State constituency. He has no congressional constituency. He does not represent any special group. He represents all the people. He is the friend of all the people.[31]

The ideal of the "president of all the people," however often articulated, has never been easy to achieve. But for Nixon, in the context of a new constellation of divisive social issues, this paradigm was even further out of reach. In the midst of this tension, Nixon offered a new definition of the president's relationship with the electorate. One year after the 1968 election, Nixon gave a speech that not only pledged to make good on his promise of "peace with honor" in Vietnam but also to heed the demands of the "silent majority." The idea of a "silent majority" signified much more than an effective foil for Vietnam protestors. It also defined the conservative position after changes of the 1960s and the Johnson presidency, tying together attitudes about both foreign policy and domestic social issues. Nixon's political advisers had thought seriously about how to cultivate support and define a conservative message with broad appeal in anticipation of the 1970 midterms. The silent majority speech was in part the product of these efforts. In the evolution of presidential mandate rhetoric, the "silent majority" idea modified the premise of the president as a national leader and adapted it to the divisions of the time. It emphasized the president's responsiveness to the needs and articulated demands of the polity. It claimed a popular mandate for conservative social ideas without explicitly referring to either and offered an alternative definition of a majority. Although the 1968 election was never received as a "mandate" in the traditional sense, the Nixon White House still saw it as appropriate and advantageous to make public statements about the meaning of the campaign and the election result. What is more, Nixon's efforts to construct a mandate from the support of a narrow segment of the electorate set a precedent on which later Republican presidents would draw as they described their relationships with the electorate.

The Troubled Second Term

After establishing his connection with a "silent majority," in 1972 Nixon won an actual majority—nearly 61 percent of the popular vote and 520 Electoral College votes. The failure of Republicans to gain control of Congress cast doubt on claims to a party mandate. Rather, the election was immediately understood as belonging to a class of personal mandates for individual presidential candidates (often running for reelection, as was the case of not only Nixon but also Bill Clinton in 1996 and Eisenhower in 1956).[32]

Media reports of the election touted the landslide and many identified it as a mandate. This interpretation was not universal. The *Sarasota Journal* cited low voter turnout and the absence of "presidential coattails" as evidence that the election had not conferred a mandate, but had created an opportunity.[33] Among sources in agreement that the election was a mandate, different perspectives emerged on what the mandate meant. One article points to the increasing power of the bipartisan "conservative coalition" in its assessment of the 1972 outcome as a "mandate for change,"[34] whereas the *New York Times* identified the election as a "mandate for more of the same."[35]

Nixon's eventual rhetoric about the mandate conferred by the 1972 election had broader institutional significance. Although not a perfect parallel to Andrew Jackson in the context of the 1832 contest and the struggle over the national bank, some elements of the situation were similar. In both cases, competing visions of the national interest, including the role of the federal government, divided the polity. Presidents with expansive visions of executive power occupied the White House and pressed at the boundaries of executive authority. At the same time, vocal opposition to executive aggrandizement countered these efforts. For Jackson, these opponents included both Whigs and Jeffersonians, and the mandate worked as an appeal to the latter group.[36] For Nixon, antigovernment sentiment emanated from a number of sources, but some of the most vocal were representatives of white working-class voters, frustrated with policy changes under Johnson and receptive to messages of populism from the right.[37] Declarations of allegiance to the "silent majority" signaled Nixon's attention to this group and its concerns. We have also already seen how Nixon invoked the pledges of the campaign in response to a number of difficult issues, including race and patronage, early on in the first term. In the second term, mandate claims were directed at a wider audience, in defense of presidential powers in the budget process, and, later, during the Watergate scandal.

Nixon's confrontation with Congress over the budget had both institutional and partisan dimensions. Tensions between the Republican president and the Democratic Congress over federal spending began in the first term and culminated with formal changes to the budget process. The Constitution assigns the duty to collect and spend revenue to Congress. Yet, the presidency, consisting of a single actor instead of a collective body of more than five hundred, had over time taken on a prominent role in the budget process. This role included impoundment, which allowed members of Congress to avoid the difficult process of reconciling expenditures and revenue.[38] Although impoundment was an accepted practice, Nixon pushed too far by impounding "funds even when legislation explicitly warned him not to do it, and he impounded funds not only for specific projects but also for entire programs he hoped to terminate."[39] In the course of the ensuing confrontation, Nixon invoked the mandate of the 1972 election. He first introduced budget issues as a matter of fulfilling the 1972 mandate in a radio address eight days after inauguration: "In the campaign last fall, I promised I would not propose any new tax increases." Similar statements were featured in the Budget Message to Congress the next day as well: "In a real sense, however, the 1974 budget is the clear evidence of the kind of change in direction demanded by the great majority of the American people." In the same Budget Message, Nixon commented, "Lethargy, habit, pride, and politics combine to resist the necessary process of change, but I am confident that the expressed will of the people will not be denied."[40] Previously undeterred, the Ninety-third Congress had proven its willingness to curb presidential power, having passed the War Powers Resolution over Nixon's veto in 1973. Now in response to the confrontation over impoundment, Congress passed legislation that prohibited impoundment without congressional consent and thus created the modern budget process.

The cases of Roosevelt, Eisenhower, and Johnson have already shown how Congress and the public often prove impervious to mandate rhetoric. Nevertheless, as the budget example illustrates, mandate rhetoric plays a recurring role during confrontations over institutional legitimacy. Contrary to expectations, the presidential mandate has only rarely been invoked to promote sweeping agendas. Rather, ideas such as popular sovereignty and electoral accountability have been used to justify the expansion of presidential power and to defend presidential behavior.

After the budget fight, defensive rhetoric became even more important to the Nixon presidency. As accusations of presidential wrongdoing in the Watergate scandal became more serious, Nixon referred to the mandate of the 1972 election as a means of defending his administration. For example, in a news conference on August 22, 1973, a reporter asked, "Sir, last week in your speech you referred to those who would exploit Watergate to keep you from doing your job. Could you specifically detail who 'those' are?" Nixon responded:

I would suggest that where the shoe fits, people should wear it. I would think that some political figures, some members of the press, perhaps, some members of the television, perhaps would exploit it. I don't impute, interestingly enough, motives, however, that are improper, because here is what is involved. There are a great number of people in this country that would prefer that I resign. There are a great number of people in this country that didn't accept the mandate of 1972. After all, I know that most of the members of the press corps were riot enthusiastic and I understand that—about either my election in '68 or '72. That is not unusual.

Frankly, if I had always followed what the press predicted or the polls predicted, I would have never been elected President. But what I am saying is this: People who did not accept the mandate of '72, who do not want the strong America that I want to build, who do not want the foreign policy leadership that I want to give, who do not want to cut down the size of this government bureaucracy that burdens us so greatly and to give more of our government back to the people, people who do not want these things, naturally, would exploit any issue—if it weren't Watergate, anything else—in order to keep the President from doing his job.[41]

Nixon's use of the presidential mandate to deflect criticism (unsuccessfully) in the lowest moment of his presidency fits the pattern established by a number of Nixon's predecessors, including Andrew Jackson and Franklin Roosevelt. The particular circumstances of Nixon's years in office added new dimensions to the concept, however. The stirrings of a polarized electorate, irreconcilably divided on social issues, inspired Nixon to direct his mandate rhetoric toward only a portion of the electorate. Although Nixon himself seemed to back away from the "silent majority" characterization in his mandate claims after the 1972 election, this idea informed subsequent formulations by later Republican presidents.

Aside from the "silent majority," Nixon's working definitions of the mandate were largely familiar. Electoral logic rhetoric served as a means of responding to political conflict both within and between parties. It also framed Nixon's attempt to push the boundaries of the presidency in terms of budget power and "executive privilege." These struggles illustrate the extent to which the structural dilemmas of the presidency have remained similar over time. They also illustrate the persistence of mandate rhetoric as a legitimacy tool. But the Nixon case shows change as well as continuity. Both the role of the federal government and the role of the president in policymaking had expanded in the modern era, a change unlikely to be reversed. Combined with polarization and skepticism about government, the political situation called for new legitimacy narratives. Nixon's idea of the silent majority was one such narrative. As the first president elected after Nixon's resignation, Jimmy Carter contended with all of these conditions as well as the repercussions of Watergate.

Carter's New Electoral Politics

Despite differences in politics and style, Carter shared Nixon's interest in reconceptualizing the presidency and its relationship with Congress. Nixon presented himself as the representative of a specific segment of the electorate, and his team fretted about dignity and treatment by the press. Carter focused on changing the image of the office; he insisted on being addressed as "Jimmy" or "Mr. Carter" rather than "Mr. President" and on dressing less formally in public appearances, including the famous speech delivered in a cardigan.[42] These changes failed to achieve the immediate goal of making the Carter presidency a political success. Despite Carter's loss in 1980, the choices he made about how to relate to the electorate had an impact on what subsequent presidents said and did. In responding to the excesses of the executive branch, Carter offered new ideas about what it could mean to be president. His incorporation of the 1976 election into governing rhetoric differed from how previous presidents had approached electoral logic.

Scholarship on the Carter presidency has mainly been devoted to explaining the administration's failures in terms of presidential choices and structural obstacles. In *Jimmy Carter and the Politics of Frustration*, Garland Haas argues that a lack of political skill and judgment fatally damaged Carter's ability to lead and persuade Congress. In particular, Haas attributes Carter's political difficulties to his failure to fully realize that "members of Congress were important people in their own right."[43] The alternative view posits that Carter's troubles stemmed from circumstances, including economic trouble and the aftermath of Vietnam and Watergate. In Skowronek's political-time schema, Carter parallels Herbert Hoover and Franklin Pierce. These "disjunctive" presidents are distinguished by their inability to respond effectively to crisis because they were indelibly connected to a disintegrating and discredited ruling coalition. Despite this parallel, Carter's public statements about the 1976 election differ sharply from Hoover's interpretations of the 1928 contest. Where Hoover had specifically referred to the Republican platform, Carter cited his own campaign promises. A combination of circumstance and style produced Carter's new approach to electoral logic.

On the surface, Carter's claims about the 1976 election result appeared deceptively ordinary, yet they were distinctive in several important ways. Carter referred to his campaign promises and justified his policy stances by labeling them "the reason I was elected." Like Nixon, he spoke about campaign promises more than previous presidents. In this sense, both presented themselves as delegates bound by their pledges. Nixon ultimately directed his delegate claims at the so-called real majority of Americans who had been on the losing end of 1960s reforms. In contrast, Carter forged an electoral logic narrative that painted him as a nonpartisan delegate. Charles O. Jones has argued that Carter imagined a "trusteeship presidency," defined by his decision to do "what is right, not what is political," without consideration for short-term electoral pressures.[44] However, when it came to invoking the 1976 election in order to justify governance, Carter was more delegate than trustee.

The 1976 victory did not compare with the landslides of 1936, 1964, or even 1972. But the same political forces that inspired Nixon to explain his presidency in terms of electoral logic acted on Carter as well. Watergate did little to alleviate public concerns about government in general and about strong presidential leadership in particular. As a result, political commentators and actors displayed heightened interest in questions of democratic legitimacy, including the presidential mandate. Before Carter commented on the election, news media began to contemplate the mandate question. Bob Wiedrich of the *Chicago Tribune* noted that although Carter did not win by a substantial margin, his leadership was unencumbered by major power brokers in the Democratic Party. This independence, according to Wiedrich, would afford the new president a measure of freedom that might allow him to take on "big government" and interrupt "business as usual" in Washington.[45] A similar assessment of the election is presented in an editorial in the *Wall Street Journal*, which calls Carter's victory as a party and Washington outsider "stunning," but questions the policy meaning of the election, arguing that it is "hard to read his election in anything but personal terms" and "hard to read into the returns a mandate for anything in particular." [46] Tom Wicker of the *New York Times* focused on the fact that Carter had won a majority of the popular vote: "Carter's mandate may not have been the greatest in history; but John F. Kennedy, for one, would have loved to have had it." [47]

Shortly after the 1976 election, pollster Pat Caddell sent Carter a long memo assessing the political circumstances after the election. This memo, now credited with introducing the concept of the "permanent campaign," also laid out a series of reasons behind Carter's election. The Caddell memo set the tone for the relationship between the election and the administration's strategies for governance. It also illustrated the idea that even elections not won by landslides held possibilities for interpretation and could impart useful lessons for governance. In assessing the reasons behind Carter's victory, Caddell suggested that the election result was attributable to three sets of factors: personal, partisan, and social and psychological. Among the latter group of factors, Caddell highlighted several ideas that informed how Carter invoked electoral logic in subsequent public argument. In addition to the oft-cited theme of change, Caddell also suggested that the "desire on the part of most Americans to 'feel good' about things" in the wake of Vietnam, Watergate, and economic problems had informed both the Carter and Ford campaigns. The memo continued by analyzing Carter's support coalition. Caddell noted that Carter had done well among traditional New Deal Democratic groups, such as Catholics, Jewish voters, and labor, but that these groups were shrinking in the broader electorate. "To make up the difference (and win the election)," Caddell noted, Carter ran well with White Protestants, educated white-collar voters, and "rural small-town voters." [48]

Caddell's analysis of the politics behind Carter's 1976 victory highlighted one of Carter's major dilemmas in developing a coherent narrative about the 1976 election. Despite his fairly orthodox Democratic issue positions, Carter's victory would have been much less likely without the support of new, traditionally non-Democratic groups. Yet, the winning coalition in 1976 was not large enough to sustain claims to a broad, bipartisan consensus. Carter addressed this lack of consensus in a news conference in May 1977. A reporter asked the president several questions about Caddell's arguments, including divisions within the Democratic Party and his comments encouraging Carter to focus on political style. Carter's response stressed his intent to restore public confidence:

> When I took office, I had not won an overwhelming victory in the general election—as you know, a couple million votes. And I believe that in the last number of years, there had been a loss of confidence in our Government, both in its integrity and also in its ability and competence.
>
> There had been a loss of confidence that the White House and Congress could work together, or that the people could have access to the decision making [sic] process, absent secrecy. So, a major commitment of mine, long before this Caddell memorandum was written, was to try to restore the confidence of the people in me.
>
> Obviously, one of those means is by frequent news conferences. Another one is by access to me in the Oval Office. Another one is the travel around our country on occasion to meet with people. And I think that this is the "style" part. I think that the walk down Pennsylvania Avenue, about which Mr. Caddell was not informed, was a good indication that I trust Washington. I didn't feel endangered, that I wanted the people to know I was one of them. I don't see anything wrong with this. I think, to the extent that I can have a good relationship with the people, it makes it easier for me to be a good President.[49]

This response set the tone for the approach to electoral logic during his presidency. Although he moved away from the idea of a mandate in the form of a sweeping election victory, Carter did not move away from electoral logic in general. Highlighting the relationship between the president and the people became a central strategy for dealing with the loss of esteem for the institution. The Carter White House incorporated this strategy into its larger narrative about how it would work to fulfill campaign promises.

One of the earliest and most prominent examples of rhetorical approach was Carter's address to the nation from the White House Library, also designated as a "fireside chat." He began the address by noting "when I was running for President, I made a number of commitments. I take them very seriously. I believe that they were the reason that I was elected. And I want you to know that I intend to carry them out. As you probably noticed already, I have acted on several of my promises."[50] The speech went on to outline plans for energy policy. The logic of campaign commitments was not limited to speeches directed at the electorate. In a communication to heads of executive branch agencies, Carter justified his zero-base budgeting plan by saying, "During the campaign, I pledged that immediately after the inauguration I would issue an order establishing zero-base budgeting throughout the Federal Government. This pledge was made because of the success of the zero-base budget system adopted by the State of Georgia under my direction as Governor."[51]

The connection between campaign promises and matters related to executive branch management did not end with zero-base budgeting. Carter presented an executive reorganization plan to Congress with a similar justification: "This is a commitment that I made in hundreds of speeches around the country during the 2-year campaign. It was one of the major reasons that I was elected."[52] After Congress had passed Carter's reorganization proposal, the campaign promise narrative resurfaced in his remarks on signing the bill. At the signing ceremony, Carter noted, "I believe it was one of the campaign issues that induced the American people to give me their support."[53] Similarly, in the official signing statement, he suggested that "this is one of the ways in which I plan to fulfill my commitment to the American people to make government more responsive, efficient, and open."[54]

The political values that Carter associated with the executive branch reorganization—responsiveness, transparency—parallel the underlying logic of using campaign promises to justify presidential action. Just as Carter's reimagination of the Democratic agenda and of executive administration encompassed the creation of new cabinet departments and agenda items, his reimagination of the presidency included a new emphasis on keeping campaign promises. This new vision of the office included both nonpartisan considerations, such as good, efficient government, and a delegate-like attention to enacting an established agenda.

New visions of presidential leadership emerged from internal struggle over the meaning of the president's role. Carter's inner circle of advisers struggled over how the president should present himself to the electorate. Shortly after the inauguration, White House communications director Jerry Rafshoon suggested that Carter should "postpone the fireside chat" scheduled for early February because "the American people like to see an active president. They see it right now on the news nightly. It is not necessary to personally intrude into the living room so soon."[55] Speechwriter Achsah Nesmith considered the question of presidential address from a different angle in a memo to fellow writer James Fallows:

I realize the phrase was his initially, but isn't there anything we can do to dispel the notion that every time the President talks to the nation, he is "going over the heads of Congress?" At this juncture, going over the many heads of Congress might be more accurate anyway. To push on, however, our founding fathers never contemplated in their day that the President would speak only to Congress and let them pass his thoughts on to the nation, and he in fact rarely spoke to Congress in those early days.[56]

These kinds of system-level concerns about how the president should relate to the electorate and to Congress occupied the White House staff alongside more immediate worries about image and message. Like Nixon's advisers in 1969, Carter's communications team puzzled about the place of the president in new political circumstances.

Concerns were not solely systemic. In the spring of 1977, the White House continued to push energy legislation and to work toward an economic plan. The speechwriting team was attuned to the political risks of these issues. Nesmith noted to Fallows her concern that "after a year of pointing out the need and then announcing, 'this is the most important problem my administration faces,' there is a real danger of asking too little."[57] Fallows expressed the fear that the economic plan would appear too much like Ford's ridiculed WIN button (an acronym for Whip Inflation Now). In the midst of these anxieties about the abstract idea of the president's place in the system and the political unease caused by crafting a new agenda and dealing with economic issues, the team fell back on electoral logic. Fallows suggested a "plot-line" for a spring speech that began in the election campaign:

The plot-line of this speech, reduced to one sentence, should be something like, "here's what we're trying to do." I would think that it should be developed in something like this sequence:

- We had several goals when we were running
- We explained them to the people, and that's why people voted
- here's what our goals are
- here's how we're starting in on them
- this is where we hope to go
- this is where we'll need your help
- this is where we'll make mistakes[58]

Nesmith suggested a similar logic in a note to White House press secretary Jody Powell in April 1978 about questions on the president's standing in the polls. Alluding to the trustee model of representation, she maintained that Carter might respond to questions about polls or image by stating, "I do what I do because, after listening to the best advice I can get, and taking into consideration all the relevant factors, it is the best thing to do for the country in my judgment. I think that's why the people elected me, and what both those who voted for me and those who voted against me want me to do every day."[59]

Carter's communications team never found winning formulas to ward off press criticism, to persuade Congress to adopt the president's preferred stances on energy policy, or to win over enough public support to earn a second term. In the context of declining political strength, the Carter White House drew on the accountability implied by campaign references. Compared to previous administrations, Carter's speechwriters and advisers made a significant effort to understand the meaning of the election result and to incorporate it into rhetoric and overall political strategy. Perhaps no one embraced this idea more than Pat Caddell, who based his initial advice to the president on the assumption that the most victory in 1976 conveyed important information about the beliefs and preferences of the electorate. As Caddell argued in his December 1976 memo, "The president was elected in part because he recognized the incompatibility of old ideological structures in truly answering or solving the concerns of most Americans today. He understood and shared the frustration of most Americans with the rhetoric of traditional liberals/conservatives which while articulate offered little guidance either toward fundamental problems like energy, the economy, cities, welfare reform, government efficiency or toward goals that express the hopes and dreams of the American people."[60]

Carter appears to have followed Caddell's advice. Despite a seemingly genuine effort to respond to perceived demand for a new approach to politics, the Carter White House never developed a compelling public argument for the 1976 election as a policy mandate. In his efforts to do so, Carter sought to revitalize a maligned institution by highlighting the potential for the president to simultaneously heed the demands of the electorate and to transcend party divisions. This balance proved politically untenable. Attempting to save the institutional legitimacy of the presidency, Carter failed to save his *own* presidency. Carter's rhetoric about keeping campaign promises and staying true to the "reasons I was elected" have enjoyed a lasting legacy, however. Subsequent presidents would also adopt these refrains. In contrast to Carter, however, their mandate rhetoric would not take such an ecumenical, nonpartisan approach. Rather, in the partisan era that began with Reagan's inauguration in 1981, presidents have followed Nixon's lead and presented themselves as delegates of a particular segment of the electorate. As we shall see in chapter 5, this rhetoric has served to reinforce, rather than transcend, ideological divisions.

The Impact of the Transition from the Modern Era to the Partisan Era

As the presidency changed in an era of skepticism, scandals, and emerging social divisions, the way presidents conceived of the relationship between elections and governance underwent its own transformation. Electoral logic, particularly campaign promises, took on a newly prominent role in presidential discourse. This shift appears to have been part of a reimagination of the presidency as old alliances and assumptions dissolved. For both Nixon and Carter, electoral logic constituted part of a larger reform narrative. Nixon cited the campaign in his promises to restore law and order, change policy on taxes and spending, and reform the Post Office. Carter, to an even greater extent, saw his presidency as a project of reform. He cited his election as evidence that the electorate sought reform. Furthermore, he used electoral logic rhetoric as a means of highlighting the values of good government: accountability, transparency, and responsiveness to the needs of the people.

In the transition period, campaign references came out not only in speeches and news conferences but also in presidential messages and remarks to members of the executive branch. These references ranged from Nixon's claims about funding for science research to Carter's plans for zero-base budgeting. Although presidential statements framed elections in terms of broad ideas and principles in previous eras, in the context of messages to specific departments or agencies, mandate rhetoric became associated with very specific plans and policy areas. This change also illustrates the extent to which electoral logic had begun to pervade presidential governance. The use of electoral logic rhetoric in messages to the executive branch also lent itself to very specific policy applications. This pervasiveness constitutes the major impact of the transition period.

Campaign references, policy specificity, and messages to the executive branch characterize electoral logic rhetoric in the transition period. At the same time, the political differences between Nixon and Carter remained evident. The major distinction, of course, is partisanship. Nixon's references to the 1968 and 1972 elections and campaigns aimed mostly at a conservative audience, constituting a step toward remaking the presidency as a representative of party constituency first and as a national leader second. Carter, in contrast, sought to maintain a separation between the presidency and partisan politics, casting about for agenda items that would resonate with the electorate. These patterns, discussed in chapter 1 and revisited in chapter 5, appear to have persisted into the partisan era.

Chapter 5

What an Election Is All About

Reagan, Bush, Obama, and the Age of Mandates

Writing in *Time* magazine after Obama's 2008 victory, Michael Grunwald posed and answered the ubiquitous postelection question: What did the result mean? He predicted, "When historians remember the 2008 election, they're going to remember that the two-term Republican president had 20 percent approval ratings, that the economy was in meltdown, and that Americans didn't want another Republican president. They'll also remember that Obama was a change candidate in a change election."[1] These comments, despite references to the specific conditions of the 2008 election, exemplify the mandate politics that characterized the partisan era. Grunwald's assessment emphasized party; although Bush could not appear on the 2008 ticket, the shortcomings of his administration contributed to the Republican candidate's defeat. Furthermore, in a move typical of the partisan era, Grunwald characterized Obama's victory as an endorsement of change.

Although the idea of a "mandate for change" may sound like a trope so generic it is nearly devoid of political meaning, statements like Grunwald's actually describe a specific approach to governing. In this version of mandate logic, a "change" candidate is obligated to deliver on a new and different set of policy promises. These premises underlie the idea of "responsible party government," yet they remain difficult to realize in the American context. Policies prove difficult to change, as Obama learned in his attempts to close the detention facility at Guantanamo Bay. The policy process remains replete with veto points, from the increasingly obstructive Senate to the entrenched bureaucracies of the federal administrative state. Yet, as these factors have become increasingly prominent in American politics, the responsible-party narrative of mandates for policy change has become ever more prevalent.

Parties and the Presidency in the Age of Mandate Politics

In the partisan era, presidential politics has been characterized by persistent, sometimes dramatic, challenges to legitimacy. These challenges are often connected to the depth of party polarization. Confrontations over legitimacy have varied in focus and in severity; they have included near-constant scandal accusations during the Clinton presidency (which culminated in impeachment proceedings), the depiction of George W. Bush as both an unqualified buffoon and a war criminal, and the questions about Barack Obama's birth certificate and possible foreign connections. These challenges have at times diminished the political status of their targets, making it more difficult for them to accomplish signature domestic agenda items or to define the meaning of their political achievements.[2] Clinton's first term was marked early on by failures in economic policy and in health care reform;[3] the second term was disrupted by the impeachment. Bush's second term, even with a Republican Congress, featured a number of high profile legislative defeats, including proposed reforms to Social Security and immigration. Obama's first term produced a number of major policy changes, but the protracted debate over health care reform revealed cracks in the foundation of Democratic unity, and backlash against the legislation left the administration politically weakened going into the 2010 midterms.[4] Presidential stumbles on key policies have in turn contributed to a sense of unfulfilled promises and expectations, further damaging presidential legitimacy.

This phenomenon was not unique to the Obama presidency; the pattern of party victory, thwarted party ambition, and backlash in the next election has recurred throughout the partisan era. Party control of Congress changed five times during the fifty-year period between 1928 and 1978.[5] In the thirty years between 1980 and 2010, Congress has undergone four partial party changes and two complete ones. The conservative victory of 1980 included a Republican takeover of the Senate, which lasted until the 1986 midterm. In 1994, Republicans, promising to counter Bill Clinton's agenda with their own Contract with America, won control of both the House and the Senate. Despite midterm losses in 1998, Republicans held onto power until the 2000 election left the Senate deadlocked. The defection of Republican James Jeffords in the summer of 2001 left the Democrats in control of the chamber until the 2002 midterms brought Republicans back to the majority. The 2004 election strengthened their numbers. Yet, after it seemed that Republicans had established a "permanent majority," Democrats roared back in 2006. Congressional Democrats picked up additional seats in 2008, only to suffer record losses in the 2010 midterms. Since 1994, in sum, American politics has experienced a dynamic in which parties win nationally in congressional and presidential elections, repudiating their opponents, only to be on the other side of the equation a few election cycles later.

The 2010 election campaign echoed the national party themes of the 1994 contests and took opposition politics a step further. Tea Party rallies featured signs declaring intent to "take our country back."[6] Candidates decried Obama as a socialist, and conservative pundits questioned his legal right to serve as president. The response to the Obama presidency represents the convergence of two phenomena that we saw during the transition period under Nixon and Carter: declining institutional status and the emergence of issues that would eventually polarize the two parties. During the 1960s and 1970s, polarization and institutional decline were distinct, separate issues. In the partisan era, they are difficult to disentangle. The emergence of "new media" and the twenty-four-hour news cycle has facilitated this convergence. New forms of media have allowed the president's detractors to transmit a continuous stream of messages reinforcing negative perspectives, from Keith Olbermann's facetious "countdown" of days since George W. Bush had declared "mission accomplished" in Iraq to the perpetuation of the "birther" movement.[7] In a study of new and traditional media, Sarah Sobieraj and Jeffrey Berry found considerable evidence of what they term "outrage"—mockery, name-calling and insults, and misrepresentation—in contemporary political discourse. Compared to more traditional forms of media, newer forms such as blogs, talk radio, and cable news more often carried commentary that challenged the legitimacy of the president and other political actors by questioning their intelligence and loyalty and painting their issue positions as extreme.[8] Furthermore, the "narrow-casting" phenomenon allowed by these new media forms meant that citizens could consume news without confronting opposing political perspectives. As Matthew Baum and Tim Groeling observe, "the increased reliance of many politically attentive Americans on partisan sites such as Daily Kos and Free Republic could potentially pose a significant challenge to American democracy."[9] Evidence suggests that the changing media environment is reflected in changing institutional norms and practices as well. Presidential leadership and public appeals strategies appear to have changed along with changes in media structure; in Jeffrey Cohen's words, "In place of building public support through appealing to the broad mass public, the president engages in a more selective approach, targeting specific groups . . . Usually presidents target friends, ginning up their enthusiasm for the president. Presidential opponents counter with appeals to opposition groups."[10] Faced with these political incentives and obstacles, presidents have invoked the election and the campaign more often than at any other juncture in the post-Progressive presidency. These campaign references, as we shall see, serve as a means for presidents to appeal to supporters. This rhetoric also allows them highlight the transparency and accountability of their leadership. Campaign references convey that the president's plans have been communicated to the public and therefore successfully placed before the electorate for approval.

Mandate rhetoric in this period is also characterized by a different approach to party and ideology. Compared with presidents of the modern era, partisan era presidents have been less likely to refer to party platforms. However, their mandate rhetoric has been more likely to invoke partisanship and ideology in other ways: references to a specific policy associated with a distinct ideological viewpoint, as in George W. Bush's 2005 mandate claims for privatizing Social Security; unfavorable comparisons with the previous administration, as in Reagan's mandate claims invoking economic change, Bill Clinton's references to change, and Barack Obama's insistence that the electorate had "rejected" Republican ideas; and outright arguments that policy positions had been the reasons behind their election victories. Combined with changes in venue and context, as described in chapter 1, mandate rhetoric in this later period appears to be aimed at supporters rather than at a broader audience.

Finally, the theme of responsibility pervades partisan era mandate rhetoric. In this context, the theme of responsibility is distinct from "responsible-party" notions of governance; rather, presidents argued that they had been elected to take responsibility for problems and not to "pass them on to the next generation." Clinton, Bush, and Obama all used this logic in explaining their policy choices. This language offers a new approach to the trusteeship model of representation, identifying the ability to tackle difficult problems as a key part of presidential leadership and yet suggesting that the justification for this leadership still derives from the will of the people.

These three changes illustrate the way in which presidents have used mandate rhetoric as a response to changes in the institutional environment. The emphasis placed on responsibility, transparency, and accountability suggests a new, more challenging presidential politics. Mandate claims have, as we have seen, been used as a defense mechanism and a response to legitimacy challenges throughout the history of the American republic. In the media and party environment of the late twentieth and early twenty-first centuries and in the wake of lasting damage to the idea of executive power, responding to such challenges has become a routine feature of presidential communication.

Three Party Victories

The three cases chosen to illustrate mandate rhetoric in the partisan era are Reagan after the 1980 election, George W. Bush after the 2004 election, and Obama after the 2008 election. These cases were selected in part for their comparability with the earlier presidential terms included in the analysis. As with the earlier cases, different categories in Skowronek's political time are represented; Reagan, like FDR, is a reconstructive leader; Bush, like Johnson, is an articulation president; and Obama, like Eisenhower, is a preemptive president.[11] Political time is not the only basis for comparison. The elections of 1980, 2004, and 2008 all produced some approximation of party victory, facilitating comparison with the earlier elections. Each of these contests—as with 1932, 1936, 1952, and 1964—ended with a majority victory for the president and significant congressional gains for the president's party. The later presidents placed greater emphasis on the mandate and defined it differently than their earlier counterparts. Where FDR, Eisenhower, and Johnson appeared to struggle with and vacillate over the question of party and nation, these presidents interpreted their elections in partisan terms.

Both the governing philosophies espoused and the political contexts faced by this later group illustrate the divergence from their modern era counterparts. For Reagan and Bush, the importance of conservatism as a driving force behind their leadership choices was apparent in their rhetoric, many of their policy actions, and also in the public's reaction to them. For Obama, this situation was more complicated. Promises of transformational and cross-partisan leadership were soon met with highly organized and vocal opposition from Republicans in Congress and in the public. Obama's approach to the presidency and to mandate claiming was less ideological than that of Reagan or of Bush, reflecting his well-documented pragmatic sensibilities.[12] Yet his leadership and language have been unmistakably rooted in partisan considerations, as we shall see in his interpretations of the 2008 election.

This distinction, driven by both political conditions and individual leadership choices, is born out in comparisons between the mandate claims of presidents serving at comparable points in political time. Reagan and FDR both promised to return the nation to its fundamental principles, but Reagan made a more explicit case for defining those values in partisan and ideological terms. The rhetorical choices facing Eisenhower and Obama illustrate change over time even more starkly: both could partially attribute their political success to their promises of a middle way. Once in office, they had to reconcile these promises with the imperatives of governing, balancing earlier high-minded bipartisanship with their decidedly partisan policy positions. Eisenhower chose to construct a mandate narrative and, in fact, a political identity around the idea of being "president of all the people." Obama, as we shall see, quickly abandoned the transcendent narrative in favor of one that reflected his polarized circumstances.

We have much less analytical distance from the Bush and Obama presidencies than from those of FDR, Eisenhower, and Johnson. Indeed, at the time of this writing, Obama's second term is ongoing. As a result, assessing these cases requires some caution, particularly without the archival sources available for earlier presidents. Yet, even at this early stage of understanding the Bush and Obama presidencies, the difference between their approach to electoral logic and that of their predecessors is apparent.

Reagan's Conservative Mandate

Initially, it seemed that Reagan might restore some of the status that had bled away from the presidency during the transitional period. Following what was widely perceived as a display of weakness on Carter's part during the Iranian hostage crisis, Reagan crafted an image of strength.[13] In his 1980 campaign, the California Republican stressed big ideas over policy details, melding a message of change with appeals to social and cultural conservatism.[14] While Carter talked about good government, Reagan promoted images of the nation's fortitude. As historian Sean Wilentz observes, "Reagan's experiences as a self-made and remade man formed the core of an American myth that became part of the substance as well as the style of his politics."[15] The 1980 campaign incorporated Reagan's story and persona into his promises for ideological and policy change.

Reagan's conservative candidacy benefited from the new nomination system. Compared to the traditional convention system, primaries tend to favor candidates who can energize audiences and deliver memorable lines. In 1976 and 1980, the new system also brought advantage to candidates whose political experience had taken place outside of national government. In this regard, Reagan's background as a governor allowed him to portray himself as an independent-thinking "outsider," as Carter had in 1976. Gerald Pomper et al. describe the new nominating system:

> A political party interested only in winning the Presidency might have given Ford more consideration [as a candidate for the Republican nomination in 1980]. The nature of the new nominating system, however, precluded this consideration. Opportunities to enter state primaries were ending rapidly, but most delegates would be selected in these primaries. While Reagan had an organization working throughout the nation, Ford had no campaign staff in the field. There were no "party bosses" to control delegations and no feasible means to delay a decision until the convention met.[16]

These circumstances also benefited the emergent conservative wing of the party, whose influence was not limited to presidential nominations. In the 1980 Republican platform, the party's long-standing support for the Equal Rights Amendment was reversed, with the new plank clarifying distaste for government involvement in society and endorsing the "traditional role" of the family.[17] In the general election campaign, Reagan reached out to religious conservatives and also used conservative messages to appeal to blue-collar and white ethnic voters.[18]

More broadly, these changes were part of a shifting political landscape in which ideology and party became more closely aligned. Reagan claimed a conservative mandate, not necessarily a Republican one. By the time of the Bush and Obama presidencies, this distinction was largely irrelevant, making mandates easier to justify and claim. For Reagan, the coalition and the claims were predominantly about ideology rather than party, a distinction we see reflected in his public rhetoric about a mandate for policy and in the comments made within the White House about the conservative mandate.

The election result appeared custom-made to frustrate mandate theorists. Reagan won just over 50 percent of the popular vote, but took more than 90 percent of the Electoral College vote share. Republicans won control of the Senate and gained 33 seats in the House of Representatives, although they fell short of winning control of that chamber.[19] The political science literature reflects this equivalence over whether the 1980 election constituted a legitimate conservative mandate. Conley identifies 1980 as one of three "popular mandates," along with 1952 and 1964, and suggests that the campaign and result allowed Reagan to pursue a conservative economic agenda in particular (alongside social and foreign policy agendas). Lawrence Grossback, David Peterson, and James Stimson similarly classify 1980 as a mandate election, along with 1964 and 1994, arguing that the unexpected magnitude of victory for Reagan as well as other Republican candidates allowed for an unusually productive—and conservative—legislative session.[20] Examining similar evidence, Charles O. Jones comes to a somewhat different conclusion. He notes that the message from voters in the 1980 contest was unclear, and that the news commentary following the election was "somewhat muted" and reflected a general sense that the victory was at least in part a result of dissatisfaction with Carter rather than preference for a conservative agenda. The idea of the 1980 election as a mandate for Reagan's agenda also inspired Robert Dahl's critique of the entire concept. Dahl notes that although Reagan won less than 51 percent of votes cast, the Reagan administration broadly touted their victory as a mandate authorizing the president to exert his preferences over those of Congress.

News media were generally optimistic about the possibilities for interpreting the election in policy terms. An op-ed piece in the *Wall Street Journal* argued that Reagan had a mandate for change and explored several possibilities for policy change: strengthening foreign policy, tax cuts, and redefining the national agenda.[21] Similarly, other pieces analyzed the election in terms of a public "endorsement" of both economic and defense agendas.[22] Still others, however, rejected the idea of a clear policy mandate. An article in the *New York Times* on November 9, 1980, presents a New York Times/CBS News Poll suggesting that Reagan voters were likely "motivated more by dissatisfaction with President Carter than any serious ideological commitment to the Republican's views." The opposite view was presented by one of Reagan's pollsters, Richard B. Wirthlin, who argued that two-thirds of Reagan's vote share was pro-Reagan rather than anti-Carter.[23] Nevertheless, Wirthlin stopped short of calling the election a "mandate" for policies derived from Reagan's ideological orientation, maintaining instead that it gave a "sanction" from the voters to some of Reagan's basic ideas. Tom Wicker's analysis cited polling data that revealed no change in the electorate's demand for government-provided public services; instead he cited foreign policy as a reason for the Republican victory. Even this interpretation did not depict the election as a policy mandate, however; the difference between the two candidates was a "matter of credibility rather than policy, since Mr. Carter made the same promise."[24]

Despite mixed reactions to the 1980 election, Reagan forged ahead with his own narrative about the conservative mandate. As Reagan constructed a "mandate for change," his electoral logic rhetoric echoed ideas from Nixon and Carter: both had routinely emphasized their campaign promises and, in the case of Nixon after the 1972 election, the mandate as a justification for strong executive power. In his efforts to jettison the baggage of the 1970s and recreate the image of the presidency, Reagan drew on arguments about the presidency that had resurged during that very period. Reagan also affirmed his commitment to the Republican platform in a way that harkened back to Progressive Era rhetoric. At his first press conference after the election, he stated, "I ran on that platform; the people voted for me on that platform; I do believe in that platform, and I think it would be very cynical and callous of me to suggest that I'm going to turn away from it."[25] This logic combined two ideas that set mandate rhetoric in the partisan era apart from that of the modern period: the depiction of the president as delegate rather than trustee and the unambiguous embrace of the president's partisan role. The use of party and ideology reflects sorting and polarization, whereas delegate language draws on a more complex dynamic. Reagan stressed a strong approach to the presidency, especially in foreign policy, yet his use of mandate language softened this stance by stressing his commitment to the electorate.

Between his inauguration in 1981 and the end of March of the same year, Reagan gave one televised national address, eight ceremonial speeches (including the inaugural address), and ten news conferences. In addition to these speeches, he sent ten messages to Congress, addressed the executive branch six times, and spoke to the National League of Cities, the National Governors Association, and a group of state legislators and county executives (twenty-two government communications in all). He also made twenty-four minor addresses and statements, and addressed Republican leaders on three occasions, including the Conservative Political Action Conference. Approximately 10.2 percent of these communications included a reference to the election or campaign of 1980. Most of these statements interpreted the election as a mandate for economic issues. In keeping with the conservative vision of smaller government, Reagan ordered a federal hiring freeze on January 22, asked all noncareer civil service employees to resign, and announced changes in travel and other similar expenditures. He justified changes in federal spending by stating in his remarks about the cuts, "And as with every other economic action we take, it's essential that we follow through on our commitments. Thus, I view the implementation of these orders as critical. The American people are determined, I believe, to have actions on the economic problems that we face. They're going to find out that we're listening to them. We're equally determined to see through every essential step that is needed to restore our economy."[26] Similarly, in the actual memorandum announcing the cuts, Reagan suggested that the new plan would "help redeem our pledge to the American people of a government that lives within its means."[27]

An instructive comparison can be made between Reagan and FDR. Sometimes compared because of their paradigm-shifting presidencies, Roosevelt and Reagan used electoral logic very differently in their communica-

tions. During the first seventy days that FDR was in office, his only reference to the 1932 election was a broad claim about "direct action" in the
Inaugural Address. For Reagan, electoral logic played a much more prominent role. In chapter two, we examined the relationships among changes in
the party system, changes in the presidency, and Roosevelt's interpretations
of the 1932 election. The first major distinction was in the status of the office. In the decades preceding Roosevelt's election, the informal role of the
presidency had grown. Furthermore, the immediacy and severity of the Great
Depression gave Roosevelt the status of a "crisis leader," boosting his authority. In 1981, conditions were quite different. Although economic issues
were important in the 1980 election, the problems did not compare to the
building unrest of the early 1930s; calls for martial law were absent in the
1980 context and, once in office, Reagan's new position did not require dras-
tic action on the level of the 1933 bank holiday. Furthermore, the presidency
had experienced a series of high-profile humiliations: Johnson's decision not
to run for reelection in 1968, Nixon's resignation in 1974, and Carter's inability to successfully reposition in the presidency or, ultimately, to win reelection. Reagan's response involved two somewhat contradictory approaches.
The conservative message of shrinking government drew on public skepticism about its role and capacity.[28] Yet his narrative was also one of reassur-
ance about the accountability and responsiveness of a new governing coalition guided by the demands of the people.[29]

As Roosevelt's mandate rhetoric reflected the politics of the transition
from the Progressive to the modern presidency, Reagan's mandate rhetoric
revealed an institution beginning to settle into a new partisan era. Despite
his investment in national mythology, Reagan's vision of the office—unlike
that of Roosevelt, Eisenhower, or Johnson—was not predicated on the idea
of transcending politics. His policy message unified disparate strains of the
conservative movement, espousing social and economic conservatism, and
anticommunism.[30] Reagan's more ideological approach was matched by a
more divided electorate. The gap between Reagan's average approval among
Democrats and Republicans in the 1981 was 45 points, the largest recorded
first-year "approval gap" for any president up to that point.[31]

The impact of changing party politics was evident beyond public opinion. By the time Reagan won the 1980 election, the conservative movement
had been building for several decades. The Reagan presidency offered the
first real chance for this movement to influence policy through the executive

branch. For example, as David Yalof has noted, the Reagan White House explicitly applied ideological criteria in judicial appointments when evaluating possible Supreme Court nominees.[32] It also shaped the Reagan White House and management of the bureaucracy. Changes to the structure of the executive branch forced bureaucrats to be more responsive to presidential directives.[33] Executive branch management, which never lived up to the ideal of "neutral competence," became even more politicized as Reagan sought to reshape policy.[34] In other words, the Reagan presidency represented a shift in the relationship between presidents and parties, and also came at a time when the influence of the conservative movement was becoming more apparent within the Republican Party.

Reagan responded to political conditions by promoting the 1980 election specifically as a mandate for conservative economic ideas. About a week after the budget announcements, Reagan refined the mandate narrative somewhat, stating in the opening remarks of a press conference that "the clear message I received in the election campaign is that we must gain control of this inflationary monster."[35] Reagan returned to budget politics in a message to Congress on March 10, 1981. In a message describing cuts to the 1982 budget, Reagan offered dramatic rhetoric: "But today's status quo is nothing more than economic stagnation coupled with high inflation. Dramatic change is needed or the situation will simply get worse, resulting in even more suffering and misery, and possibly the destruction of traditional American values." The argument for budget changes did not end there. Reagan also connected the budget to his vision of the 1980 mandate, contending "when considering the economic recovery package, I urge the Members of Congress to remember that last November the American people's message was loud and clear. The mandate for change, expressed by the American people, was not my mandate; it was our mandate. Together we must remember that our primary responsibility is to the Nation as a whole and that there is nothing more important than putting America's economic house in order."[36]

White House staff also invoked the mandate when challenged in less public forms of communication. Representative Patricia Schroeder (D-CO) wrote a letter urging the administration to call for a deferral of the pay raise scheduled for members of Congress and top federal executives. White House aide Max Friedersdorf's reply, which was in agreement with Schroeder's suggestion, emphasizes that the President's intended course of action was "consistent with the mandate he received in last November's election."[37] In an exchange between Reagan aide Lyn Nofziger and Patsy Mink of the Americans for Democratic Action (ADA), the 1980 mandate was also invoked. A letter from Mink, representing the views of the ADA, raises reservations about Reagan's proposed spending cuts and acknowledges an electoral mandate to improve economic conditions while calling into question the methods the administration plans to employ. Nofziger's response dismisses the previous interpretation of the election with a reminder that "as you must recognize, many of the proposals that you criticize in your letter are precisely the measures that President Reagan used as the basis for his campaign last November."[38] This argument sounds much like the "responsible-party" model of government. At the same time, it further underscores the defensive character of mandate claims. When confronted with views of the other side, the Reagan White House reminded opponents that the conservative policy platform had been the winning one in the election.

Reagan's approach to electoral logic in 1981 reflected the crosscurrent of developments in the party system and the presidency at that time. As such, he drew heavily on the idea of an electoral mandate in order to justify governing choices. Historian Gil Troy has observed that the Reagan mandate, although artificially "manufactured" by his communications team, "was central to the Reaganites' success."[39] But, as we have seen, the mandate is not a fixed concept. Reagan and his staffers took care to construct a particular kind of mandate that addressed the presidency at the time. The focus on a single-issue area, the economy, lent coherence to the narrative.[40] References to the transparency and responsiveness to the will of the people can be understood as a response to the decline in institutional prestige following Watergate and Vietnam. The emphasis on conservative themes reflects the infusion of ideology into party politics and the transformation of presidential politics into a more prime-ministerial approach. Like Nixon's idea of the "silent majority" in 1969, the Reagan White House offered a narrative of a mandate that reflected the needs and preferences of a specific group within the electorate: those who had voted for them. Presidents have never been able to avoid what George Washington famously denounced as "partisan entanglements"—even Washington found himself taking Alexander Hamilton's side on major policy disagreements with Madison and Jefferson.[41] But transcending partisanship was at least an aspiration for modern presidents such as Eisenhower and Johnson, an impulse with pragmatic motivations and philosophical implications. As parties become more internally homogenous, and the fault lines dividing the two parties became more pronounced, the notion of the "president above politics" has proven even more elusive. In constructing the mandate of 1980, the Reagan White House appears to have given the nonpartisan ideal little thought. As a short-term strategy, this generally yielded good results. As a point in the development of the presidency, Reagan's claims to a 1980 conservative mandate anticipated the later function of mandate rhetoric: affirming and reinforcing polarized political discourse. Reagan's choices also reinforced a delegate definition of the mandate, presenting the president as a follower rather than a leader and as a representative of a specific segment of the public.

Through political skill and strategy, Reagan avoided the pitfalls of being seen as a follower. Strong rhetoric about defense and national security helped him maintain the appearance of strength and leadership. The Reagan White House skillfully used what Bruce Miroff calls "spectacle" in order to project an image of "potency."[42] This approach required mastery of imagery and rhetoric in order to be successful, but the political context created scope conditions. The current of individualized, candidate-centered politics that swept through politics in the early 1980s allowed Reagan to cite the people's will as the main impetus for his decisions, yet still appear to be a strong, decisive leader.

Bush Plays to the Base

By 2004, George W. Bush's self-description as a "compassionate conservative" had deteriorated from bumper sticker slogan to punch line. Political scientist Gary Jacobson proclaimed Bush a "divider, not a uniter," inverting another 2000 campaign slogan.[43] By June 2004, the president's approval ratings were strongly polarized—nearly 90 percent among Republicans and as low as 12 percent among Democrats.[44] The emergent cable news media contributed to this political environment as well. Keith Olbermann, who would later call Bush a "murderous fascist" on his MSNBC show, reported on election "irregularities" after the 2004 contest had concluded, prompting criticism from his counterparts on the right.[45]

Early interpretations of the 2004 election in the traditional news media also demonstrated Bush's polarizing impact. For example, conservative columnist Charles Krauthammer developed an extensive definition of the presidential mandate that took into account the number of popular votes by which Bush won reelection, suggesting that the 3.5 million vote margin was a "serious majority" (conflating "margin of victory" and "majority").[46] Skepticism about the magnitude of the election victory to clear a mandate threshold came from Krauthammer's liberal colleague E. J. Dionne, who maintained that, "A 51–48 percent victory is *not* a mandate."[47] Doubts came from conservatives as well. In a piece urging the Bush administration not to confuse a rejection of the Kerry campaign with a mandate for conservative policies, former Reagan aide Lyn Nofziger asserted, "The president and his people are deluding themselves if they think his victory signified general approval of his record."[48] The *Christian Science Monitor* published an analysis that pointed out the growing divisions within the party over social issues that accompanied conservative victories on same-sex marriage ballot initiatives in 2004.[49]

As they contemplated the meaning of the election outcome, journalists also questioned whether Bush would stress the issue priorities of conservatives or reach beyond the party base. On November 4, 2004, the *New York Times* contributed to this interpretation and assessed the importance of social issues on the election result by suggesting that the president's supporters "anticipated a revolution."[50] In another article, *New York Times* writer Todd S. Purdum posed the question, "So what next? If even a one-vote margin is a mandate, as John F. Kennedy once said, what might a real mandate look like for Mr. Bush? Will he pursue his course undaunted, whatever the opposition may do? Or once again seek, as he promised four years ago, to 'change the tone' in Washington, and reach out to the one-quarter of voters in the electorate who described themselves as angry at his administration?"[51] In debating over the meaning of the 2004 election, journalists presented their audiences with the classic presidential dilemma: Would—and should—the newly reelected Bush administration take the "responsible-party" direction, or would the second term turn toward a more national and inclusive vision?

These remarks also highlight the general lack of consensus about the meaning of the term "presidential mandate" in 2004. In a country deeply divided, what did it mean for the Republican Party to win the presidency and gain seats in both houses of Congress? The concept of responsible-party government has never been entirely compatible with the American system of separated powers. But after the election of 2004, it seemed that many of the elements were in place. The distinct positions of the two parties were readily evident. The campaign had brought out differences on economic issues, entitlement reform, social issues, and foreign policy. On domestic policy, Bush and the Republicans offered further tax cuts, a plan to privatize Social Security, and opposition to abortion and same-sex marriage.[52] In the highly salient debate over foreign policy, they promised to stay the course in Iraq, while Democratic presidential candidate John Kerry denounced the administration's actions. After both sides made their positions clear, one side won.

The margin of victory was slim, however. If an important characteristic of a mandate election is an extraordinary result, then 2004 fell short. Compared with historic landslide elections such as 1932 and 1964, the Bush victory appeared quite modest. In other words, like many elections, the 2004 results were ambiguous. The raw facts revealed by the voting returns appear not to have shaped Bush's response to the election. Instead, Bush's construction of the 2004 mandate reflects the polarized state of the party system and the need to establish and bolster the legitimacy of the Bush presidency.

Bush emphasized the election and the campaign far more than either Franklin Roosevelt or Lyndon Johnson, despite winning a much more modest victory. More than 28 percent of presidential communications in the spring of 2005 included mandate rhetoric. After the election, Bush had declared that his "political capital" would be applied to a variety of problems, including the terrorism and foreign policy issues that had dominated much of the policy agenda since 2001.[53] But in 2005, the newly reelected president constructed the mandate narrative almost exclusively around the issue of Social Security reform. Bush's mandate rhetoric also emphasized the fulfillment of campaign promises, as in an address at a Republican National Committee Dinner on March 15. Explaining the intent to continue to cut taxes, the president remarked, "In the 2004 elections, we ran on large issues. We campaigned on a platform of big ideas. We discussed those ideas at every campaign stop, and the American people responded. And now it is our turn to respond and do what they expect."[54] Alongside rhetoric about decisiveness and presidential power, Bush offered delegate-style claims about campaign promises.

As the signature domestic issue, Social Security must have seemed like a natural choice for mandate rhetoric. Journalist Robert Draper explains that

Bush had "littered the campaign trail with references to Social Security private accounts" and thus believed that since he had been reelected in 2004, this position must have been the reason—despite evidence to the contrary. Draper notes, "No one in the White House reminded him that the election had been framed as a Choice, Not a Referendum, the Steady Leadership versus the Flip-flopping Windsurfer."[55] Fiona Ross calls Bush's effort to persuade voters and legislators on the Social Security issue "a spectacularly unsuccessful investment of political capital" and cites "the naïve faith that the administration placed in the power of communications, and even particular phrases such as 'choice' and 'ownership' to change public opinion" as part of the problem.[56] Nevertheless, framing the issue in terms of the putative party mandate followed established political tactics. In the 2004 race, the campaign had focused heavily on mobilizing the conservative base.[57] Campaign strategy quickly became governing logic. Lou Cannon and Carl Cannon describe how "Bush and [Karl] Rove worked overtime to keep the base mollified."[58] Social Security reform fit into the strategy of base politics, with much higher favorability ratings among Republicans than Democrats. A Gallup Poll in December 2004 found that almost 70 percent of Republican respondents favored the president's proposed reforms, while only 26 percent of Democrats favored them.[59]

The challenge of transforming these numbers into a working coalition in Congress did not deter the administration from constructing the 2004 mandate almost exclusively around the issue of Social Security. Bush toured the nation to promote his plan, stopping in a number of states where he won in 2004—Arizona, Colorado, Louisiana, Iowa, Indiana, New Mexico, and North Carolina—as well as a handful in which he lost, including Pennsylvania, New Jersey, and Maryland. The mandate rhetoric in these speeches emphasized that the president had run on the issue of Social Security reform. For example, in Tucson, giving an address on strengthening Social Security, Bush made this statement during the question-and-answer portion of the presentation:

> Well, let me tell you my theory on this—not my theory; my view. [Applause] Thank you all, but here's what I believe. I know the Senator believes this—I know Senators believe it; I know Members—these Members of the House believe it. Our job is not to pass problems on to future Presidents or future Congresses. That's not why we ran for office. We ran for office, and we said

to the people, "When we see a problem, in good faith we will work together to solve it." That's what we said. This is a problem; now is the time for members of both political parties to work together to solve the problem so that a person like Jack [an audience member who had asked a question] says to Members of the Congress, both parties, "Job well done, you've done what we expected you to do." [60]

In Notre Dame, Indiana, on March 4, 2005, Bush similarly argued, during the question-and-answer period:

> The fundamental question facing our society and facing our Congress is, are we willing to worry about taxpayers that have yet to come close to retirement? That's really what we're talking about. I campaigned on this issue. I said, "Vote for me, and I'm going to bring forth interesting ideas to make the Social Security system sound." I believe people appreciate a candid approach to issues and want people to work together to solve problems. [61]

Despite this effort to shore up support among the Republican base, the privatization plan never gained traction in Congress. Democrats as well as Republicans in marginal districts had little incentive to advocate for the reforms, which were unpopular with the electorate as a whole. Rove's strategy had met its limits. Aside from its ineffectiveness in this instance, what does this story tell us about mandate rhetoric in the twenty-first century?

By claiming a mandate on the basis of a clear, distinct party platform and a slim majority (as Reagan had in 1980 and Bush had in 2004), Reagan and Bush may have served to reinforce divisions in the electorate rather than to reconcile them. In the first term, Bush had been involved in several important bipartisan initiatives: No Child Left Behind, on which he collaborated with Senator Edward Kennedy (D-MA), and Medicare reform that won support across party lines. However, in the second term, Bush's overall message changed. By focusing his communications efforts on areas friendly to the administration and to conservative views, Bush underscored the idea that his presidency represented only a certain segment of the nation. Karl Rove's "base" strategy for campaigning and governance was a defining feature of the Bush presidency. [62] But at least where mandate rhetoric is concerned, this stategy seems to be part of a larger development in Republican presidential politics. Engaging the core support coalition also fit the political circumstances of the era. Surveyed a few days before the inauguration in

2005, 91 percent of Republicans reported the expectation that Bush would be an above average or outstanding president, versus 4 percent who expected that he would be below average or poor. In contrast, 74 percent of Democrats and 49 percent of independents expected Bush to be a below average or poor president. Democrats and independents were also much less likely to report the expectation of greatness—22 and 44 percent, respectively.[63] In this context, appealing to supporters may have seemed the safest strategy.

The main lesson from the Bush case appears to be that appealing to the party base did not produce political or policy success. During the first two years of Bush's second term, his efforts to govern from the right were not successful, as we have seen in the case of Social Security reform. Neither were his efforts to move to the center with an immigration reform plan that attracted some Democrats but repelled the conservative wing of Bush's own party.[64] The experience of the Bush presidency following the 2004 elections exemplifies a powerful discrepancy between ideas about governing and the reality of policymaking. The responsible-party ideal shaped Bush's thought and rhetoric after his reelection; ideological distance between the parties and the idea of appeasing the party's base informed this approach. However, the responsible-party ideal came up against some of the most consequential realities of American government: the difficulty of changing policy and the broad coalitions required by the legislative process.

Politically, the 2006 midterms brought Democrats back to power in Congress, reducing the final years of Bush's second term to a series of partisan struggles. The Democratic majorities passed laws calling for the withdrawal of troops from Iraq, supporting stem-cell research, and expanding programs to provide health care to needy children. The president vetoed these measures. Although these measures did not appear to hurt his standing with Republicans, the support of the base was not enough to save his political status.[65] Standing by the letter of conservative principles proved more difficult after the banking collapse in fall 2008. Bush backed government plans to "bail out" troubled financial institutions in order to forestall further problems. This decision inspired criticism from conservatives, including Republican presidential candidate John McCain.[66] McCain missed his opportunity to experience the cross-pressures of presidential leadership, however. The 2008 election delivered a majority to the Democratic candidate, Barack Obama.

Rejecting the Politics of the Past

On November 4, 2008, Barack Obama addressed the nation for the first time as the president-elect, offering a plea and a promise: "Let us resist the temptation to fall back on the same partisanship and pettiness and immaturity that has poisoned our politics for so long . . . And to those Americans whose support I have yet to earn—I may not have won your vote, but I hear your voices, I need your help, and I will be your President too." [67] Obama's vows to "change the tone in Washington" date back to the speech at the 2004 Democratic National Convention that launched him onto the national stage. Confronting culture war stereotypes, Obama declared, "We worship an awesome God in the blue states, and we don't like federal agents poking around our libraries in the red states. We coach little league in the blue states and, yes, we've got some gay friends in the red states." [68] Nevertheless, during the 2008 campaign—first during the primaries and then in the general election—Obama emphasized the differences between his positions and those of the incumbent Republican administration. Throughout the campaign, he cited his consistent record of opposition to the war in Iraq and promised to end American military involvement. [69] The Obama campaign also differentiated itself from the Bush administration on domestic issues, especially the economy. Whereas the 2004 election had focused on the party base, [70] the Obama campaign (in coordination with the Democratic National Committee, chaired by 2004 presidential hopeful Howard Dean) employed a "fifty-state strategy." [71] By reaching beyond the typical "blue" pockets along the coasts and in the upper Midwest, the campaign comfortably cleared the threshold for Electoral College victory by winning in states such as Virginia, North Carolina, and Indiana. This gave the appearance of a new, broad coalition—even though the Obama campaign drew substantial support from traditional Democratic groups, such as African Americans and lower-income voters. [72]

The success of the fifty-state strategy, along with promises to find common ground between Republicans and Democrats, created expectations of a "postpartisan" presidency. At the same time, Obama's pledges for policy change signaled intent to repudiate Republican ideas, not accommodate them. In this way, Obama set himself up for a difficult time constructing a single, coherent narrative for the interpretation of the 2008 election. But the problem was not entirely attributable to Obama's previous rhetoric. A polarized polity meant that Republican opposition to Obama was strong and unified. His favorability ratings with Republicans never reached above 41 percent during the first year; by the end of 2009, they were below 20 percent.[73]

As in 2004, media interpretations of the election were mixed. The *San Francisco Chronicle* featured several articles that took on the debate about the partisan implications of the election contest and result. One article quotes Senate majority leader Harry Reid insisting that, "it is not a mandate for any political party or any ideology, but a mandate to get over those things that divide us and focus on getting things done,"[74] whereas another casts the election as a clear choice between the competing legacies of Ronald Reagan and Franklin Delano Roosevelt.[75] Echoing Reid's sentiment about the meaning of the election, an opinion piece in the *Los Angeles Times* argued that the president was charged with the responsibility of reuniting the country. The same piece maintained that he "must repair the United States' international relations and renew our ties to the multilateral organizations that President Bush neglected. He must repair the damage inflicted by the so-called war on terror, which has alienated the United States from many friends. Closing the detention facility at Guantanamo Bay, Cuba, would be a welcome and symbolic start."[76] *Forbes* magazine took the position that the election result signaled "the electorate's deep desire for change." In the context of his own mixed campaign messages and an unevenly polarized political environment, Obama tended toward a partisan interpretation of the election. This position was not unreasonable; Democrats had shown even more strength in the 2008 contest than Republicans had in 2004. However, in contrast with Reagan and Bush, Obama did not create a unified narrative about the party's values and the message of the election. Between January 20 and March 31, he linked the election to three main policy areas: good government, the rejection of Republican economic ideas, and changes in the conduct of the war on terrorism.

Obama's high approval ratings in early 2009 belied the complicated politics of his presidency. The new president's struggles to establish legitimacy were in some ways typical of the politics of the era. Efforts to bring House Republicans on board with the economic stimulus bill were unsuccessful, portending other highly partisan votes and negotiations;[77] congressional polarization had emerged long before Obama took office.[78] This development affected the presidencies of George H. W. Bush, Bill Clinton, and

George W. Bush, hindering their ability to work across the aisle and increasing their reliance on their own partisans in Congress.[79]

Yet Obama's particular situation also brought on unique legitimacy challenges. Bert Rockman notes that although Senate norms about filibusters and "holds"—rules designed to empower the minority party—had changed well before Obama took office, the Republican opposition took their use to a new level during the first term of the Obama presidency.[80] From the 2009 stimulus bill to the Patient Protection Act to the debt negotiations of 2011, Obama contended with a particularly focused—if not always necessarily unified—opposition party. The political objectives of this strategy were brought into stark relief with Senate minority leader Mitch McConnell's famous statement that his primary legislative objective was "for President Obama to be a one-term president."[81]

In addition to legislative opposition, Obama's presidency also became the target of a growing and active new media effort. As with congressional opposition, the difference between Bush and Obama constituted one of degree more than kind. The proliferation of blogs and other new media sources allowed for Obama's critics—as well as his supporters—to add their ideas to the media narrative and to shape the discourse. A dedicated and vocal opposition had begun to form even before Obama's inauguration. For example, Fox News host Glenn Beck told audiences on January 12 that "I do believe Obama is a socialist. He may be a full-fledged Marxist. He has surrounded himself by Marxists his whole life."[82] A few days before the inauguration ceremony, radio personality Rush Limbaugh famously announced, "I hope he fails," in response to a putative request of a statement on his "hopes" for the Obama presidency.[83] Conservative blogs also took aim at the president and his supporters; for example, the blog Wonkette referred to supporters as "Obamatards."[84] It remains to be seen whether these patterns of media incivility and legitimacy challenges will persist beyond the Obama presidency; as Obama's second term unfolds, there exists scant evidence of their abatement.

In the early months of 2009, Obama's use of mandate rhetoric reflected the need to establish legitimacy and to deflect criticism. In major addresses, statements, and news conferences, we observe Obama using the logic of campaign promises and telling audiences that he was, in essence, doing what he was elected to do. These claims interpreted the 2008 election in expansive, yet specific, policy terms. The president not only cited his campaign as a means of justifying his agenda and anticipating and responding to criticism but also used mandate language to criticize political opponents by suggesting that their ideas had been rejected by the people.

On January 21, Obama notified the White House senior staff that in addition to a salary freeze, he would also issue an executive order restricting the ability of White House staff to work as lobbyists after leaving their posts. The new president introduced these changes by citing campaign promises:

> But the American people deserve more than simply an assurance that those who are coming to Washington will serve their interests. They also deserve to know that there are rules on the books to keep it that way. They deserve a Government that is truly of, by, and for the people. As I often said during the campaign, we need to make the White House the people's house. And we need to close the revolving door that lets lobbyists come into Government freely and lets them use their time in public service as a way to promote their own interests over the interests of the American people when they leave. So today we are taking a major step towards fulfilling this campaign promise. The Executive order on ethics I will sign shortly represents a clean break from business as usual.[85]

The connection between campaign promises and improving government ethics recall Carter's promises to provide better, more honest practices in government. Obama also linked these ideas to the now-familiar theme of deficit reduction, stating at a Fiscal Responsibility Summit on February 23:

> In the end, however, if we want to rebuild our economy and restore discipline and honesty to our budget, we will need to change the way we do business here in Washington. We're not going to be able to fall back into the same old habits and make the same inexcusable mistakes: the repeated failure to act as our economy spiraled deeper into crisis; the casual dishonesty of hiding irresponsible spending with clever accounting tricks; the costly overruns, the fraud and abuse, the endless excuses. This is exactly what the American people rejected when they went to the polls.

Three days later, in remarks on the federal budget, Obama offered a similar sentiment:

> Now, I know that this will not always sit well with the special interests and their lobbyists here in Washington, who think our budget and tax system is

just fine as it is. No wonder; it works for them. I don't think that we can continue on our current course. I work for the American people, and I'm determined to bring the change that the people voted for last November. And that means cutting what we don't need to pay for what we do.

More than thirty years before Obama took office, Jimmy Carter demonstrated the risks involved in claiming a mandate for good government. Although touting improvements to the system has intuitive appeal, such claims can set an impossible standard for the administration.[86] Entering its fourth year at the time of this writing, the Obama administration has thus far avoided any major scandals involving high-ranking Cabinet officials or White House staff. However, the watchdog organization PolitiFact has identified the rule against working for lobbyists as a "promise broken," citing a provision in the order that allows former lobbyists to serve in the administration.[87] Thus far, Obama's criticism from the left has emphasized issues other than lobbyists and the power of special interests. However, with seven out of ten Americans reporting the belief that "lobbyists have too much power,"[88] it seems possible that this issue may gain greater salience.

Obama's mandate rhetoric about the economic situation and about foreign policy took the "change" idea even further. These messages differed from the populist and reform themes developed elsewhere, instead stressing partisanship and campaign promises, following a similar pattern to that of Reagan and Bush. Obama succinctly summarized this approach in a comment to then-House minority whip Eric Cantor, who criticized the president's tax policy. The president responded, "I won."[89] As he presented economic plans to Congress and the public, Obama repeatedly framed the 2008 election as a rejection of Republican economic ideas. For example, on February 4, in remarks on the national economy, Obama interpreted the 2008 election in partisan policy terms:

> I've heard criticisms that this plan is somehow wanting, and these criticisms echo the very same failed economic theories that led us into this crisis in the first place: the notion that tax cuts alone will solve all our problems; that we can ignore fundamental challenges like energy independence and the high cost of health care; that we can somehow deal with this in a piecemeal fashion and still expect our economy and our country to thrive.
>
> I reject those theories, and so did the American people when they went to the polls in November and voted resoundingly for change. So I urge Mem-

bers of Congress to act without delay. No plan is perfect, and we should
work to make it stronger. No one is more committed to making it stronger
than me. But let's not make the perfect the enemy of the essential. Let's show
people all over the country who are looking for leadership in this difficult
time that we are equal to the task.[90]

Obama's mandate rhetoric resembles Bush's rhetoric about the 2004 election and Social Security in the sense that it invokes the campaign and presents the president as a responsible-party leader or a partisan delegate. An
innovation all Obama's own, however, is the depiction of the 2008 election
as a negative event.[91] Other elections have featured considerable negative
advertising or been decided by negative evaluations of the incumbent. However, Obama appears to be the first to embrace negativity in his mandate
rhetoric, referring to the 2008 election more than once as a "rejection" of
Republican economic philosophy.

As with economic policy, Obama drew distinctions between his ideas
about foreign policy and those of his predecessor. In February 2009, Obama
announced plans to gradually withdraw the U.S. military from Iraq. In a
speech announcing these plans at Camp Lejeune, North Carolina, Obama
put the decision in the context of earlier campaign promises:

> The first part of this strategy is therefore the responsible removal of our
> combat brigades from Iraq. As a candidate for President, I made clear my
> support for a timeline of 16 months to carry out this drawdown, while pledg-
> ing to consult closely with our military commanders upon taking office to
> ensure that we preserve the gains we've made and to protect our troops.
> These consultations are now complete, and I have chosen a timeline that will
> remove our combat brigades over the next 18 months.[92]

Despite its softer language—especially compared to the rhetoric about
"overwhelming" rejection of Republican economic ideas—Obama's statement about the withdrawal represented a departure from previous practice:
previous presidents had rarely invoked electoral logic to deal with foreign
issues, and never for one as central as the Iraq invasion. The difficulties associated with such claims are illustrated in Obama's interview with Jim
Lehrer on the same day. In a discussion about Obama's announcement at
Camp Lejeune, Lehrer asked the president about the withdrawal timeline:
"You've caught some heat as you know, Mr. President, today from some of

your Democratic colleagues in Congress saying wait a minute, we're not supposed to have 50,000 troops still there or whatever. What is your—the criticism being that the withdrawal is too slow and it isn't as dramatic as they had expected, your colleagues, your supporters had expected. How do you answer that?"

Obama's initial reaction went immediately back to campaign logic, stating:

> Well, what I would say that is that they maybe weren't paying attention to what I said during the campaign. I said that we were going to take 16 months to withdraw our combat troops from Iraq. We are now taking 18 months rather than 16. I said that we would have a residual force—a transition force that could continue to stand up Iraqi security forces, provide them logistical support and training and also make sure that we are protecting U.S. civilian and military personnel.
>
> I said that we would have a counterterrorism capacity to make sure that al Qaeda or other extremist organizations did not try to take advantage of a diminished U.S. presence there. So everything that I said I would do during the campaign I am now doing.

Lehrer pressed the president further on the partisan dimensions of his decision, noting that, "John McCain and John Boehner—the Republican leader of the House—have praised your plan while the Democrats are criticizing it?" In Obama's response, the electoral logic began to unravel, with an initial statement, "You know, I don't—I don't make these decisions based on polls or popularity. I make the decisions based on what I think is best," followed by a reiteration that, "This is consistent with what I said during the campaign. The fact—if anything I think people should be interested in the fact that there's been a movement in the direction of what I thought was going to be the right plan in the first place."[93]

These statements illustrate the mismatch between mandate logic and the kinds of reasons that presidents usually invoke for issues of war and peace. The first incongruence involves the familiar tension between party and national leadership. When Obama first denounced the war in Iraq as a "dumb" mistake, he was an Illinois state Senator.[94] Later, as a candidate for the presidency, contending first to win the Democratic primaries and then to garner enough votes to win office, Obama continued to assert his position. After assuming office, the president contended with the challenge of fulfilling his promises without diminishing the sacrifice or accomplishments of the U.S. military (which Obama also noted in his exchange with Lehrer). Reconciling the difference between candidate and commander-in-chief was not the only pitfall of using electoral logic rhetoric to justify defense policy, however. Obama's own words acknowledge that making decisions in response to public opinion—acting as a delegate—stands at odds with using one's best judgment about a situation—acting as a trustee. Traditionally, presidents have justified foreign policy in terms of national security. Bush's address to the nation before invading Iraq relied heavily on arguments about national security, stating that "the danger is clear" and asserting that "the United States of America has the sovereign authority to use force in assuring its own national security."[95] Human, civil, and political rights have also formed the basis for foreign policy rationales. Bill Clinton declared in his 1999 State of the Union address that, "You know, no nation in history has had the opportunity and the responsibility we now have to shape a world that is more peaceful, more secure, more free. All Americans can be proud that our leadership helped to bring peace in Northern Ireland. All Americans can be proud that our leadership has put Bosnia on the path to peace. And with our NATO allies, we are pressing the Serbian Government to stop its brutal repression in Kosovo, to bring those responsible to justice, and to give the people of Kosovo the self-government they deserve."[96] Even Eisenhower's statements about withdrawal from Korea, a major subject in the 1952 campaign, did not draw explicitly on electoral logic.

Obama's decision to frame his first major defense decision in terms of campaign promises suggests the depths of delegate logic in twenty-first century presidential politics. In some respects, this choice represents the natural extension of the trend that began in the transition period. It has become standard for presidents to present themselves as delegates, particularly in response to objections against their actions or proposals. The Iraq withdrawal timeline challenged some of the fundamental commitments of the Obama presidency. Obama's opposition to the war had informed his candidacy against Hillary Clinton for the nomination, positioning the Illinois Senator as the more progressive candidate in the race. By proposing a gradual timeline, Obama strained his credibility with antiwar Democrats, as Jim Lehrer pointed out in the PBS interview in February 2009. At the same time, the move hardly won favor with conservatives; in a Gallup Poll about a month later, only 29 percent of Republicans reported approval of the president's handling of foreign affairs, compared with 64 percent of independents and 85 percent of Democrats. Faced with challenges from the left and the right and confronted with a new political identity as president rather than candidate, Obama turned to campaign promises to legitimize his approach.

On this particular policy, the stress placed on transparency and deliberation may have been a strategic choice on Obama's part. This approach contrasts with the decision-making process for which his predecessor had been famous (or infamous, depending on whom one asked). Decisions in the Bush White House had a reputation for being, in Thomas Langston's words, "made by instinct, without deliberation or consultation."[97] This perceived preference for quick and instinctual decisions was matched by his beliefs about the expansive nature of presidential power. Obama's rhetoric about campaign promises and the beginning of the Iraq withdrawal thus represents a distinction from Bush, not only in the substance of the policy itself but also in presidential style.

Obama's efforts to link the 2008 election result to good government, economic policy, and foreign policy meant that by the time debate began on the issue of health care reform, several mandate narratives had already been tried. Contrary to Reagan and Bush, whose efforts to construct mandates had focused on a few related issues, Obama had tried to justify a wide array of seemingly unconnected issues in terms of the election and campaign. Carter and Clinton had fallen into this pattern as well. More than either Carter or Clinton, however, Obama invoked partisan logic in his mandate rhetoric, echoing existing divisions. By claiming that the 2008 election had been the electorate's rejection of Republican ideas, yet not offering a clear set of alternative economic ideas, Obama left himself vulnerable. Such pronouncements provided little incentive for Republicans, already disinclined, to cooperate with the administration. Yet they also fell short of offering a vision to unify the fissiparous Democratic congressional caucus, inviting detraction from the more conservative wing of the party during the long health care debate.

If voters had rejected Republicans ideas in 2008, this rejection was short lived. The 2010 midterms returned the House of Representatives to Republican control, and Republicans gained five seats in the Senate. The victory of Tea Party candidates in congressional races enhanced the sense of programmatic party politics. As part of a national movement, these highly conservative candidates held clear positions on taxation and federal spending. The movement also borrowed heavily from the 1994 congressional campaign, issuing a ten-point formal agenda under the label "Contract from America." During budget debates in 2011, members of the House Tea Party caucus held fast to their promises, refusing to compromise during a protracted negotiation over raising the federal debt ceiling and reducing the deficit. Although their behavior was often decried as anything but responsible, members of the Tea Party clearly conceptualized politics as a game of winning elections on an agenda, and then adhering to their promises. Thus far, the combination of divided party government and agenda-driven politics has produced a series of near-crises and subsequent compromises, further serving to undermine governing legitimacy.

Challenging Obama's authority also appeared to be a more explicit goal of the Tea Party movement. Denouncement of the president and his policies as "socialist" constituted a central idea of the movement.[98] In the summer of 2010, a group in Iowa created a billboard comparing the forty-fourth president to Adolf Hitler and Vladimir Lenin.[99] Speaking at a Tea Party event, former representative Tom Tancredo (R-CO) emphasized the president's middle name, Hussein, and made jokes about his birth certificate.[100] Controversy exists over the extent to which Tea Party activists embraced the "birther" movement that questioned the validity of Obama's citizenship; a systematic study showed that a quarter of signs at a Tea Party rally expressed anger directed at the president, and only 5 percent mentioned race or religion.[101] Regardless of the specific role of racism and xenophobia in the movement, the Tea Party's electoral success in 2010 illustrates the extent to which presidents in the partisan era have become vulnerable to legitimacy challenges.

The Partisan Era from Reagan to Obama

Reagan's controversial use of mandate rhetoric set the tone for the partisan era in several ways. By clearly and consistently interpreting the 1980 election as a conservative mandate, Reagan fused the roles of chief executive and conservative movement leader. The message of conservative movement politics also worked to undermine the legitimacy of government by suggesting that "government is the problem." The implications of this rejection are apparent in mandate rhetoric throughout the partisan era: Bush sought to construct a mandate to transform Social Security from a federal entitlement to a private investment program; Obama defended his plans for government action in terms of the electoral mandate.

Bush's Social Security failure and Obama's struggles with the Tea Party illustrate how the responsible-party ideal undermines governing legitimacy. Once largely saved for major institutional confrontations such as Jackson's Bank War, Roosevelt's court packing, or Nixon's impoundments of funds, mandate rhetoric has now become a standard frame for presidential agendas. Deepening divisions between the two parties have inspired presidents to direct their mandate rhetoric at their supporters, claiming mandates for party agenda items. Yet, even after party victories in 2004 and 2008, the veto points of the American system thwart the responsible-party model. Bush failed to rally his own party around the Social Security plan, and Obama's accomplishments, although considerable, inspired a powerful backlash. Mandate claims, often considered a means for presidents to bolster their persuasive power, appear instead to be, at best, irrelevant to governing, and at worst, part of a cycle of policy disappointment and crumbling legitimacy.

CONCLUSION

Delivering the People's Message

In order to become the master, the politician poses as the servant.
—CHARLES DE GAULLE

Presidential elections are open to multiple interpretations. For nearly any election result, politicians, pundits, and scholars can point to arguments both for and against the idea of "a mandate." Presidents can and do interpret elections as both calls for unity and popular endorsement of their party's signature policy issues, as arguments for sweeping change and for adjustments to arcane regulatory practices. They may also choose to eschew public interpretations of elections altogether. Choices are abundant, and nearly all can be supported through selective use of facts and arguments. The main contention of this research, however, has been that these choices are not idiosyncratic. Nor are they linked closely to measurable features of elections, such as margins of victory or shares won in the popular vote or the Electoral College. Instead, the findings presented in this work suggest that presidential language about elections and campaigns reflects the political circumstances that they face, both long and short term.

This study of presidential mandate rhetoric has revealed three major areas of change. First, presidential efforts to justify their actions with electoral logic have become more frequent since the Nixon presidency, reverting to patterns more typical of the Progressive Era. Used primarily in symbolic speeches, mandate rhetoric was relatively rare between 1941 and 1965, even among presidents who had won in landslide elections. Second, the content of mandate rhetoric has also changed in ways that reflect broader institutional development. Presidents have used election results to explain their commitments to very specific policies as well as to broad agendas, and more often for partisan positions. The way that mandate rhetoric presents presidential leadership has also shifted from a trusteeship model toward a delegate-style approach to representation. Finally, the context of mandate rhetoric has changed; these claims have become less frequent in major national addresses and ceremonial speeches such as the inaugural address. Minor addresses, media exchanges, and communications with other members of the government account for expansion of mandate rhetoric over time.

These developments in mandate rhetoric can be attributed to changes in the long-term institutional environment. In examining changes in mandate rhetoric from 1929 through 2009, we have seen that the more polarized the political environment, the more likely it is that the president will employ mandate rhetoric as a substantial part of the communication strategy. Mandate claims also appear to have an inverse relationship with the institutional status of the presidency; as public approval ratings have dropped overall, mandate rhetoric has become more prominent. We have also seen that some of the factors often linked to mandate claims, such as the magnitude of the president's victory and the performance of his party in congressional races, appear unrelated to the prominence of mandate claims in presidential rhetoric after taking office.

The president's ability to transcend partisan politics and act as a representative of the national interest has always been more of an ideal than a description of political reality. But for Roosevelt, Eisenhower, and Johnson, this ideal influenced how they thought about the presidency as an office. It also, in turn, shaped how they spoke about the elections that brought them to office. The nonpartisan ideal began to fade during the transition to the partisan era. More than his modern-era predecessors, Richard Nixon suggested that his presidency would be responsive to his supporters, the "silent majority" of Americans. Jimmy Carter rejected this brand of mandate rhetoric and sought to link the 1976 election to less partisan themes such as good governance, sensible budget politics, and environmental protection. Later leaders, however, picked up where Nixon left off. Reagan interpreted the 1980 election as a conservative mandate, and George W. Bush attempted to construct the 2004 election as a mandate for Social Security reform. In the final case study, we saw how Barack Obama focused his mandate references after the 2008 election on three major differences between his administration and the previous one: government accountability, economic policy, and foreign policy.

The contrast between presidents in the partisan era and their earlier counterparts also illustrates how party politics shape mandate claims. Polarization has exacerbated legitimacy problems. A related but distinct development has been an understanding of the presidency in a more "prime-ministerial" light. Reagan's efforts to establish a conservative mandate illustrate how a president can merge the role of chief executive with that of ideological movement leader. Bush's repeated emphasis on the fact that he had "campaigned" on Social Security reform showcases one effort to frame domestic politics as a "responsible-party" model of governance. Finally, Obama's references to "failed" Republican ideas demonstrate how contemporary presidents can interpret elections in ways that reflect, rather than reframe, the contours of partisan disagreement.

Although much of the theory presented in this work focuses on change, we also observe continuity in the way that presidents use mandate rhetoric throughout the post–Progressive period. In the modern and partisan eras alike, presidents have used mandate rhetoric in response to major challenges to their authority. Such instances include Roosevelt's attempt to restructure the Supreme Court and Richard Nixon's confrontation with Congress over the impoundment of appropriated funds. In addition to major confrontations over the boundaries of presidential power, mandate rhetoric has also consistently played a role in responses to more mundane challenges. When reporters questioned Eisenhower's approach to farm price supports, he responded with a reference to the campaign and the Republican platform. Similarly, when Nixon faced objections from his own party for plans to reform the U.S. Post Office Department, he framed his actions as the fulfillment of campaign promises. Memoranda from Carter's speechwriters explicitly make this connection, suggesting that the president should cite campaign promises in its interactions with critical reporters or other detractors.

Although short-term challenges to presidential authority have occurred throughout American history, they have become more common in the partisan era. On average, public approval ratings have dropped, particularly during the first weeks of each term in office. Recent presidents have also experienced a much wider partisan "gap" between approval from citizens who share their party label and those who affiliate with the opposite party. In this political environment, electoral logic has served as a means for presidents to defend their choices to skeptical audiences. Furthermore, it has provided a language for continuing appeals to core supporters. We have seen this in the Reagan White House, where the logic of the conservative mandate pervaded not only public speeches but also internal communications and responses to political rivals. After the 2004 election, George W. Bush sought to frame the contest as a mandate for an idea that appealed only to serious conservatives: the privatization of Social Security; and he offered this argument to supportive audiences throughout the country. Barack Obama interpreted the 2008 election as a "rejection" of Republican economic ideas. However, Obama also invoked campaign promises in response to criticisms from the left about his timetable for the removal of troops from Iraq.

Institutional Change, Party Politics, and Presidential Rhetoric

One of the key implications of this research is that changes in presidential rhetoric occur at the intersection of change across multiple institutions. These findings challenge several long-held assumptions about presidential mandates. Presidential mandate claims do not appear to be exclusively about policy opportunism; more often they are used in a defensive context. Furthermore, similarities in mandate claiming exist among presidents whose terms were proximate in time, despite differences in party, ideology, and contextual factors such as divided government and the state of the economy.

The evolution of mandate claiming among Democratic and Republican presidents has not been identical. During the modern era, in which the Democratic Party was electorally dominant, Democratic presidents' mandate claims were focused on large issues and rooted in a trusteeship vision of presidential representation. On the rare occasions that Roosevelt, Truman, and Johnson spoke about election results, they invoked broad ideas of freedom, equality, and consensus. However, Carter, Clinton, and Obama have all taken a different approach. With the exception of Clinton's second term, each of these leaders spoke about the campaign and the election with some frequency—not unlike their Republican counterparts during the same period. They also claimed electoral mandates for a wide range of issues, often minor and technocratic, alongside major policy initiatives and ideas.

Among Republicans, the pattern has been reversed, with partisan-era presidents using mandate rhetoric to explain cohesive policy agendas. In the modern era, Eisenhower was the only Republican to serve as president, making patterns difficult to discern. Despite significant differences in their elections and political circumstances, Nixon, Reagan, and Bush shared a common approach to mandate rhetoric. All three tended to use mandate narratives for distinctly partisan positions. For Nixon, usage included promoting "law-and-order" issues and cuts to the federal budget and taxes— mixed in with a range of other issues such as science funding and post office reform. For Reagan and Bush, the partisan dimensions of the mandate narrative were more pronounced and highly focused, with Reagan emphasizing economic issues in 1981 and Bush emphasizing Social Security reform in 2005. Both Reagan and Bush stated that they saw election victories as endorsements for their issue positions and intended to carry out their promises. They also emphasized the difference between their positions and those of their opponents, and claimed electoral mandates to dismantle parts of the federal government that had been built up by Democrats. Attacking Social Security constituted a sound rejection of the accomplishments and values of the other side. Traces of this adversarial approach can be found in Franklin Roosevelt's mandate rhetoric, but not in that of Eisenhower or Johnson. In other words, this approach to interpreting elections appears to have emerged through the transition into the partisan era and to have reflected shifting priorities in a period of Republican dominance.

Bush's failure to unify the party around the privatization plan illustrates the structural dilemma of Republican presidential philosophy in the partisan era. The tug-of-war between party and nation has long shaped the way presidents set priorities, choose political strategies, and attempt to construct mandates. Republican presidents after 1981 have used mandate rhetoric to present a governing philosophy and to appeal to a distinct ideological base. In contrast, Democratic presidents have connected their mandate rhetoric to a range of policies, without integrating them into a central governing philosophy.

Change over time and divergence between parties seems to underscore the importance of cross-institutional relationships. Although mandates have traditionally been considered to be functions of party performance in the short term, presidential mandate rhetoric actually reflects the longer-term status of the parties. Both the change and the divergence suggest that prolific and varied use of mandate rhetoric was part of the Democratic strategy to establish legitimacy and justification for policy in the post–New Deal era. Republican presidents have used mandate rhetoric with equal frequency, yet their messages were substantially more focused. This divergence may simply reflect the Democrats' decline and the Republicans' ascendance. But it may also reflect different relationships between presidents and their parties' ideological bases.

Finally, the use of mandate rhetoric not only suggests that the strategic concern and leadership style of individual presidents is important but also reflects more durable ideas about the presidency as an office. Presidential rhetoric is indicative of immediate concerns and of larger conceptualizations about the meaning and significance of the office, and its relationship with the rest of the political system. In this sense, the research presented in this work constitutes a call for scholarship on mandates to focus not only on individual presidents, but on the presidency as an institution.

The Age of Mandate Politics

The age of mandate politics overlaps with other institutional structures and expectations that shape presidential behavior and use of power. These phenomena include the "permanent campaign" and the plebiscitary presidency; the persistence of the original constitutional system, which presents veto points and obstacles to the "prime-ministerial" approach to the presidency; and the growth of the unilateral presidency.

The Permanent Campaign and the Plebiscitary Presidency

Presidential mandate claims have often been grouped with the rhetoric and ideas of the plebiscitary presidency. Yet an examination of presidential mandate rhetoric shows that this classification is not as apt as it might seem on the surface. The defensive, and often partisan, character of mandate rhetoric distinguishes it from more plebiscitary forms of discourse.

Mandate politics also bear similarity to, but are distinct from, the politics of the permanent campaign. This idea, introduced in Sidney Blumenthal's 1982 book,[1] suggests that the politics of the presidency have been permanently altered by perpetual engagement in electoral activities.[2] The logic of the permanent campaign, as journalist Joe Klein explains, has led presidents to govern "from a political consultant's eye view."[3] Simultaneously, however, in the age of mandate politics, we observe a logic of governance that inverts the permanent campaign. Although campaign considerations inform governing, governing decisions are also justified in terms of campaign promises. In other words, the logic of mandates is one of following and fulfilling promises. The governing implications of this logic are related to the questions over trusteeship and delegate forms of representation, or what Hanna Pitkin terms the "mandate-independence" controversy. This problem is not purely theoretical, and its normative manifestations can be observed in the presidential politics of the partisan era. The question of whether the president should behave more like a trustee or more like a delegate is as persistent as it is intractable; presidents must, of course, take public attitudes into account while they exercise independent leadership and judgment. In the age of mandate politics, we observe that presidents increasingly explain their choices to fellow governing elites, journalists, and citizen audiences in terms of campaign promises and public promises rather than their own independent judgment. In sum, the rise of mandate politics is not defined by the president's efforts to connect with the public or by the convergence of governing and campaigning. Rather, it is a distinct governing logic that connects policy action to elections that have already happened and that implicates public opinion, not as a bargaining tool but as a means of justifying action.

The Constitutional System

Although the changing politics of the presidential mandate may indicate that presidents understand the preferences of their party bases and seek to represent them, this idea is normatively problematic to the extent that presidents are expected to represent the interests of the entire nation. Throughout the history of the American republic, presidents have balanced the needs of nation and party and have pursued policy in line with their own ideology and party priorities. Yet, the shift toward more partisan and ideological mandate rhetoric suggests an attendant shift in presidents' conceptualization of their core constituencies. The comparison between comments in the Eisenhower White House about acting as president of all the people and in the Reagan White House about fulfilling the conservative mandate of 1980 illustrates this point. In practice, presidential action almost always balances a number of countervailing forces: the preferences of the party's core constituency, the opinion of the broader public, the governing imperatives posed by policy problems, and pressures from organized interests. It is the shift in the way that presidents imagine their constituencies and obligation that indicates an altered logic of governance.

These changes in context and perspective engage directly with the meaning of representative democracy. In one respect, the relationship between mandate rhetoric and party change indicate the potential for high quality in presidential representation. That is, over time, presidents have drawn accurate inferences about their supporters, and these inferences have influenced their rhetorical choices. In contrast, however, the nature of presidential representation remains vulnerable to the criticism that the presidency was not designed to represent narrow partisan or ideological concerns.

What is more, the expectations that come along with a more prime-ministerial role can very difficult for American presidents to fulfill. Although Reagan, Bush, and Obama all presented themselves, to some extent, as responsible-party leaders, their ability to deliver on the promises of their respective party platforms has been mixed. Reagan and Bush succeeded in their efforts to enact tax cuts, but delivered relatively little for social conservatives despite much rhetoric. Obama's first two years in office produced considerable policy success, including major health care reform. Yet his ability to define and publicly explain these policies proved quite limited. In other cases, prime-ministerial efforts have simply failed. After its key role in Bush's 2004 victory, the conservative base expected him to deliver policy. Mandate rhetoric has the potential to reinforce these expectations. Yet it appears to be unhelpful in delivering real policy change; even energized partisans are often stymied by systemic constraints. Despite Bush's efforts to interpret the 2004 election as a mandate for conservative policies, he proved unable to shape the party's domestic agenda.

The Rise of Unilateral Presidential Power

Finally, the narrative of transparency that partisan-era presidents embrace with their words about promises and commitments is a false one. Executive branch decision making has become less transparent, not more. The unilateral power of presidents to make decisions free of interference from Congress, the courts, the media, or the public has been of central importance to the Bush and Obama administrations.[4] Signing statements and executive orders remain important for domestic policymaking.[5] The use of mandate rhetoric has not alleviated these problems; it may even have exacerbated them. Stephen Hartnett and Jennifer Mercieca maintain that contemporary presidential rhetoric leaves citizens "awash in white noise," preventing them from deliberating important policy questions and thus facilitating the continued rise of the "imperial presidency." [6] Mandate rhetoric, employed widely and frequently, has the potential to constitute such "white noise." Campaign-oriented mandate rhetoric can either distract from or substitute for explanation of the merits of major energy policy, Social Security reform, or the timeline for withdrawal of troops from Iraq (to name a few examples). In this way, the age of mandate rhetoric has contributed to what Marc Landy and Sidney Milkis lament as the decline in the "civic education" component of presidential discourse and helped to produce a false sense of transparency surrounding the presidency.

The Future of Presidential Mandate Rhetoric

Barack Obama won reelection in 2012 in a tight but decisive contest. As with George W. Bush's reelection in 2004, Obama won just over 51 percent of the popular vote, with 47 percent for his Republican opponent, Mitt Romney. As with Reagan's victory in 1980, Obama's small popular majority was matched by a much stronger showing in the Electoral College (although, at 61 percent, still smaller than Reagan's 90 percent of Electoral College votes). As with every election in the partisan era, the interpretation of the 2012 election results has received considerable attention from politicians and pundits and yet has defied simple classification.

During the first postelection news conference, a week after the election, Obama fielded a question about whether the election had been a policy mandate. The newly reelected president responded with a statement that both reflected and contradicted the mandate logic typical of the partisan era:

> I've got one mandate. I've got a mandate to help middle class families and families that are working hard to try to get into the middle class. That's my mandate. That's what the American people said. They said: Work really hard to help us. Don't worry about the politics of it, don't worry about the party interests, don't worry about the special interests. Just work really hard to see if you can help us get ahead, because we're working really hard out here and we're still struggling, a lot of us. That's my mandate.[7]

This part of the statement taps into familiar themes: it makes a strong claim to an electoral mandate, reminiscent of Reagan's rhetoric in 1981 and Clinton's in 1993; and it draws implicitly on criticisms levied against the infamous statements made by his Republican opponent, Mitt Romney, about the "47 percent" of Americans who would never break their dependence on government and the controversial comments of vice-presidential candidate Paul Ryan about "makers and takers." In its partisanship, its commitment to mandate logic, and its emphasis on listening to the demands of the people, this statement fits the general mold of partisan-era mandate rhetoric.

However, in the same news conference, Obama followed the statement with remarks that suggested an evolving perspective on mandate logic and rhetoric:

> I don't presume that because I won an election that everybody suddenly agrees with me on everything. I'm more than familiar with all the literature about Presidential overreach in second terms. We are very cautious about that. On the other hand, I didn't get reelected just to bask in reelection. I got elected to do work on behalf of American families and small businesses all across the country who are still recovering from a really bad recession, but are hopeful about the future.

Obama's reflection on the 2012 results differed from both his conciliatory statements in 2004 about red states and blue states and his 2009 "I won" approach. His remarks attempted to find meaning in the election result while avoiding direct statements about issue positions. In terms of political context, the electorate has remained polarized and Obama's approval ratings, while above 50 percent, remain approximately 20 points lower than Eisenhower's at the beginning of 1957, at the start of his second term.[8] Despite the polarized electorate, the 113th Congress began its session with a bipartisan effort in the Senate to promote immigration reform. House Speaker John Boehner appears to be more willing to rebuff the most conservative legislators in his party caucus, suggesting a possible change in the tenor of party politics in that chamber. At the same time, Obama's inaugural address suggested an end to conciliatory efforts toward the other party and instead focused on issues important to the party base, such as the preservation of the social safety net and the rights of lesbian, gay, bisexual, and transgender Americans.

The pervasiveness of the idea of party mandates can be seen in the emergence of a group called Use Your Mandate, formed in January 2013. This group attempted to connect the 2012 election result to its objection to the controversial nomination of former Senator Chuck Hagel (R-NE) for Secretary of Defense. The group's advertisements urged audiences to tell their senators to oppose Hagel and asked, "What did we fight this election for?" Use Your Mandate also circulated mailers that point to Hagel's record on gay rights, along with the statement, "This isn't what we voted for in November." In a bizarre twist, however, the group, whose membership remains undisclosed, is reputed to be a front for conservative opponents of Hagel's nomination.

After the 2012 election, Obama's public speeches have embraced the priorities of the Democratic base, and he has not hesitated to assign blame to Republicans for obstructing policy change. His interpretations of the 2012 campaign and results have stressed economic issues and occasionally other themes such as immigration. At the same time, his 2013 State of the Union address mentioned bipartisanship four times. Facing a divided government, prime-ministerial rhetoric is even less likely to succeed.

Directions for Further Research

For every tentative answer and implication generated by this research, new questions arise. One of the main normative and theoretical implications of this research concerns the relationship between president and party. Further study of how mandate rhetoric influences the ideas and behavior of different audiences is needed in order to understand the politics of the age of mandates. We have seen the effects of changing party politics on presidential mandate rhetoric—its tone and content as well as the frequency and context of its use. We observe that, in the partisan era, presidents use mandate rhetoric with fellow partisans, with members of the executive branch, and with citizen audiences who are likely to be supportive. They also use mandate rhetoric in contexts with broader audiences—news conferences and occasionally in major speeches. However, understanding how these different audiences absorb the mandate message and react to the use of mandate logic, as opposed to other forms of argumentation, remains beyond the scope of this study. Inquiry into these responses would illuminate how mandate rhetoric fits into contemporary presidential governance and particularly how it shapes and is shaped by partisan polarization.

This study also highlights the need for further research into other forms of presidential argumentation and governing logic. We know that mandate rhetoric has increased as a percentage of presidential rhetoric. However, this research does not assess whether this change has occurred at the expense of other forms of governing appeals—constitutional, problem solving—or alongside the use of these appeals. In other words, as presidents have spoken more about elections and campaigns, have they spoken less about other forms of justification for their choices? This question is directly relevant to our understanding of how presidential rhetoric has evolved in response to a changing institutional environment and is deserving of further study.

Finally, this research opens up questions about the depth of the connection between presidential legitimacy and the political environment of the twenty-first century. The analysis in chapter 5 links the decline in the institutional prestige of the presidency to the rise of the new partisan media as well as to the legacies of Vietnam and Watergate. The questions that remain concern whether these developments are permanent, and whether the status of the presidency will ever rebound to its pre-1965 levels. Furthermore, if the developments in the media and revelations about the dangers posed by executive excess have done permanent damage to the status of the office, should we expect mandate language to continue to serve as a defense mechanism? In sum, we observe a dynamic pattern in presidential legitimacy throughout the post–Progressive Era, with both expansions and contractions, and resulting changes in mandate rhetoric. Yet, whether the forces that have contributed to the erosion of presidential legitimacy will persist remains an open question.

The main lesson to be taken from this research is that presidential mandate rhetoric is indicative of much more than the circumstances of any particular election. The way that presidents interpret elections is shaped by their perceptions of their own authority and constraints, the political obstacles they face, and their relationships with the party system. Far from being idiosyncratic or individualized, presidential mandate rhetoric tends to conform to temporal patterns. As the presidency and the party system have changed, presidential mandate rhetoric has changed.

In this spirit, scholars of the presidency can cautiously predict that future presidents will rely more on mandate rhetoric—regardless of election results—when they face challenging institutional circumstances. In order to understand how presidents interpret elections, we should look beyond polling numbers and election results to broad institutional conditions. When they are less popular, when they face confrontations with Congress over institutional boundaries, when opposition from the other party is most vocal, we should expect to see presidents incorporate more mandate language. Mandate claims are rhetorical tools not of strength but of survival.

NOTES

Introduction

1. Ramesh Ponnuru, "He'll Make a Mandate," *Washington Post*, October 31, 2004; Jeffrey M. Jones, "Low Trust in Federal Government Rivals Watergate Levels," Gallup News Service, September 26, 2007. http://www.gallup.com/poll/28795/low-trust-fed eral-government-rivals-watergate-era-levels.aspx.

2. Matthew Levendusky, *The Partisan Sort: How Liberals Became Democrats and Conservatives Became Republicans* (Chicago: University of Chicago Press, 2009), 1–5.

3. Richard M. Skinner, "George W. Bush and the Partisan Presidency," *Political Science Quarterly* 123, no. 4 (2009): 606–607.

4. See Shanto Iyengar and Kyu S. Hahn, "Red Media, Blue Media: Evidence of Ideological Selectivity in Media Use," *Journal of Communication* 59, no. 1 (2009): 19–39.

5. As scholars (including myself) have noted elsewhere, the dilemma between the president's competing roles is structural and has been persistent over time, although its impact has been particularly profound during times of high polarization. Julia R. Azari, Lara M. Brown, and Zim G. Nwokora, *The Presidential Leadership Dilemma: Between the Constitution and a Political Parity* (Albany: State University of New York Press, 2013).

6. John H. Aldrich, *Why Parties? The Origin and Transformation of Parties in America* (Chicago: University of Chicago Press, 1995), 10–11.

7. Paul R. Abramson, John H. Aldrich, and David W. Rohde, *Change and Continuity in the 2004 Elections* (Washington, DC: CQ Press, 2006), 48.

8. Patricia Heidotting Conley, *Presidential Mandates: How Elections Shape the National Agenda* (Chicago: University of Chicago, 2001), 17.

9. Charles O. Jones, *The Presidency in a Separated System* (Washington, DC: Brookings Institution Press, 2005), 185.

10. Lawrence Grossback, David A. M. Peterson, and James Stimson, *Mandate Politics* (New York: Cambridge University Press, 2006), 28.

11. Woodrow Wilson, who theorized extensively about the role of the popular mandate in presidential politics, never won a majority of the popular vote; see also, Terri Bimes and Quinn Mulroy, "The Rise and Decline of Presidential Populism," *Studies in American Political Development* 18 (Fall 2004): 136–159.

12. Stephen Skowronek, *The Politics Presidents Make: Leadership from John Adams to Bill Clinton* (Cambridge, MA: Belknap Press, 1997), 6.

13. William G. Howell, *Power without Persuasion: The Politics of Direct Presidential Action* (Princeton, NJ: Princeton University Press, 2003), 26–27.

14. David Zarefsky, "Presidential Rhetoric and the Power of Definition," *Presidential Studies Quarterly* 34, no. 3 (2004): 607–619; Jeffrey K. Tulis, *The Rhetorical Presidency* (Princeton, NJ: Princeton University Press, 1988).

15. Conley, *Presidential Mandates*, 3; Jones, *Presidency in a Separated System*, 181; Richard J. Ellis and Stephen Kirk, "Presidential Mandates in the Nineteenth Century: Conceptual Change and Institutional Development," *Studies in American Political Development* 9 (Spring 1995): 117–186.

16. Samuel Kernell, *Going Public: New Strategies of Presidential Leadership* (Washington, DC: CQ Press, 1997), 21; Brandice Canes-Wrone, *Who Leads Whom? Presidents, Policy and the Public* (Chicago: University of Chicago Press, 2006), 22–23; see also, Brandon Rottinghaus, "Strategic Leaders: Identifying Successful Momentary Presidential Leadership of Public Opinion," *Political Communication* 26, no. 3 (2009): 296–316.

17. Robert Dahl, "The Myth of the Presidential Mandate," *Political Science Quarterly* 105, no. 3 (1990): 355–372; Kernell, *Going Public*.

18. Theodore J. Lowi, *The Personal Presidency: Power Invested and Promise Unfulfilled* (Ithaca, NY: Cornell University Press, 1985), 79.

19. Skowronek, *Politics Presidents Make*, 20.

20. U.S. Const. art. II, § 3.

21. Denise Bostdorff, *The Presidency and the Rhetoric of Foreign Crisis* (Columbia: University of South Carolina Press, 1994), 5–7.

22. Skowronek, *Politics Presidents Make*, 18.

23. Ibid., 248.

24. Victoria Farrar-Myers, *Scripted for Change: The Institutionalization of the American Presidency* (College Station: Texas A&M University Press, 2006), 15.

25. Adam D. Sheingate, "Political Entrepreneurship, Institutional Change, and American Political Development," *Studies in American Political Development* 17, no. 2 (2003): 193.

26. Ellis and Kirk, "Presidential Mandates in the Nineteenth Century," 119.

27. Daniel Walker Howe, *What God Hath Wrought: The Transformation of America, 1814–1848* (New York: Oxford University Press, 2007), 367.

28. Ellis and Kirk, "Presidential Mandates in the Nineteenth Century," 180.

29. Ibid., 137.

30. Donald Cole, *The Presidency of Andrew Jackson* (Lawrence: University Press of Kansas, 1999), 145.

31. Andrew Rudalevige, *The New Imperial Presidency: Renewing Presidential Power after Watergate* (Ann Arbor: University of Michigan Press, 2005), 102.

32. Marc Karnis Landy and Sidney M. Milkis, *Presidential Greatness* (Lawrence: University Press of Kansas, 2000), 38

33. Sidney Milkis, *The President and the Parties: The Transformation of the American Party System since the New Deal* (New York: Oxford University Press, 1993), 57.

34. Richard E. Neustadt, *Presidential Power and the Modern Presidents* (New York: Free Press, 1990), 29.

35. Lara M. Brown, *Jockeying for the American Presidency: The Political Opportunism of Aspirants* (New York: Cambria Press, 2010), 20.

36. Daniel J. Galvin, *Presidential Party-building: Dwight D. Eisenhower to George W. Bush* (Princeton, NJ: Princeton University Press, 2010), 20.

37. Richard M. Skinner, "George W. Bush and the Partisan Presidency," *Political Science Quarterly* 123, no. 4 (2009): 608.

38. Stephanie Condon, "Boehner Resists Budget Deal as Tea Partier Seeks His Ouster," CBS News, March 31, 2011.

39. Matt Bai, "A Mandate? Not Really," *New York Times*, July 9, 2011.

40. David Mayhew, *Electoral Realignments: A Critique of an American Genre* (New Haven, CT: Yale University Press, 2004), 39.

41. The logic behind the inclusion of Nixon's first term also reflects the idea of "causal process observation," whereas the other case studies draw more on the logic of a "most similar," comparative case-study design. Henry E. Brady, David Collier, and Jason Seawright, "Refocusing the Discussion of Methodology," in *Rethinking Social Inquiry: Diverse Tools, Shared Standards*, ed. Henry E. Brady and David Collier, 2nd ed. (Lanham, MD: Rowman & Littlefield, 2010); see also Gary King, Robert O. Keohane, and Sidney Verba, *Designing Social Inquiry: Scientific Inference in Qualitative Research* (Princeton, NJ: Princeton University Press, 1994); Adam Przeworski and Henry Teune, *The Logic of Comparative Social Inquiry* (New York: Wiley Interscience, 1970).

42. Jonathan Alter, *The Defining Moment: FDR's Hundred Days and the Triumph of Hope* (New York: Simon & Schuster, 2006), 273.

43. Milkis, *President and the Parties*, 52.

44. Landy and Milkis, *Presidential Greatness*, 178.

45. Aaron Wildavsky, "The Two Presidencies," *Trans-Action* 4 (1966): 7–14.

46. Thomas E. Mann and Norman J. Ornstein, *The Broken Branch: How Congress Is Failing America and How to Get It Back on Track* (New York: Oxford University Press, 2008), 60–61.

47. Jeffrey M. Jones, "Obama's Approval Most Polarized for First-Year President," Gallup News Service, January 25, 2010.

48. Daniel Walker Howe, *The Political Culture of the American Whigs* (Chicago: University of Chicago Press, 1979), 87–88.

49. The 2008 Democratic platform reads, "We reject the use of national security letters to spy on citizens who are not suspected of a crime. We reject the tracking of citizens who do nothing more than protest a misguided war. We reject torture. We reject sweeping claims of 'inherent' presidential power. We will revisit the Patriot Act and overturn unconstitutional executive decisions issued during the past eight years. We will not use signing statements to nullify or undermine duly enacted law." Democratic Party Platform, August 25, 2008, American Presidency Project [hereafter cited as APP].

50. Walter Dean Burnham, *Critical Elections and the Mainsprings of American Politics* (New York: Norton, 1970), 9–10.

51. Stephen Skowronek, *Politics Presidents Make*, 38.

Chapter 1

1. Robert A. Dahl, "The Myth of the Presidential Mandate," *Political Science Quarterly* 105, no. 3 (Autumn 1990): 355–372; Douglas A. Hibbs, "President Reagan's Mandate from the 1980 Elections," *American Politics Research* 10, no. 2 (October 1982): 387–420.

2. Gallup Poll #639, Gallup News Service, December 6, 1960.

3. Gallup Poll #720, Gallup News Service, November 16, 1965; Gallup Poll #773, Gallup News Service, January 1–6, 1969.

4. Gallup Poll #970, Gallup News Service, March 18–21, 1977; Gallup Poll #168G, Gallup News Service, January 27, 1981; Gallup Poll #249G, January 25–28, 1985; Gallup Poll January Wave 1, January 8–11, 1993; Gallup Poll, January Wave 2, January 10–13, 1997; "The Mood of the Nation," Gallup News Service, January 10–14, 2001; "The Mood of the Nation," Gallup News Service, January 1–5, 2005; Jeffrey M. Jones, "Domestic Problems Top Americans' To-Do List for Obama," Gallup News Service, January 19, 2009.

5. In April 2004, more than a quarter of respondents out of a total of 1,014 told the Gallup Poll that the Iraq War was the most important problem facing the nation; terrorism accounted for another 13 percent of responses. Joseph Carroll and Frank Newport, "A Quarter of Americans Say Iraq Nation's Most Important Problem," Gallup News Service, April 15, 2004. http://www.gallup.com/poll/11368/quarter-americans -say-iraq-nations-most-important-problem.aspx.

6. James E. Campbell, "Why Bush Won the Presidential Election of 2004: Incumbency, Ideology, Terrorism, and Turnout," *Political Science Quarterly* 120, no. 2 (2005): 219–241, 225; D. Sunshine Hillygus and Todd G. Shields, "Moral Issues and Voter Decision-making in the 2004 Election," *PS: Political Science and Politics* (April 2005): 201–209. Hillygus and Shields find that 86 percent of voters who listed terrorism as the most important issue voted for Bush, as opposed to 14 percent of such voters who preferred Kerry (202).

7. Keith T. Poole and Howard Rosenthal, "D-NOMINATE After 10 Years: A Comparative Update to Congress: A Political-Economic History of Roll-Call Voting," *Legislative Studies Quarterly* 25, no. 1 (February 2001): 5–29.

8. For this measure, I used the scores from the Congresses that began when the president took office.

9. Karlyn Kohrs Campbell and Kathleen Hall Jamieson, *Presidents Creating the Presidency: Deeds Done in Words* (Chicago: University of Chicago Press, 2008), 138.

10. The major address category also includes radio addresses along with State of the Union messages and other televised national speeches. In this sense, the "major speech" label may be somewhat more complicated to apply to later presidents in the data set. Ronald Reagan began a tradition of weekly presidential radio addresses in 1982, and all presidents since, with the exception of George H. W. Bush, have continued this practice. Although the weekly Saturday radio address was designed with Franklin Roosevelt's fireside chats in mind, it is not clear that contemporary presidential radio addresses have ever reached that level of influence.

11. Samuel Kernell, *Going Public: New Strategies of Presidential Leadership*, 2nd ed. (Washington, DC: Congressional Quarterly Press, 1993), 92, 105. Kernell observes that presidents have devoted more time to domestic travel in order to make local appearances and given more minor addresses since the late 1970s. The Public Papers of the President [hereafter cited as PPP] data are consistent with this finding. See also Jeffrey Cohen, *Going Local: Presidential Leadership in the Post-Broadcast Age* (New York: Cambridge University Press, 2009).

12. See Matthew Eshbaugh-Soha, "Presidential Press Conferences over Time," *American Journal of Political Science* 47, no. 2 (April 2003): 348–353; Cohen, *The Presidency in the Era of 24-Hour News* (Princeton, NJ: Princeton University Press, 2008); Martha Kumar, "Presidential Press Conferences: The Importance and Evolution of an Enduring Forum," *Presidential Studies Quarterly* 35, no. 1 (March 2005): 166–192.

13. A typical convention holds that the State of the Union will be delivered by a president who has been in office for at least once year. However, in the case of 1953, Truman chose not to deliver a final State of the Union before leaving office in January. Gerhard Peters, State of the Union Addresses and Messages, PPP.

14. George H. W. Bush, Address on Administration Goals before a Joint Session of Congress, February 9, 1989, PPP.

15. Bill Clinton, Address before a Joint Session of Congress on the State of the Union, February 4, 1997, PPP.

16. George W. Bush, Remarks prior to a Meeting with Bipartisan Congressional Leaders and an Exchange with Reporters, January 24, 2001, PPP.

17. George H. W. Bush, Remarks to Members of the Senior Executive Service, January 26, 1989, PPP.

18. Bill Clinton, Remarks on Arrival in Detroit, Michigan, February 10, 1993, PPP.

19. Harry Truman, Address at the Jefferson-Jackson Day Dinner, February 24, 1949, PPP.

20. Ibid.

21. George W. Bush, Remarks at the National Republican Congressional Committee Dinner, March 15, 2005, PPP.

22. Harry Truman, Address at the Jefferson-Jackson Day Dinner, February 24, 1949, PPP.

23. Barack Obama, Remarks at the Department of Energy, February 5, 2009, PPP.

24. For more about congressional polarization, see Sean Theriault, *Party Polarization in Congress* (New York: Cambridge University Press, 2008).

25. Richard Nixon, President's News Conference, March 15, 1973, PPP.

26. Tables 1.6 and 1.7 show the breakdown for each individual term in order to note which terms began under divided government, which we might expect to affect choices about partisan rhetoric.

27. Stephen Skowronek, *The Politics Presidents Make: Leadership from John Adams to Bill Clinton* (Cambridge, MA: Belknap Press, 1997), 46.

28. Jonathan Alter, *The Promise: President Obama, Year One* (New York: Simon & Schuster, 2010), 117.

29. Ronald Reagan, Memorandum Requesting the Resignation of Non-career Federal Employees, January 21, 1981, PPP.

30. Barack Obama, Remarks to White House Senior Staff, January 21, 2009, PPP.

31. George H. W. Bush, Address on Administration Goals before a Joint Session of Congress, February 8, 1989, PPP; George W. Bush, Remarks at the Tax Family Reunion and an Exchange with Reporters, February 7, 2001, PPP.

32. Richard J. Ellis and Stephen Kirk, "Presidential Mandates in the Nineteenth Century: Conceptual Change and Institutional Development," *Studies in American Political Development* 9 (Spring 1995): 117–186.

33. Jeffrey Tulis, *The Rhetorical Presidency* (Princeton, NJ: Princeton University Press, 1988), 128.

34. Edmund Burke, "Speech to the Electors of Bristol," cf. Stanley Kelley, *Interpreting Elections* (Princeton, NJ: Princeton University Press, 1983), 129.

35. Dwight Eisenhower, Annual Message to the Congress on the State of the Union, February 2, 1953, PPP.

36. Ronald Reagan, Inaugural Address, January 20, 1985, PPP.

37. Lyndon Johnson, Remarks upon Receiving the Anti-Defamation League Award, February 3, 1965; Johnson, Remarks to the Press Following a Meeting with Congressional Leaders to Discuss Medical Care Legislation, March 26, 1965, PPP.

38. Barack Obama, Remarks on the Federal Budget, March 17, 2009, PPP.

39. Barack Obama, Remarks at the Democratic National Committee Fundraiser, March 25, 2009, PPP.

40. Ralph Ketcham, *Presidents Above Party: The First American Presidency, 1789–1829* (Chapel Hill: University of North Carolina Press, 1987), 89.

41. Andrew Rehfeld, *The Concept of Constituency: Political Representation, Democratic Legitimacy, and Institutional Design* (New York: Cambridge University Press, 2005), 203.

42. George W. Bush, Remarks in a Discussion on Strengthening Social Security in Westfield, New Jersey, March 4, 2005, PPP.

43. George H. W. Bush, Statement on Proposed Child-Care Legislation, March 15, 1989, PPP; Jimmy Carter, Zero-Base Budgeting for the Fiscal Year 1979, Budget Memorandum to the Heads of Executive Departments and Agencies, February 14, 1977, PPP.

44. B. Dan Wood, *The Myth of Presidential Representation* (New York: Cambridge University Press, 2009), 25.

45. Thomas E. Cronin and Michael A. Genovese, *The Paradoxes of the American Presidency* (New York: Oxford University Press, 2004), 116.

Chapter 2

1. Telegraph to the President, March 4, 1933, Collection, box 6, president's personal file 200, public reaction folder, Franklin D. Roosevelt Presidential Library, Hyde Park, New York, [hereafter cited as FDR].

2. CSPAN Historians Presidential Leadership Survey, 2009, http://legacy.c-span.org/PresidentialSurvey/Overall-Ranking.aspx; Arthur M. Schlesinger, Jr., "Rating the Presidents: Washington to Clinton," *Political Science Quarterly* 112, no. 2 (Summer 1997): 179–190.

3. Stephen Skowronek, *Politics Presidents Make: Leadership from John Adams to Bill Clinton*, 2nd ed. (Cambridge MA: Belknap Press, 1997), 299.

4. Daniel P. Klinghard, "Grover Cleveland, William McKinley, and the Emergence of the President as Party Leader," *Presidential Studies Quarterly* 35, no. 4 (2005): 736.

5. This range diverges from the usual cutoff point for the Progressive Era. My range suggests that the presidents in the 1920s were still influenced by Progressive ideas about governance and the presidency—if only in their opposition to them.

6. Victoria Farrar-Myers, *Scripted for Change: The Institutionalization of the American Presidency* (College Station: Texas A&M Press, 2006), 6, 12.

7. Jeffrey K. Tulis, *The Rhetorical Presidency* (Princeton, NJ: Princeton University Press, 1988), 128

8. Peri E. Arnold, *Remaking the Presidency: Roosevelt, Taft and Wilson, 1901–1916* (Lawrence: University Press of Kansas, 2009), 167.

9. Sarah Watts, *Rough Rider in the White House* (Chicago: University of Chicago Press, 2003), 64.

10. Ibid., 65.

11. Kathleen Dalton, *Theodore Roosevelt: A Strenuous Life* (New York: Knopf Doubleday, 2002), 281.

12. Arnold, *Remaking the Presidency*, 68.

13. Tulis, *Rhetorical Presidency*, 102–103.

14. Ibid., 106.

15. Arnold, *Remaking the Presidency*, 167.

16. Tulis, *Rhetorical Presidency*, 122; James Ceaser, *Presidential Selection: Theory and Development* (Princeton, NJ: Princeton University Press, 1979), 171.

17. Daniel Stid, *The President as Statesman: Woodrow Wilson and the Constitution* (Lawrence: University Press of Kansas, 1998), 91.

18. Tulis, *Rhetorical Presidency*, 123.

19. Farrar-Myers, *Scripted for Change*, 143.

20. Tulis, *Rhetorical Presidency*, 128.

21. Ibid., 96; Colleen Shogan, *The Moral Rhetoric of American Presidents* (College Station: Texas A&M University Press, 2006), 64.

22. Tulis, *Rhetorical Presidency*, 148.

23. Stephen Skowronek, *Building a New American State* (New York: Cambridge University Press, 1982), 29; see also Martin Shefter, *Political Parties and the State: The American Historical Experience* (Princeton, NJ: Princeton University Press, 1993), 160–161.

24. Klinghard, "Emergence of the President as Party Leader," 749.

25. Saladin Ambar, *How Governors Built the Modern American Presidency* (Philadelphia: University of Pennsylvania Press, 2012), 49–54.

26. Dalton, *Theodore Roosevelt*, 203.

27. Ibid., 291, for a description of Roosevelt's disagreements with Henry Cabot Lodge.

28. Skowronek, *Politics Presidents Make*, 247. Italics in the original.

29. Sidney Milkis, *Theodore Roosevelt, the Progressive Party, and the Transformation of American Democracy* (Lawrence: University Press of Kansas, 2009).

30. Jules Witcover, *Party of the People: A History of the Democrats* (New York: Random House, 2003), 303.

31. Stid, *President as Statesman*, 49–50.

32. Robert A. Dahl, "The Myth of the Presidential Mandate," *Political Science Quarterly* 105, no. 3 (1990): 359–360.

33. Daniel Scroop, *Mr. Democrat: Jim Farley, the New Deal, and the Making of Modern American Politics* (Ann Arbor: University of Michigan Press, 2006), 57–58.

34. Ibid.

35. Ibid., 54.

36. Donald Ritchie, *Electing FDR: The New Deal Campaign of 1932* (Lawrence: University Press of Kansas, 2009), 138.

37. John Gerring, *Party Ideologies in America, 1828–1996* (New York: Cambridge University Press, 1998), 192–193.

38. Ritchie, *Electing FDR*, 138.

39. Roosevelt Campaign Speeches, FDR. July 30, 1932.

40. Grover Cleveland, Second Inaugural Address, March 4, 1893, American Presidency Project [hereafter cited as APP].

41. Klinghard, "Emergence of the President as Party Leader," 754.

42. Milkis, *Theodore Roosevelt*, 44.

43. Shogan, *Moral Rhetoric of American Presidents*, 60.

44. Woodrow Wilson, Inaugural Address, March 4, 1913, PPP.

45. Lewis L. Gould, *Grand Old Party* (New York: Random House, 2003), 243.

46. Calvin Coolidge, Inaugural Address, March 4, 1925, PPP.

47. Joan Hoff Wilson, *Herbert Hoover: Forgotten Progressive* (Long Grove, IL: Waveland Press), 128.

48. Skowronek, *Politics Presidents Make*, 270.

49. Wilson, *Herbert Hoover*, 144.

50. Ceaser, *Presidential Selection*, 174.

51. Skowronek, *Politics Presidents Make*, 299; see also Bruce Ackerman, *Transformations*, vol. 2 of *We the People* (Cambridge, MA: Belknap Press, 2000).

52. "McBride Scoffs at 'Beer Mandate,'" *New York Times*, November 11, 1932.

53. "Nation's Press, Analyzing Election, Calls for Harmony of All Factions," *New York Times*, November 10, 1932. (This article features election commentary from a variety of newspapers.)

54. Charles Hurd, "The Week in America: Democrats Sweep Nation," *New York Times*, November 13, 1932.

55. Thomas F. Woodlock, " 'Liberal' Victory," *Wall Street Journal*, November 28, 1932.

56. The data sample presented in chapter 1 has FDR making one mandate claim in thirty-two communications (approximately 3 percent), which falls to 2 percent when we look at the rest of 1933.

57. Ritchie, *Electing FDR*, 138.

58. Elvin T. Lim, "The Lion and the Lamb: Demythologizing Franklin Roosevelt's Fireside Chats," *Rhetoric and Public Affairs* 6, no. 3 (2003): 448.

59. Franklin Roosevelt, Remarks to Relief Administrators, June 14, 1933, PPP.

60. Franklin Roosevelt, Letter to Leon McCord, July 8, 1933, PPP.

61. Franklin Roosevelt, Annual Message to Congress, January 1934, PPP.

62. William Borah in William E. Leuchtenburg, "When the People Spoke, What Did They Say? The 1936 Election and the Ackerman Thesis," *Yale Law Journal* 108, no. 8 (June 1999): 2077–2114.

63. William E. Leuchtenburg, *Franklin D. Roosevelt and the New Deal, 1932–1940* (New York: Harper Perennial, 2009), 175.

64. Witcover, *Party of the People*, 371.

65. Jean Edward Smith, *FDR* (New York: Random House, 2008), 372.

66. Roosevelt, "Greeting to the Third National Conference on Labor Legislation," November 7, 1936, PPP.

67. Marc Landy and Sidney Milkis, *Presidential Greatness* (Lawrence: University Press of Kansas, 2000), 180.

68. Jeffrey Shesol, *Supreme Power: Franklin Roosevelt and the Supreme Court* (New York: Norton, 2010), 42.

69. Richard J. Ellis and Stephen Kirk, "Presidential Mandates in the Nineteenth Century: Conceptual Change and Institutional Development," *Studies in American Political Development* 9, no. 1 (1995): 140.

70. Leuchtenburg, "When the People Spoke," 2082.

71. Conrad Black, *Franklin Delano Roosevelt: Champion of Freedom* (New York: PublicAffairs, 2005), 408.

72. Ibid., 409.

73. Leuchtenburg, *Franklin D. Roosevelt*, 235.

74. Franklin Roosevelt, Message to Congress on the Reorganization of the Judicial Branch of the Government, February 5, 1937, PPP.

75. John W. Sloan, *FDR and Reagan* (Lawrence: University Press of Kansas, 2008), 279.

76. Leuchtenburg, *Franklin D. Roosevelt*, 237.

77. Sloan, *FDR and Reagan*, 276.

78. Landy and Milkis, *Presidential Greatness*, 174.

79. Ibid., 180.

80. Ibid., 178.

81. Sloan, *FDR and Reagan*, 260.

Chapter 3

1. Charles O. Jones, *The Presidency in a Separated System* (Washington, DC: Brookings Institution Press (2005), 185.

2. Patricia Heidotting Conley, *Presidential Mandates: How Elections Shape the National Agenda* (Chicago: University of Chicago Press, 2001), 89–90.

3. Lawrence Grossback, David A. M. Peterson, and James A. Stimson, *Mandate Politics* (New York: Cambridge University Press, 2006), 4–5.

4. Harry Truman, Inaugural Address, January 20, 1949, Public Papers of the Presidents [hereafter cited as PPP].

5. George C. Edwards III, *The Strategic President: Persuasion and Opportunity in Presidential Leadership* (Princeton, NJ: Princeton University Press, 2009), 83.

6. Adam Przeworski and Henry Teune, *The Logic of Comparative Social Inquiry* (New York: Wiley Interscience, 1970), 35.

7. Daniel J. Galvin, *Presidential Party-building: Dwight D. Eisenhower to George W. Bush* (Princeton, NJ: Princeton University Press, 2010), 42.

8. For a brief overview of Johnson's pre-presidential life, see "American President: A Reference Resource," Miller Center. http://millercenter.org/president/lbjohnson/essays /biography/2.

9. For example, see William E. Leuchtenburg, *In the Shadow of FDR: From Harry Truman to George W. Bush* (Ithaca, NY: Cornell University Press, 2001).

10. Richard E. Neustadt, *Presidential Power and the Modern Presidents* (New York: Free Press, 1990), 31–33.

11. Jeffrey M. Jones, "Obama's Approval Ratings More Polarized in Year 2 Than Year 1," Gallup News Service, February 4, 2011.

12. See Brendan Nyhan, "Why the Death Panel Myth Wouldn't Die," *The Forum* 8, no. 1 (2010); Matthew A. Baum and Tim Groeling, "New Media and the Polarization of American Discourse," *Political Communication* 25 (2008): 345–365.

13. Jim Newton, *Eisenhower: The White House Years* (New York: Doubleday, 2011), 141.

14. Sidney Milkis, *The President and the Parties* (New York: Oxford University Press, 1993), 168.

15. See Hahrie Han and David Brady, "A Delayed Return to Historical Norms: Congressional Party Polarization after the Second World War," *British Journal of Political Science* 37 (2007), 505–531.

16. Robert Mason, *The Republican Party and American Politics from Hoover to Reagan* (New York: Cambridge University Press, 2012), 162–163.

17. Sean J. Savage, *JFK, LBJ, and the Democratic Party* (Albany: State University of New York Press, 2004), 183.

18. Robert Dallek, *Flawed Giant: Lyndon Johnson and His Times, 1961–1973* (New York: Oxford University Press, 1999), 108.

19. Stephen Skowronek, *The Politics Presidents Make: Presidential Leadership from John Adams to Bill Clinton*, 2nd ed. (Cambridge: Belknap Press, 1997), 345.

20. Skowronek, *The Politics Presidents Make*, 46.

21. Galvin, *Presidential Party-building*, 42.

22. Newton, *Eisenhower*, 60.

23. Skowronek, *Politics Presidents Make*, 450.

24. Lewis L. Gould, *Grand Old Party: A History of the Republicans* (New York: Random House, 2003), 327.

25. Fred I. Greenstein, *The Hidden-Hand Presidency: Eisenhower as Leader* (Baltimore, MD: Johns Hopkins University Press, 1994), 5.

26. Jim Hagerty, Memo to the President, n.d., Hagerty Papers, box 7, staff files, Dwight D. Eisenhower Presidential Library, Abilene, Kansas [hereafter cited as DDE].

27. Michael Korzi, *Presidential Term Limits in American History: Power, Principles, and Politics* (College Station: Texas A&M University Press, 2011), 146.

28. Bryce Harlow, Memorandum: Report to the Nation, Legislative Achievements 2, August 6, 1953, Bryce Harlow Records, box 32, speech folder, DDE.

29. Bryce Harlow, Memorandum to C. D. Jackson: Report to the People, TV Broadcast, January 4, 1954, Bryce Harlow Records, box 33, speech folder, DDE.

30. Bill Moyers, Memo to McGeorge Bundy, Bill Moyers Papers, box 29, speech drafts folder, Lyndon Baines Johnson Library, Austin, Texas, [hereafter cited as LBJ].

31. Richard Goodwin, Memo to McGeorge Bundy, n.d. Harry McPherson Collection, box 15, proposed presidential trips/speeches folder, LBJ.

32. Doris Kearns Goodwin, *Lyndon Johnson and the American Dream*, 2nd ed. (New York: St. Martin's Griffin, 1991), 216, 245.

33. Bill Moyers, Memo to Walt Rostow: Themes for Presidential Speeches, September 24, 1964, Bill Moyers Papers, box 31, suggestions for speeches folder, LBJ.

34. Conley, *Presidential Mandates*, 85.

35. Walter Trohan, "Landslide for Ike," *Chicago Tribune*, November 5, 1952.

36. Associated Press, "Change Begins," *New York Times*, November 9, 1952.

37. "The Landslide," *New York Times*, November 6, 1952.

38. Stephen Benedict, Memo to the President, November 13, 1952. Stephen Benedict Papers, box 10, staff memoranda, Citizens for Eisenhower folder, DDE.

39. Harold Stassen, Memo to Emmet Hughes: State of the Union 1953, December 30, 1952. Bryce Harlow Records, box 9, outline and drafts folder, DDE.

40. Draft No. 1: State of the Union 1953, n.d. Bryce Harlow Records, box 9, outline and drafts folder, DDE.

41. Speech draft: State of the Union 1953, n.d. Bryce Harlow Records, box 9, outline and drafts folder, DDE.

42. Dwight Eisenhower, Annual Message to the Congress on the State of the Union, February 2, 1953, PPP.

43. For a more extensive account of Eisenhower's involvement in the speechwriting process, see Kurt Ritter and Martin J. Medhurst, *Presidential Speechwriting: From the New Deal to the Reagan Revolution and Beyond* (College Station: Texas A&M University Press, 2004), chap. 3.

44. 1952 Republican Party Platform, July 7, 1952, PPP.

45. Schapsmeier and Schapsmeier, "Eisenhower and Agricultural Reform: Ike's Farm Policy Legacy Appraised," *American Journal of Economics and Sociology* 51, no. 2 (1992): 147–160.

46. Dwight Eisenhower, "Personal and Confidential to Edgar Newton Eisenhower," November 8, 1954, in *The Presidential Papers of Dwight D. Eisenhower*, eds. L. Galambos and D. van Ee (Baltimore, MD: Johns Hopkins University Press), doc. 1147, http://www.eisenhowermemorial.org/presidential-papers/first-term/documents/1147.cfm; cf. Greenstein, *Hidden-Hand Presidency*, 50.

47. Schapsmeier and Schapsmeier, "Eisenhower and Agricultural Reform," 150; Newton, *Eisenhower*, 142.

48. Greenstein, *Hidden-Hand Presidency*, 67.

49. Gould, *Grand Old Party*, 334

50. Skowronek, *Politics Presidents Make*, 287.

51. David A. Crockett, *The Opposition Presidency: Leadership and the Constraints of History* (College Station: Texas A&M University Press, 2002), 131.

52. Paul Conkin, *Big Daddy from the Pedernales: Lyndon Baines Johnson* (Boston: Twayne, 1986), 190.

53. Douglass Cater, Memo to the President, October 1, 1964. Douglass Cater Papers, box 13, memos to the president folder, LBJ.

54. Douglass Cater, Memo to the President, October 2–October 28, 1964. Douglass Cater Papers, box 13, memos to the president folder, LBJ.

55. "After the Vote," *New York Times*, November 15, 1964.

56. James Reston. "How Will the President React to His Victory?," *New York Times*, November 4, 1964.

57. Willard Edwards, "Johnson Gets Big Majority in Congress," *Chicago Tribune*, November 5, 1964.

58. "The Johnson Landslide," *New York Times*, November 5, 1964.

59. Marc Landy and Sidney Milkis, *Presidential Greatness* (Lawrence: University Press of Kansas, 2000), 231.

60. Dallek, *Flawed Giant*, 190.

61. Goodwin, *Lyndon Johnson and the American Dream*, 216.

62. Lyndon Johnson, Address before a Joint Session of Congress on the State of the Union, January 4, 1965, PPP.

63. Lyndon Johnson, Statement by the President Following Passage of the Medicare Bill by the Senate, July 9, 1965, PPP.

64. Lyndon Johnson, Memorandum, n.d. Horace Busby Collection, box 34, miscellaneous memos folder, LBJ.

65. Horace Busby, Memorandum for Dick Goodwin, January 4, 1965, Annual Message on the State of the Union 2, January 4, 1965, Statements of Lyndon B. Johnson Collection, LBJ. The irony of Busby's identification of LBJ as the first "unity" president is that, as chap. 3 shows, Eisenhower and his aides conceived the presidency in much the same way.

66. Which was given before January 20 and thus is not in the data set presented in chap. 2.

67. Johnson's statement about the election and policy toward the Soviet Union—which reads, "Last fall I asked the American people to choose that course"—could be interpreted a number of ways. However, contextual cues found elsewhere in the documents about foreign policy and the 1964 campaign suggest that the Johnson team conceptualized this stance as a matter of widespread social consensus rather than as an enduring difference between the parties.

68. Presidential Job Approval, January 12, 1965–December 16, 1965, American Presidency Project; Jeffrey Jones, "Obama's Approval Ratings More Polarized in Year 2 than Year 1," February 4, 2011. The "gap" between Johnson's approval among Democrats and among Republicans in 1965 was 31 percent, the second lowest of all second-year presidents since 1953.

69. David Zarefsky, "Presidential Rhetoric and the Power of Definition," *Presidential Studies Quarterly* 34, no. 3 (2004): 616.

70. Tulis, *Rhetorical Presidency*, 164–165.

71. Landy and Milkis, *Presidential Greatness*, 210–211.

72. Maurice Isserman and Michael Kazin, *America Divided: The Civil War of the 1960s* (New York: Oxford University Press, 2000), 199.

73. Dallek, *Flawed Giant*, 406.

74. Ibid.

75. Landy and Milkis, *Presidential Greatness*, 212.

76. Skowronek, *Politics Presidents Make*, 358.

77. Draft of Speech for Harrisburg Fund-raising Dinner, September 1964, Bill Moyers Papers, box 23, LBJ.

78. Gallup Political Index, Public Relations Collection, box 395, White House central files, LBJ.

79. Mary Dovel, Letter to the President, box 8, White House administration files, folder WH May 14, 1965–September 7, 1965, LBJ.

Chapter 4

1. Len Garment, Memorandum to H. R. Haldeman, Ehrlichman Papers, box 31, numerical subject file folder, domestic plans 2 of 2, Richard M. Nixon Presidential Library, Yorba Linda, California [hereafter cited as RMN].

2. Gary Orren, "Fall from Grace, the Public's Loss of Faith in Government," in *Why People Don't Trust Government*, eds. Joseph S. Nye Jr., Philip D. Zelikow, and David C. King (Cambridge, MA: Harvard University Press, 1997), 78.

3. Andrew Rudalevige, *The New Imperial Presidency: Renewing Presidential Power after Watergate* (Ann Arbor: University of Michigan Press, 2005), 58.

4. Orren, "Fall from Grace," 81.

5. Melvin Small, *The Presidency of Richard Nixon* (Lawrence: University Press of Kansas, 1999), 155.

6. Patricia Heidotting Conley, *Presidential Mandates: How Elections Shape the National Agenda*, (Chicago: University of Chicago Press, 2001), 156–157.

7. Martin P. Wattenberg, *The Rise of Candidate-Centered Politics* (Cambridge, MA: Harvard University Press, 1991).

8. Morris P. Fiorina, "The Decline of Collective Responsibility in American Politics," *Daedelus* 109, no. 3 (1980): 25–45; Russell J. Dalton, "The Decline of Party Identifications," in *Parties Without Partisans*, eds. Russell J. Dalton and Martin P. Wattenberg (New York: Oxford University Press, 2002), 23.

9. Robert Mason, *Richard Nixon and the Quest for a New Majority* (Chapel Hill: University of North Carolina Press, 2004), 83.

10. Mason, *Richard Nixon and the Quest*, 145–146.

11. Bruce Miroff, *The Liberal's Moment: The McGovern Insurgency and the Identity Crisis of the Democratic Party*, 2nd ed. (Lawrence: University Press of Kansas, 2009), 124.

12. Stephen Skowronek, *The Politics Presidents Make: Presidential Leadership from John Adams to Bill Clinton* (Cambridge, MA: Belknap Press, 1997), 366.

13. Skowronek, *Politics Presidents Make*, 362.

14. For example, the Supreme Court had curtailed Truman's use of presidential war power to seize steel mills, but this action did little to prevent an overall expansion of these powers. After Truman's actions in Korea, Senate Republicans unsuccessfully pursued the Bricker Amendment as a way to curb presidential capacity to initiate military conflict.

15. Mason, *Richard Nixon and the Quest,* 18.

16. Len Garment, Memorandum to James Keogh, February 21, 1969, Len Garment Papers, White House Memos Collection, box 1, January–June 1969 folder, RMN.

17. Daniel Moynihan, Memorandum to President Nixon, July 17, 1969, John Ehrlichman Papers, box 31 numerical subject file folder, domestic plans group, RMN.

18. Mason, *Richard Nixon and the Quest*, 40–41.

19. John McClaughry, Memorandum to Len Garment and Bryce Harlow, April 2, 1969, Ehrlichman Papers, box 31, numerical subject file folder, domestic policy 2 of 2, RMN.

20. James Reston, "From Promise to Policy," *New York Times*, November 7, 1968.

21. Associated Press, "The World's Week," (Fredericksburg, Virginia) *Free Lance-Star*, November 9, 1968.

22. "Mr. Nixon's Challenge," (Owosso, Michigan) *Argus Press,* November 9, 1968.

23. "The Post-Election Letdown," *Chicago Tribune*, November 10, 1968.

24. Robert J. Donovan, "The Man in the Center," *St. Petersburg Times*, November 7, 1968.

25. "There Is No Mandate," *Daytona Beach Morning Journal*, November 7, 1968.

26. Richard Nixon, Remarks about a New Policy on Appointment of Postmasters, February 5, 1969, PPP.

27. Nyle Jackson, Memorandum to Harry Dent, Harry Dent Papers, memoranda and department records, 1969 Jackson memos folder, RMN.

28. Richard Nixon, President's News Conference, January 27, 1969, PPP.

29. Richard Nixon, Address Accepting the Presidential Nomination at the Republican National Convention in Miami, Florida, August 8, 1968, PPP.

30. Melvin Small, *The Presidency of Richard Nixon* (Lawrence: University Press of Kansas, 2003), 163.

31. Richard Nixon, President's News Conference, February 6, 1969, PPP.

32. Charles O. Jones, *The Presidency in a Separated System* (Washington, DC: Brookings Institution Press, 2005), 188.

33. Ernest B. Furguson, "It's an Opportunity if Not a Mandate," *Sarasota Journal*, November 15, 1972.

34. "Mandate for Change," *Tri-City Herald*, November 14, 1972.

35. R. W. Apple Jr., "A Vote for More of the Same," *New York Times*, November 12, 1972.

36. Richard J. Ellis and Stephen Kirk, "Presidential Mandates in the Nineteenth Century: Conceptual Change and Institutional Development," *Studies in American Political Development* 9, no. 1 (1995): 182.

37. James T. Patterson, *Freedom Is Not Enough: The Moynihan Report and America's Struggle over Black Family Life from LBJ to Obama* (New York: Basic Books, 2010), 90; Marc Landy and Sidney Milkis, *Presidential Greatness* (Lawrence: University Press of Kansas, 2000), 212–213.

38. Rudalevige, *New Imperial Presidency*, 87–88.

39. Small, *Presidency of Richard Nixon*, 200.

40. Richard Nixon, Annual Budget Message to the Congress, Fiscal Year 1974, January 29, 1973, PPP.

41. Richard Nixon, President's News Conference, August 22, 1973, PPP.

42. Jim Fallows, Memorandum to the President, February 11, 1977, Speechwriters Collection, Fallows, box 6, presidential memos folder, January 28, 1977–November 30, 1977, Jimmy Carter Presidential Library, Atlanta, Georgia [hereafter cited as JEC].

43. Garland Haas, *Jimmy Carter and the Politics of Frustration* (Jefferson, NC: McFarland, 1992), 65.

44. Charles O. Jones, *The Trusteeship Presidency: Jimmy Carter and the United States Congress* (Baton Rouge: Louisiana State Press, 1988), 2–6.

45. Bob Wiedrich, "Carter Can Be His Own Man, If He Will," *Chicago Tribune*, November 21, 1976.

46. "A Change, But What Kind?," *Wall Street Journal*, November 4, 1976.

47. Tom Wicker, "Mr. Carter's Mandate," *New York Times*, November 7, 1976.

48. Patrick Caddell, Initial Working Paper on Political Strategy, Jody Powell Collection, box 4, memoranda folder, Pat Caddell, December 10, 1976–December 21, 1976, JEC.

49. Jimmy Carter, President's News Conference, May 12, 1977, PPP.

50. Jimmy Carter, Report to the America People: Remarks from the White House Library, February 2, 1977, PPP.

51. Jimmy Carter, Zero-Base Budgeting for the Fiscal Year 1979, Budget Memorandum to the Heads of Executive Departments and Agencies, February 14, 1977, PPP.

52. Jimmy Carter, Reorganization Plan Authority, Remarks on Transmitting Proposed Legislation to the Congress, February 4, 1977, PPP.

53. Jimmy Carter, Reorganization Act of 1977, Remarks at Signing Ceremony, April 6, 1977, PPP.

54. Jimmy Carter, Reorganization Act of 1977, Statement Signing S. 626 into Law, April 6, 1977, PPP.

55. Jerry Rafshoon, Memorandum to the President, January 25, 1977, White House Office subject file, Press Office - Powell, box 49, Fireside Chats 1977 folder, JEC.

56. Achsah Nesmith, Memorandum to James Fallows, Speechwriters Collection, Nesmith, box 4, in-house memos and drafts folder, March 8–June 8, 1977, JEC.

57. Achsah Nesmith, Memorandum to James Fallows, Speechwriters Collection, Nesmith, box 4, in-house memos and drafts folder, March 8–June 8, 1977, JEC.

58. James Fallows, Memorandum to Achsah Nesmith, Speechwriters Subject File Collection, box 42, Memoranda, Fallows, Jim January 21–May 20, 1977, JEC.

59. Achsah Nesmith, Memorandum to Jody Powell, April 17, 1978. Speechwriters Collection, Nesmith, box 4, in-house memos and drafts folder, March 8–June 8, 1977, JEC.

60. Patrick Caddell, Initial Working Paper on Political Strategy, December 10, 1976, Jody Powell Collection, box 4, memoranda folder, Pat Caddell, December 10–December 21, 1976, JEC.

Chapter 5

1. Michael Grunwald, "Obama Elected President with Mandate for Change," *Time*, November 4, 2008.

2. Skowronek has referred to the period beginning with the Reagan presidency as "a state of perpetual preemption," which would "offer reasonable prospects for presidents to get things done and shake things up, but little hope for disarming potential critics." Skowronek, *Politics Presidents Make*, 444. His subsequent work has suggested that the patterns of political time persist into the twenty-first century. The approach in this book has been to decouple the institutional legitimacy of the presidency from the cycle of political time, which allows both observations to be true: the oppositional environment in which later presidents operate is more challenging, and presidents continue to follow the basic predictions of political time.

3. Raymond Tatalovich and John Frendreis, "Clinton, Class, and Economic Policy," in *The Postmodern Presidency: Bill Clinton's Legacy in U.S. Politics*, ed. Steven E. Schier (Pittsburgh, PA: University of Pittsburgh Press, 2000), 48; Bruce Miroff, "Courting the Public: Bill Clinton's Postmodern Education," in Schier, *Postmodern Presidency*, 114–116.

4. The Patient Protection and Affordable Care Act of 2010 caused considerable disunity among congressional Democrats, most notably with regard to the bill's provisions for federal subsidies for abortion coverage, led in the House of Representatives by Bart Stupak (D-MI) and in the Senate by Ben Nelson (D-NE). Jonathan Weisman, "Stupak: 15–20 Dems Can't Back Obama Health Plan," *Wall Street Journal*, February 24, 2010; Jodi Kantor, "Congressman Defies Party on Health Care Bill," *New York Times*, January 6, 2010; Paul Kane, "To Sway Nelson, a Hard-Won Compromise on Abortion Issue," *Washington Post*, December 20, 2009.

5. The Great Depression ended the Republican majority elected in 1928, with the House falling to the Democrats in the 1930 midterm and the Senate following in 1932. Democrats lost control of Congress in 1946, regained it in 1948, and lost again in 1952.

Republicans found themselves relegated once again to the minority in the 1954 midterms, a status they would maintain in the Senate until 1980 and in the House until 1994.

6. Theda Skocpol and Vanessa Williamson, *The Tea Party and the Remaking of American Conservatism* (New York: Oxford University Press, 2012), 3.

7. For example, see Michael D. Shear, "Huckabee Questions Obama Birth Certificate," *New York Times*, March 1, 2011.

8. Sarah Sobieraj and Jeffrey M. Berry, "From Incivility to Outrage: Political Discourse in Blogs, Talk Radio, and Cable News," *Political Communication* 28, no. 1 (2011): 19–41.

9. Matthew Baum and Tim Groeling, "New Media and American Political Discourse," *Political Communication* 25, no. 4 (2008): 345–365, 359.

10. Jeffrey Cohen, "If the News Is So Bad, Why Are Presidential Polls So High? Presidents, the News Media, and the Mass Public in an Era of New Media," *Presidential Studies Quarterly* 34, no. 3 (2004): 512.

11. In Skowronek's essay "Leadership by Definition: First Term Reflections on George W. Bush's Leadership Stance," in *Presidential Leadership and Political Time: Reprise and Reappraisal*, 2nd ed. (Lawrence: University Press of Kansas, 2011), he elucidates the ways in which the presidency of George W. Bush exhibits the characteristics of articulation, or "orthodox innovator" leadership. A different essay in the same volume explores the "reconstructive" potential of the Obama administration, weighing this possibility against the likelihood of a "preemptive" presidency. In particular, comparison between Obama and earlier preemptive leaders Wilson and Nixon suggests that opposition leaders who emerge later in the political order often have the opportunity to be "more strident in (their) assaults on the established regime and a bit more forthright in (their) attempts to replace it" (177). Furthermore, the political order initiated by Reagan has yet to experience a disjunctive presidency in the mold of Herbert Hoover or Jimmy Carter, distinguished not only by political failure but also by its "candid" recognition of the "deep-seated problems within the older order" (178). With this distinction in mind, I have placed Obama in the preemptive category for comparison purposes.

12. See Stephen J. Wayne, "Obama's Personality and Performance," in *Obama in Office*, ed. James Thurber (Boulder, CO: Paradigm), 2011.

13. See Andrew E. Busch, *Ronald Reagan and the Politics of Freedom* (Lanham, MD: Rowman & Littlefield, 2001), chap. 3; Bruce Miroff, "The Presidential Spectacle," in *The Presidency and the Political System*, ed. Michael Nelson (Washington, DC: CQ Press, 2008).

14. Andrew E. Busch, *Reagan's Victory: The Presidential Election of 1980 and the Rise of the Right* (Lawrence: University Press of Kansas, 2005), 106.

15. Sean Wilentz, *The Age of Reagan: A History, 1974–2008* (New York: Random House, 2009), 129.

16. Gerald M. Pomper, Ross K. Baker, Kathleen A. Frankovic, Charles E. Jacob, Wilson Carey McWilliams, and Henry A. Plotkin, *The Election of 1980* (Chatham, New Jersey: Chatham House Publishers, 1981), 14.

17. 1980 Republican Platform, July 15, 1980 American Presidency Project [hereafter cited as APP], www.presidency.ucsb.edu.

18. Wilentz, *Age of Reagan*, 122.

19. In their analysis of the election, Paul R. Abramson, John H. Aldrich, and David W. Rohde point out that the House of Representatives became considerably more conservative based on which legislators kept their seats and which individuals retired or lost their reelection bids. Abramson, Aldrich, and Rohde, *Change and Continuity in the 1980 Elections*, rev. ed. (Washington, DC: CQ Press, 1983), 204.

20. Lawrence Grossback, David A. M. Peterson, and James Stimson, *Mandate Politics* (New York: Cambridge University Press, 2006), 150.

21. "Mandate for Change," *Wall Street Journal*, November 6, 1980.

22. James M. Perry and Albert R. Hunt, "GOP Mandate," *Wall Street Journal*, November 5, 1980; Gene G. Marcial, "Defense Issues Explode as Reagan's Landslide Is Seen as Assuring Increased Spending for Arms," *Wall Street Journal*, November 6, 1980.

23. Adam Clymer, "Presidential Pollsters Are Breeds Apart: Not a Mandate, but a Sanction," *New York Times*, December 14, 1980.

24. Tom Wicker, "Mandate and Burden," *New York Times*, January 20, 1981. The polling data cited in this article are both from the New York Times/CBS poll and from the Gallup Poll.

25. Gail E. S. Yoshitani, *Reagan on War: A Reappraisal of the Weinberger Doctrine, 1980–1984* (College Station: Texas A&M University Press, 2012), 8.

26. Ronald Reagan, Remarks Signing a Memorandum Directing Reductions in Federal Spending, January 22, 1981. Public Papers of the Presidents [hereafter cited as PPP].

27. Ronald Reagan, Memorandum Directing Reductions in Federal Spending, January 22, 1981.

28. See Skowronek, *Politics Presidents Make*, 414.

29. This approach appears to have worked, at least temporarily. See Marc J. Hetherington, *Why Trust Matters: Declining Political Trust and the Demise of American Liberalism* (Princeton, NJ; Princeton University Press, 2006), 23.

30. Busch, *Reagan's Victory*, 23.

31. Jeffrey M. Jones, "Obama's Approval Most Polarized for First-Year President," Gallup News Service, January 25, 2010.

32. David Yalof, "The Presidency and the Judiciary," in *The Presidency and the Political System*, ed. Michael Nelson (Washington, DC: CQ Press, 2009), 450. Although Roosevelt's approach to the court was certainly political, his appointment strategy could be seen as a reaction to court decisions. In contrast, Reagan's strategy, as described by Yalof, constituted an important opportunity for what Steven Teles has described as the "conservative legal movement." Steven Teles, "Transformative Bureaucracy: Reagan's Lawyers and the Dynamics of Political Investment," *Studies in American Political Development* 23 (April 2009): 61–83.

33. Shirley Anne Warshaw, "The Other Reagan Revolution," *The Reagan Presidency*, eds. Paul Kengor and Peter Schweizer (New York: Rowman & Littlefield, 2005), 148–149.

34. For a summary of politicization and its roots in the Nixon and Reagan administrations, see David E. Lewis, *The Politics of Presidential Appointments: Political Control*

and Bureaucratic Performance (Princeton, NJ: Princeton University Press, 2008), chap. 3 and 97–100.

35. Ronald Reagan, President's News Conference, January 29, 1981, PPP.

36. Ronald Reagan, Message to Congress, March 10, 1981, PPP.

37. Max L. Friedersdorf, Letter to Patricia Schroeder, March 19, 1981, White House Office of Records Management [hereafter abbreviated WHORM] Subject Files, SP 281-05, box 63, Economic Recovery Address before Congress February 18, 1981 – Begin 008984 folder, Ronald Reagan Presidential Library, Simi Valley, California [hereafter abbreviated RWR].

38. Lyn Nofziger, Letter to Patsy Mink, February 1981, WHORM Public Relations Collection, 002—Complaints about the Administration, box 11, folder 000001-05999, RWR.

39. Gil Troy, *Morning in America: How Ronald Reagan Invented the 1980s* (Princeton, NJ: Princeton University Press, 2007), 53.

40. The emphasis on economic, rather than social, issues also helped the story of a conservative mandate to gain wider acceptance and to forestall counterclaims. As Geoffrey Kabaservice describes, Reagan's early successes can be partially attributed to the fact that "the White House decided to prioritize the economic issues that most moderates agreed with over the social issues they did not." Geoffrey Kabaservice, *Rule and Ruin: The Downfall of Moderation and the Destruction of the Republican Party, from Eisenhower to the Tea Party Era* (New York: Oxford University Press, 2012), 364.

41. Marc Landy and Sidney Milkis, *Presidential Greatness* (Lawrence: University Press of Kansas, 2000), 38.

42. Bruce Miroff, "The Presidential Spectacle," 216.

43. Gary C. Jacobson, *A Divider, Not a Uniter: George W. Bush and the American People*, 2nd ed. Great Questions in Politics Series, ed. George C. Edwards III (New York: Pearson Longman, 2011).

44. Jeffrey M. Jones, "Bush Ratings Show Historical Levels of Polarization," Gallup News Service, June 4, 2004.

45. Jeremy Cluchey, "Conservatives Rail Against MSNBC's Olbermann for Reporting Election Irregularities," *Media Matters*, November 16, 2004.

46. Charles Krauthammer, "Using All of a Mandate," *Washington Post*, November 5, 2004.

47. E. J. Dionne, "He Didn't Get It," *Washington Post*, November 5, 2004.

48. Lyn Nofziger, "Bush's Trouble Ahead," *New York Times*, November 7, 2004.

49. Dante Chinni, "Is the Red Post-Election Tinge a Mandate? Don't Bet on It," *Christian Science Monitor*, November 4, 2004.

50. David D. Kirkpatrick, "Some Bush Supporters Say They Anticipate a 'Revolution,'" *New York Times*, November 4, 2004.

51. Todd S. Purdum, "President Seems Poised to Claim New Mandate," *New York Times*, November 3, 2004.

52. 2008 Republican Party Platform, August 25, 2008, APP.

53. George W. Bush, President's News Conference, November 4, 2004, PPP.

54. George W. Bush, Remarks at a Republican National Committee Dinner, March 15, 2005, PPP.

55. Robert Draper, *Dead Certain: The Presidency of George W. Bush* (New York: Simon & Schuster, 2008), 297.

56. Fiona Ross, "Reforming Social Security," in *The Polarized Presidency of George W. Bush*, ed. George C. Edwards III and Desmond King (New York, Oxford University Press, 2007), 423.

57. Lou Cannon and Carl M. Cannon, *Reagan's Disciple: George W. Bush's Troubled Quest for a Presidential Legacy* (New York: Public Affairs, 2008), 83.

58. Ibid., 84.

59. Alec M. Gallup and Frank Newport, *The Gallup Poll: Public Opinion 2005* (New York: Rowman & Littlefield, 2006), 5.

60. George W. Bush, "Remarks in a Discussion on Strengthening Social Security in Tucson," March 21, 2005, PPP.

61. George W. Bush, "Remarks in a Discussion on Strengthening Social Security in Notre Dame, Indiana," March 4, 2005, PPP.

62. Edwards and King, *Polarized Presidency*, 20.

63. Frank Newport and Joseph Carroll, "Pre-inauguration Attitudes Reveal Unmet Expectations, Hopes for Second Term," Gallup News Service, January 20, 2005.

64. Michael A. Fletcher, "Bush Immigration Plan Meets GOP Opposition," *Washington Post*, January 2, 2005.

65. Joseph Carroll, "Bush Job Approval Near Its Low Point," Gallup News Service, June 19, 2007.

66. "Bush Hails Financial Rescue Plan," BBC News, September 20, 2008.

67. Barack Obama, "Address in Chicago Accepting Election as the 44th President of the United States," November 4, 2008, Campaign Documents, APP.

68. Barack Obama, "Illinois Senate Candidate" (transcript), *Washington Post*, July 27, 2004.

69. Robert P. Saldin, "Foreign Affairs and the 2008 Election," *The Forum* 6, no. 4 (2008): 8.

70. To say that Bush's 2004 strategy was oriented toward the Republican base is not to deny that the campaign sought to expand beyond its usual coalition. Indeed, the 2004 campaign did relatively well with Latino voters, garnering 44 percent to the 31 percent won by the Bush-Cheney ticket in 2000. However, political scientists David Leal, Matt Barreto, Jongh Lee, and Rodolfo de la Garza challenge this exit poll–based estimate. Furthermore, they and others provide evidence that "moral values" issues, including abortion and same-sex marriage, influenced the Hispanic vote for Bush. Marisa Abrajano, R. Michael Alvarez, and Jonathan Nagler find that "Hispanic voters who ranked moral values or terrorism as their most important issue, rather than taxes, were more likely to vote for Bush, controlling for other factors in the model." This effect existed among white voters for terrorism, but not for moral values. Abrajano, Alvarez, and Nagler, "The Hispanic Vote in the 2004 Presidential Election: Insecurity and Moral Concerns," *Journal of Politics* 70, no. 2 (2008): 375. Leal and others find a religion gap among Latino voters, with Bush doing considerably better among Latino "evangelical or born-again Christians" as compared to Catholics, mainline Protestants or secular voters who self-identified as Latino. Leal, Barreto, Lee, and de la Garza, "The Latino Voter in the 2004 Election," *PS: Political Science and Politics* 38, no. 1 (2005): 41–49.

71. Daniel J. Galvin, "Changing Course: Reversing the Organizational Trajectory of the Democratic Party from Bill Clinton to Barack Obama," *Forum* 6, no. 2 (2008): 2.

72. Paul R. Abramson, John H. Aldrich, and David W. Rohde, *Change and Continuity in the 2008 Elections* (Washington, DC: CQ Press, 2010), 118.

73. Jeffrey M. Jones, "Obama Most Polarized First-Year Presidency," Gallup News Service, January 25, 2010.

74. Carolyn Lochhead, "Debate Opens on Obama's Mandate," *San Francisco Chronicle*, November 6, 2008.

75. David Sirota, "Mandate '08: Reagan vs. FDR," *San Francisco Chronicle*, October 31, 2008.

76. Editorial, "Obama's Victory is a Mandate for Change," *Los Angeles Times*, November 5, 2008; see also Brian Wingfield, "A Clear Mandate for Obama," *Forbes*, November 5, 2008.

77. Jackie Calmes, "House Passes Stimulus with No GOP Votes," *New York Times*, January 28, 2009.

78. See Sean Theriault, *Party Polarization in Congress* (New York: Cambridge University Press, 2008); Marc Hetherington and Bruce Larson, *Parties, Politics, and Public Policy in America*, 11th ed. (Washington, DC: CQ Press, 2009).

79. Richard M. Skinner, "George W. Bush and the Partisan Presidency," *Political Science Quarterly* 123, no. 4 (2009), 614–615.

80. Bert Rockman, "The Obama Presidency: Hope, Change and Reality," *Social Science Quarterly* 93, no. 5 (2012): 1075.

81. Major Garrett, "Top GOP Priority: Make Obama a One-Term President," *National Journal*, October 23, 2010.

82. "Days after decrying those who say Democrats are 'trying to turn us into Communist Russia,' Beck claimed 'Obama has Marxist tendencies,'" Greg Lewis, Media Matters for America, January 14, 2009.

83. Rush Limbaugh, *The Rush Limbaugh Show* (transcript), January 16, 2009.

84. Sara K. Smith, "Eager Obamatards Waiting Patiently for Jobs They Won't Get," Wonkette.com, March 17, 2009. http://wonkette.com/407041/eager-obamatards-waiting-patiently-for-jobs-they-wont-get.

85. Barack Obama, Remarks to Senior White House Staff, January 21, 2009, PPP.

86. Carter experienced backlash when his longtime friend and head of the Office of Management and Budget, Bert Lance, was accused of improper behavior. After emphasizing his "commitment to the highest ethical standards in government," Carter's defense of Lance damaged his credibility. Burton I. Kaufman and Scott Kaufman, *The Presidency of James Earl Carter*, 2nd ed. (Lawrence: University Press of Kansas, 2006), 73.

87. Angie Drobnic Holan, "Obama's Lobbyist Rule: Promise Broken," PolitiFact, March 17, 2009.

88. Frank Newport, "Seven in Ten Americans Say Lobbyists Have Too Much Power," Gallup News Service, April 11, 2011.

89. Jonathan Alter, *The Promise: President Obama, Year One* (New York: Simon & Schuster, 2010), 147.

90. Barack Obama, Remarks on the National Economy, February 4, 2009, PPP.

91. Obama's negativity in describing the 2008 election stands out even in contrast with Bill Clinton, who had actually defeated the incumbent president, George H. W. Bush. Clinton's mandate references in early 1993 stressed the theme of change (Remarks at a Town Meeting in Detroit, February 10, 1993, PPP; President's Radio Address, March 20, 1993; President's News Conference, March 23, 1993, PPP) and stressed his promises to end gridlock (Remarks at the Democratic Governors Association Dinner, February 1, 1993, PPP), decrease the size of the White House Staff (Remarks on Reduction and Reorganization of the White House Staff, February 9, 1993, PPP). However, these statements contrast with Obama's in two important ways. First, they lack Obama's emphasis on voters' "rejection" of the previous administration's policies; they frame the same process in positive rather than negative terms. Furthermore, Clinton's rhetoric is devoid of statements condemning the governing philosophy of his predecessor; he cites policy and results rather than ideas.

92. Barack Obama, "Remarks on Military Operations in Iraq at Camp Lejeune, North Carolina," February 27, 2009, PPP.

93. Barack Obama, Interview with PBS' Jim Lehrer, February 27, 2009, PPP.

94. See George E. Condon Jr. "Fort Bragg Speech Evokes Memories of Another Iraq War Speech," *National Journal*, December 14, 2011.

95. George W. Bush, Address to the Nation on Iraq, March 17, 2003, PPP.

96. Bill Clinton, Address before a Joint Session of the Congress on the State of the Union, January 19, 1999, PPP.

97. Thomas Langston, " 'The Decider's' Path to War in Iraq and the Importance of Personality," in Edwards and King, *Polarized Presidency*, 166.

98. Kate Zernike, *Boiling Mad: Inside Tea Party America* (New York: Times Books/Henry Holt, 2011), 78.

99. "Iowa Tea Party Group's Sign Links Obama, Hitler," Associated Press, July 13, 2010.

100. Zernike, *Boiling Mad*, 95–96.

101. Amy Gardner, "Few Signs at Tea Party Rally Expressed Racially Charged Anti-Obama Themes," *Washington Post*, October 14, 2010.

Conclusion

1. Sidney Blumenthal, *The Permanent Campaign* (New York: Simon & Schuster, 1982).

2. See also Brendan Doherty, *The Rise of the President's Permanent Campaign* (Lawrence: University Press of Kansas, 2012).

3. Joe Klein, "The Perils of the Permanent Campaign," *Time*, October 30, 2005.

4. Stephen Hartnett and Jennifer Mercieca, " 'A Discovered Dissembler Can Achieve Nothing Great': or Four Theses on the Death of Presidential Rhetoric in an Age of Empire," *Presidential Studies Quarterly* 37, no. 4 (2007): 599–621; Andrew Rudalevige, *The New Imperial Presidency: Renewing Presidential Power after Watergate* (Ann Arbor: University of Michigan Press, 2005).

5. See Christopher S. Kelley and Bryan W. Marshall, "The Last Word: Presidential Power and the Role of Signing Statements," *Presidential Studies Quarterly* 38, no. 2 (2008): 248–267; Philip J. Cooper, *By Order of the President: The Use and Abuse of Executive Direct Action* (Lawrence: University Press of Kansas, 2002).

6. Hartnett and Mercieca, "'A Discovered Dissembler Can Achieve Nothing Great,'" 604.

7. Barack Obama, President's News Conference, November 14, 2012, PPP.

8. Jeffrey M. Jones, "Obama's Fourth Year in Office Ties as Most Polarized Ever," Gallup News Service, January 24, 2013. It is also worth noting that Obama is one of only three presidents who have won reelection with a smaller share of the popular vote than in their earlier elections. The only other presidents to lose vote share and still win reelection were Grover Cleveland (who won the popular vote in 1888 and 1892, both times with less than his original vote share in 1884) and Franklin Roosevelt (who lost vote share in his third and fourth reelections).

Index